Weed Land

The publisher gratefully acknowledges the generous support of the General Endowment Fund of the University of California Press Foundation.

Weed Land

INSIDE AMERICA'S MARIJUANA EPICENTER
AND HOW POT WENT LEGIT

Peter Hecht

UNIVERSITY OF CALIFORNIA PRESS

BERKELEY LOS ANGELES LONDON

University of California Press, one of the most distinguished university presses in the United States, enriches lives around the world by advancing scholarship in the humanities, social sciences, and natural sciences. Its activities are supported by the UC Press Foundation and by philanthropic contributions from individuals and institutions. For more information, visit www.ucpress.edu.

University of California Press
Berkeley and Los Angeles, California

University of California Press, Ltd.
London, England

Library of Congress Cataloging-in-Publication Data

Hecht, Peter, 1956–
    Weed land : inside America's marijuana epicenter and how pot went legit / Peter Hecht.
        pages   cm
    Includes bibliographical references and index.
    ISBN 978-0-520-27543-0 (pbk. : alk. paper) —
    ISBN 978-0-520-95824-1 (e-book)
    1. Marijuana—California.   2. Marijuana—Therapeutic use—California.   3. Marijuana—Law and legislation—California.   4. Marijuana industry—California.   I. Title.
    HV5822.M3H43   2014
    363.4509794—dc23

                                    2013043271

Manufactured in the United States of America

23   22   21   20   19   18   17   16   15   14
10   9   8   7   6   5   4   3   2   1

In keeping with a commitment to support environmentally responsible and sustainable printing practices, UC Press has printed this book on Natures Natural, a fiber that contains 30% post-consumer waste and meets the minimum requirements of ANSI / NISO Z39.48-1992 (R 1997) (*permanence of Paper*).

In memory of my mother, Susan Sullivan Hecht, the writer in the family, 1923–2012

CONTENTS

1. · The Way It Was Supposed to Be 1

2. · Oaksterdam 15

3. · Kush Rush 30

4. · Reefer Research 45

5. · The Pot Docs 64

6. · L.A. Excess 79

7. · Wafting Widely 92

8. · Courting Compassion 106

9. · Martyrdom for the Missionaries 121

10. · Campaign for Cannabis 138

11. · A Mile High and Beyond 156

12. · Cultivating Trouble 170

13. · Return of the Feds 186

14. · Back to the Garden 203

Acknowledgments 215
Notes 217
Index 239

ONE

The Way It Was Supposed to Be

For the California medical marijuana movement, this was its siege at Wounded Knee. Early in the morning of September 5, 2002, dozens of Drug Enforcement Administration agents, camouflaged and heavily armed, surged into the Santa Cruz Mountains. Their black-windowed four-wheel-drive vehicles, followed by a U-Haul truck, rumbled into the forest and up a winding road, climbing to a crescent-shaped ridge shrouded by coastal redwoods and eucalyptus. Beneath the ridge was a terraced marijuana garden—a medicinal and spiritual refuge for the sick and dying.

Mike Corral, cofounder and supervising gardener for the Wo/Men's Alliance for Medical Marijuana, had just arisen. He heard the vehicles lurch to a stop at 6:45 outside his board-and-batten cottage, which had a grooved fiberglass roof and a solar heat collector. Corral had stayed there while his wife, Valerie Corral, and two female friends had gone to a James Joyce reading in Santa Cruz by local author and philosopher Robert Anton Wilson. The women were in the upper house on the property, a rustic, angular lodge perpetually under construction. They had gone to bed after sitting up until 3 A.M. wrestling with ideas for a hospice care program for terminally ill friends who used marijuana to quiet the searing pains from cancer or AIDS as they readied for their final journeys.

Mike Corral looked out a window to the clearing between his cottage and the WAMM garden, a flowering orchard of 167 marijuana plants, arranged with paths for wheelchairs and a welcoming sign: Love Grows Here. He saw agents bolting out with automatic weapons and then scurrying to assemble a battering ram. Corral ran to leash his Belgian sheepdog, Ebo, fearing they might shoot the dog if it were loose. He grabbed his cell phone, dialing the first five digits of Valerie's number before the officers burst inside.

"Where are you?" they yelled.

They headed toward the stairs, their assault rifles leading the way. Corral moved toward the top of the staircase.

"I'm not violent. This is medical marijuana," he hollered. "I've got a phone in my hand. I'm not going to resist."

Shirtless and wearing a pair of sweat pants, he started down the stairs and was hit immediately with blinding floodlights. Agents grabbed him, forced him facedown at the base of the stairs, and cuffed him. Corral saw a rifle barrel inches from his left eye—and sensed another half dozen weapons trained on him.

"Where's Valerie?" the agents demanded.

The DEA task force was being led by agent Patrick Kelly, a thirty-one-year-old former U.S. Marine Corps captain fresh from an assignment as an air marshal after the September 11, 2001, attacks on the World Trade Center and the Pentagon. On loan from the DEA, Kelly had guarded flights in and out of Washington, D.C., and the 2002 Winter Olympics in Salt Lake City from would-be international terrorists. Now he was working for Group 2—the marijuana unit—in the DEA's San Francisco office. He was soon to become California supervisor of the DEA's Domestic Cannabis Eradication/Suppression Program, charged with targeting major drug traffickers and destroying illicit gardens of sometimes tens of thousands of plants. But Kelly didn't know that he was about to carry out the smallest raid, in plant number, of his career, or that it would trigger a backlash for the DEA for destroying a garden that alleviated the suffering of severely and terminally ill people. He didn't fathom the political flak the agency would take for unknowingly sending armed agents to the bed of a polio patient or for arresting a husband/caregiver, Mike Corral, and his wife, Valerie, an accident victim whom the marijuana movement and the media would cast as the Mother Teresa of medicinal cannabis.

Years earlier, Valerie had suffered head trauma in a bizarre car crash, in which a low-flying World War II–era P-51 Mustang training in the Nevada desert for an air show caused a Volkswagen Beetle she was riding in to tumble off a highway. The 1973 accident left Valerie with often uncontrollable grand mal seizures, triggering confusion, loss of muscle control, convulsions, and fainting. Mike, who married Valerie in 1978, would sometimes notice her eyes go blank in midconversation. She would touch the right side of her injured skull. Her body would shake. He would wrap his arms around her to keep her from wildly flailing or grab her before she hit the floor. A couple of times the seizures struck when they were at a restaurant. He scooped her up and carried her out.

Valerie had been a premed student at the time of her accident, but then she became a prisoner of the seizures and the multitude of prescription medicines meant to combat them. The drugs left her feeling listless, as if she were "living under water," she would say. Mike Corral, a son of an IBM computer technician, had quit a tech job to become a nature photographer and then started reading up on marijuana. Drawn to a medical journal article on cannabis treating seizures in rats, he urged Valerie to try marijuana. In 1986, eight years after they were married, the couple moved to the wooded sanctuary north of Santa Cruz and Mike started growing a few plants on the property. Over time, pot reduced the intensity of Valerie's seizures—so much so that Mike soon took to leaving prerolled joints in every room of the house. He lit one and brought it to her mouth each time she got the "aura," that blank, fearful look signaling an attack coming on. Ultimately, marijuana succeeded in nearly quashing Valerie's seizures altogether, weaned her from prescription meds, and gave her back her life.

In 1993, local authorities raided the Corral's five-plant garden, stirring protests from marijuana advocates. Mike Corral accepted drug treatment in lieu of prosecution for pot cultivation, only to aggravate his counselors by bringing in articles on the healing benefits of marijuana. Valerie filed California's first-known medical necessity defense for marijuana. With her case set for trial, the Santa Cruz County district attorney abruptly dismissed charges against her. The same year, Mike and Valerie founded the Wo/Men's Alliance for Medical Marijuana. The Santa Cruz refuge for medicinal cultivation quickly drew in the sickest of the sick.

Area oncologists gently suggested to patients who couldn't stomach their chemotherapy that they get in touch with WAMM. The group attracted people seeking pain relief, therapy, and fellowship in the final stages of life. Valerie Corral emerged as a nurturing caregiver and a meticulous administrator for a marijuana-growing collective that parceled out its harvest, sharing the medicine at weekly Tuesday night meetings at a rented hall in downtown Santa Cruz. Up in the mountains, Mike Corral oversaw the communal garden. He directed WAMM volunteers—patients growing their own medicine—in raising seedlings in greenhouses before the first full moon in spring, putting the plants into the ground before the summer solstice, and usually harvesting by the first full moon in fall.

The crop was a few weeks from harvest on September 5, 2002, when the DEA team moved from the lower house, where Mike Corral was handcuffed, to the guest room adjoining the upper house, where they rousted a sleeping Suzanne Pfeil.

"Get up!" the officers barked.

Trained for armed and dangerous drug criminals, they didn't realize this suspect was a woman with a leg badly shriveled from childhood polio who used a motorized wheelchair or moved tepidly with leg braces and crutches.

"Get up!"

Pfeil fumbled to remove the respirator that helped her weakened lungs function while she slept. She tried to explain she couldn't rise. She gestured toward the crutches and braces at the bedside, seized by a sudden fear the agents might mistake them for weapons.

"Get up!"

The officers pulled back the covers, revealing her atrophied leg. Pfeil managed to sit up enough for them to handcuff her from behind. They left her in bed with a couple of officers standing guard.

"Stay here!" one of the departing agents said as they moved in formation back out to the deck and into the house. Pfeil, a Santa Cruz watercolor artist who used marijuana to ease pain from muscle failure and damage to her nervous system, wondered where exactly they thought she might go.

The morning raid was happening a decade after 77 percent of voters in liberal Santa Cruz County passed a local initiative endorsing the use of marijuana for medical conditions. It was nearly six years after California voters approved Proposition 215, the Compassionate Use Act for Medical Marijuana. In 1996, Californians made their state the first in America to legalize marijuana as medicine in a vote driven by sympathetic images of cancer patients quelling nausea with cannabis, and AIDS sufferers keeping themselves from wasting away by boosting their appetites with weed.

Proposition 215, allowing physicians to recommend marijuana "in the treatment of cancer, anorexia, AIDS, chronic pain, spasticity, glaucoma, arthritis, migraine or *any other illness for which marijuana provides relief,*" would eventually give birth to an unbridled medical marijuana market. By the late 2000s, purportedly nonprofit patient "collectives" sprouted wildly in California cities and counties as retail-style medical pot stores. They raked in millions of dollars in marijuana transactions with people declaring a medical need for relief from anything from restless legs syndrome to psoriasis, sleep apnea to menopause, social anxiety to diarrhea. By early 2010, the State Board of Equalization taxation agency estimated medical marijuana dispensaries—patient networks accepting "reimbursement" for the costs of cannabis cultivation—were annually producing up to $1.3 billion in over-the-counter transactions and more than $100 million in state sales taxes. A burgeoning support industry of pot doctors, hydroponics supply stores, lawyers, property managers, and public relations specialists cashed in on the boom.

And yet, in its patient-run garden in the mountains and its modest office and lounge at a downtown Santa Cruz warehouse, there was WAMM. Mike Corral liked to say the pot-growing community of some 200 to 250 patient-members at any given time lived on as a "socialist organization trying to exist in a capitalist world." It was more. Founded three years before Proposition 215, WAMM, with its members battling symptoms that were anything but benign, shared the crop based on medical need. Most members got their medicine for free. Others paid a fraction of what medical marijuana consumers doled out for designer weed brands at bustling dispensaries in California's urban centers. The Wo/Men's Alliance for Medical Marijuana, with a couple of office workers, modest salaries for Mike and Valerie, and a legion of patient volunteers, operated perpetually on the verge of insolvency.

People such as Harry Wain, a former Lockheed engineer with terminal pancreatic cancer, came to WAMM for companionship. He had never tried marijuana. After a while, he told Valerie Corral that the pot the community gave him "opened a portal to accept death, to engage the unknown." He summoned her to his bedside in his final days. "Come sit with me in the exquisiteness of this moment," he would say. "You can feel it. Exquisite. Isn't it?" Harold Allen, a tattoo-sporting construction contractor with a roaring Harley became one of WAMM's first members. He turned to Valerie as he surrendered to cancer and HIV-related illnesses. "Humor me, I'm dying," he said.

Maria Lucinda "Lucy" Garcia, a Santa Cruz hairdresser and makeup artist, endured her ovarian cancer though the company of members of WAMM. She long hid her marijuana use from her teenage daughter, unable to admit pot kept her upbeat and functional. Lucy was an animated presence in the garden. She packed lunches, relaxed by making collages out of gum wrappers, and boosted the spirits of fellow members with constant banter. When she began to lose her grasp on life, WAMM members such as Dianne Dias, a breast cancer patient and former nurse, administered morphine and puffed on joints, blowing smoke over Lucy's bed. When Lucy died, Valerie Corral dressed her in a long red gown for her funeral and did her hair and nails. Corral later adopted Lucy's daughter, Shana Conte Garcia. Over nearly eighteen years, more than 220 WAMM members succumbed to their illnesses, with others to follow. Many had their ashes scattered on the hillside above the garden, their lives and resting places commemorated by painted stones and Buddha figurines.

On the night before the DEA raid, Corral and Pfeil sat up sipping coffee and smoking joints while sharing ideas for a WAMM bedside vigil and around-the-clock support system the group would later call its Design for Dying Project. Corral's other houseguest, Alice Smith, a WAMM volunteer who didn't consume marijuana, stuck with coffee as she joined in the brainstorming. Four hours later, Valerie and Alice were awoken by the commotion in Suzanne's room. Valerie slipped out of the master bedroom, walked around a deck, and confronted the agents in the entryway.

"What are you doing in my house? Get out!"

Having just ordered Pfeil to get up, the agents told Valerie to hit the floor. She refused. Valerie sat on a bench, surrounded by hanging plants and more Buddha figures, and demanded to see the search warrant. The agents brought her facedown onto the deck. Pfeil watched from her bed as they cuffed Valerie at gunpoint. Other agents then emerged from the master bedroom, leading out Alice Smith, who was wrapped in a towel. The DEA team walked Valerie and Alice down a path to the lower house, where Mike Corral was being held. Agents loaded Pfeil into an SUV to drive her there.

It was on the walk that Valerie Corral introduced herself to Patrick Kelly. She stridently started in on the operation commander about the Wo/Men's Alliance for Medical Marijuana and its garden that soothed the dying. Kelly was half-listening. He wanted to get her to the lower house to read her her Miranda rights and to interrogate his detainees about marijuana cultivation and the illegal distribution of a prohibited narcotic. To Kelly, he was simply there to enforce Title 21 of the 1970 U.S. Controlled Substances Act. He had a crime scene to process. He was in radio contact with agents in the garden, and with others holding Mike Corral and securing the expansive mountain property.

At the lower house, after agents moved Valerie's handcuffs from behind her back to her front, she offered the officers tea. And every question they asked after Mirandizing her, she deflected by spinning the WAMM narrative. For hours, she talked so passionately about its healing mission to Kelly that the by-the-book DEA agent sensed the strangeness of getting lectured by a woman who came across as some sort of angel of cannabis, as "a true believer" in medical marijuana.

"I want you to remember me," Valerie told him. "I want you to remember what happens here, that this is a garden that brings peace into people's lives."

"I don't think I'll remember you," Kelly answered as he tried to get on with his duties.

But he would. He would also remember Mike Corral's terraced garden. Kelly had never seen anything like it. The main stems of the marijuana plants were staked down on the ground sideways with wire hooks so that the side branches grew vertically as the plants expanded horizontally. Branches extended up and out through wide-holed netting that supported the heavy limbs bursting with marijuana buds. Single plants, giant bushes more than twelve feet high, filled a hundred square feet of ground each. It would take agents with chainsaws, machetes, and loppers several hours to take them down.

Despite the passage of Proposition 215, marijuana—medical or otherwise—remained a federal crime, with the 1970 Controlled Substances Act declaring that marijuana had no accepted medical use and a high potential for abuse. In the six years after the initiative's approval, government agents raided cannabis shops serving sick patients in Oakland, Los Angeles, and West Hollywood. Marijuana-growing guru and author Ed Rosenthal spent a day in jail after agents seized plants grown for his Harm Reduction Center, a San Francisco facility serving HIV and hepatitis patients. Authorities raided the San Francisco Cannabis Buyers Club of Dennis Peron, who had coauthored California's medical marijuana initiative and championed its passage by invoking the name of his lover, Jonathan West, who had died of complications from AIDS. The cases all stirred media attention. Yet it was at the garden of the Wo/Men's Alliance for Medical Marijuana, in the presence of the living and the dead, that a federal raid would inspire unprecedented compassion and acceptance for medicinal cannabis in California.

The word got out because of Suzanne Pfeil and her hypertension that went into overdrive. As Kelly directed questioning of the detainees at the lower house, Pfeil became light-headed. Her chest was pounding.

"I'm not well," she told Valerie Corral.

Valerie checked her blood pressure. It was surging. Pfeil was sweaty and pale.

"May I leave?" Pfeil asked the DEA agents. They told her no.

"Well then, you need to call an ambulance. Because if I stroke out, it's going to be bad news."

A young agent, one of those who had stormed her bedside, looked at Pfeil with concern. She asked him to get her purse, which contained her blood pressure pills. She didn't mention that it also had a phone. Pfeil was struck by the agent's apparent compassion as he went to retrieve her bag. She felt sorry for him. When he gets home, she thought, he's going to have to tell somebody he held a gun on a cripple.

Kelly decided getting an ambulance up to the remote property was not an option. He told Alice Smith, by now dressed, she could leave to drive Pfeil to the hospital. Pfeil gulped down three blood pressure pills. Her leg braces strapped on, she rode in the passenger seat as Smith navigated the narrow, pothole-ridden road out of the forest, down the mountain, and into cell phone range. Pfeil, WAMM's vice president, had helped organize the group's emergency "phone tree," developed after the 1993 local raid on Mike and Valerie's garden. The plan was to have WAMM members immediately alert the media if they were raided and call six members each to get a crowd to the site to rally public support.

Her blood pressure medication kicking in, Pfeil started dialing. She called WAMM's lawyers, Santa Cruz attorney Ben Rice and Santa Clara University School of Law professor Gerald Uelemen. She called television stations in San Francisco and Santa Cruz. She called Americans for Safe Access, an Oakland-based advocacy group for medical marijuana patients. She called Dale Gieringer, the California director of the National Organization for the Reform of Marijuana Laws and one of the architects of Proposition 215.

"This is an outrage," Gieringer thundered. "This time, they've gone too far. This means war!"

Pfeil then summoned Harold "Hal" Margolin, a seventy-year-old Korean War veteran and a former Santa Cruz clothing manufacturer, to start the WAMM phone tree. "Oh my God, Hal, the DEA is raiding the place!" she told him. They met him at WAMM's offices in downtown Santa Cruz to get out the next round of media calls. Pfeil never made it to the hospital. "She took advantage of my good nature," Kelly would reflect, dryly, years later, on her role in alerting the outside world. "Imagine that."

With the raid under way, Hal Margolin drove up to the mountain property, hoping his presence there could somehow save WAMM as it had saved him. Margolin had been a WAMM member for nearly a decade—since a disastrous spinal surgery left him in such pain that friends told him to seek out the local medical marijuana group. He was dubious about joining. He didn't want to be involved with "a bunch of potheads." But he went to a WAMM meeting. He then showed up for a second one. Just as he was entering the room, he collapsed from a heart attack. Members caught him before he hit the ground. They put him in a chair, bathed his face with moist towels, and got him to the hospital.

The bespectacled man with a thin white beard was the only member to reach the garden. He saw agents grinding away at the plants with chainsaws. Two armed officers sternly waved Margolin back, ordering him to retreat down the mountains. They glared at him, Margolin thought, as if they were looking at the enemy. Margolin, known around the WAMM commune for his eloquent storytelling, for his ever-wise counsel, began to cry. Years later, in intensive care after a second heart attack, a broken hip, and late-stage leukemia, Margolin recalled that the agents "came with a heavy hand to show us that we were not going to be able to do this. They were teaching us a lesson." But the pot patients were to deliver one of their own.

Margolin dropped back to the edge of the property as dozens of WAMM members and scores of supporters swarmed to the heavy metal gate at the entrance. That's when somebody got an idea: they closed the gate and padlocked it, locking the federal agents' vehicles inside.

By then, the Associated Press and most every major regional newspaper and news station was on the story. Some WAMM members smoked joints, or sobbed, at the gate as supporters directed a torrent of shouts at officers near the entrance. Before television cameras and a press gathering that would turn the raid on the Santa Cruz medical marijuana patients into a national story for days afterward, they refused to allow the government convoy—and its U-Haul of seized pot—to leave. They demanded word on the fate of Mike and Valerie Corral.

Agents on-site told crowd members the couple was still on the property. But Mike and Valerie had already been transported to a federal detention facility in San Jose for arrest and processing.

At the garden, with the remaining DEA vehicles lined up in a convoy preparing to leave, Kelly got word of the clamor at the gate. The task force commander was worried. The last thing he wanted was a confrontation, with people jumping the fence and his agents having to respond. Kelly contacted the Santa Cruz County Sheriff's Department, which hadn't been notified about the raid. "We need some marked units up here," Kelly said, asking the sheriff to clear the crowd from the road. Sheriff Mark Tracy, who had long been a public supporter of WAMM, sent deputies to the entrance. But neither the sheriff nor his officers were eager to add to the media spectacle by dispersing angry pot patients. Instead, sheriff's officers became a conduit for tense negotiations to end the standoff.

At the San Jose Federal Building, Mike and Valerie were placed in side-by-side walled cells. Mike tapped on the partition to let her know he was okay. She tapped back, signaling she was there. They communicated updates that way as they were alternately brought in and out, photographed, fingerprinted, and booked. Eventually, they heard a rustle of activity outside. Agents came in, removed both from their cells and brought them into an office.

"We've got a problem," one of the DEA officers said. "There are a hundred people at the gate. They've got the exits blocked and we can't leave."

Mike Corral started to laugh.

The agents asked them to tell the crowd to stand down.

"No, take us there and we'll diffuse the situation," Mike said. He was feeling angry now. He wanted to go back, get in the face of the officers who had brought on this raid, put rifles to his head, and upset so many people. But that wasn't going to happen. The DEA didn't want to bring Mike and Val to the crowd.

At the gate, Danny Rodrigues, a San Francisco barkeep who had lived with AIDS for nearly three decades, who had survived quadruple-bypass heart surgery, let it be known to sheriff's deputies that neither he nor the crowd would be going anywhere until Mike and Valerie were free. A sheriff's officer relayed word to the DEA. Valerie refused agents' requests to tell Danny to unlock the gate.

By then, the agents in San Jose had processed the couple. They knew they weren't going to hold them. "We're going to let you go," they announced.

"So is this like a hostage exchange?" responded Mike Corral.

"Yeah," one of the agents said with an anxious laugh. "Please calm things down."

Valerie agreed to speak with Danny Rodrigues, who had been furnished with a phone by the sheriff's department. She asked him if the media was there. She could hear people shouting in the background and feel their anger. She feared a confrontation could backfire on WAMM, could diminish public outrage over the federal raid and move the eyes of the media "away from something that was unjust."

"Danny, tell people to calm down," she said. "Tell everyone to let them pass—and don't be rude."

Rodrigues and another WAMM member took a pair of bolt cutters and cut the chain to the locked gate. At the garden, Kelly got word by radio that the DEA caravan could leave.

"Please let them go," Rodrigues directed the crowd, his voice raw. "Don't do anything that would create violence in any manner."

The DEA vehicles swooped down the mountains, through the gate, and past the jeering crowd. For the moment, it was over.

Twelve days after the raid, with the marijuana crop hacked down and hauled off, WAMM members and supporters massed outside Santa Cruz City Hall, openly smoking pot and distributing a stored stash of medicine the feds had missed. Before still more television cameras, a procession of sick people, including patients in wheelchairs, passed a table, picking up marijuana muffins and cannabis tinctures. One by one, they spoke out, declaring, "I am not a criminal." Dr. Arnold Leff, a Santa Cruz physician with a beard smothered by his walruslike mustache, took to the microphone. Leff was a former associate director of the White House Office of Drug Abuse Prevention under President Richard Nixon. He had been treating patients suffering from AIDS and HIV since 1985. Dozens of his patients found their way to WAMM. Leff became a mainstay at the organization's downtown office, treating and counseling the sick until their photos joined the vast wall of tributes honoring the dead. Leff never visited the WAMM garden. He feared that even venturing near it might cause the DEA to come after his medical license. But he stood at city hall, where he angrily spoke to the cameras and publicly decried "an outrageous example of a government without compassion."

Days later, Valerie and Mike Corral came to the steps of the California capitol building in Sacramento. Valerie looked out over a throng of supporters, welcoming them "to the center of the cyclone" and to a space of reflection on a militaristic raid on sick people cultivating marijuana. "I also want to welcome the DEA agents who may be here," she said. "I want to welcome the agents behind the masks, the wardens of injustice who carry the guns that point at our heads, who cuff the ill, who steal our medicine. . . . I hope they feel what we feel. I hope they have seen what we have seen, because you can't be brought to experience the truth without having it touch you, without having it change who you are."

California's top law enforcement officer, state attorney general Bill Lockyer, demanded an explanation for the federal raid. In Washington, D.C., DEA administrator Asa Hutchinson answered that the agency had appropriately enforced U.S. law against illegal marijuana cultivation and distribution. "The DEA's responsibility is to enforce our controlled substances laws, and one of them is marijuana. Someone could stand up and say one of those marijuana plants is designed for someone who is sick, but under federal law, there's no distinction," Hutchinson said. But it was a PR disaster. No criminal charges were filed.

WAMM sued federal authorities over the raid. Hal Margolin signed up as one of the plaintiffs. "By God, I had to do it," he said. The city and county of Santa Cruz joined in the lawsuit. "The DEA was out of its mind. We had wars going on and violent crime and they were raiding people in pain," declared state senator John Vasconcellos.

Months after the raid, Vasconcellos opened hearings at the capitol to draft a new California law setting rules for the distribution of marijuana for medical purposes. Senate Bill 420—given the numeric nickname for pot—allowed patient-run "collectives" to collect money to cover costs of cultivating and distributing medical marijuana to members. Valerie and Mike Corral testified at the hearings. They thought the legislation, referred to after its passage as the Medical Marijuana Program Act, would help protect patient groups such as WAMM in cultivating marijuana and sharing the medicine. They were naive in thinking that's what the bill would lead to. With the feds easing off, leery of another misstep, many medical marijuana providers—and speculators—saw Senate Bill 420 as safe cover to accelerate a legal cannabis market.

In 2004, U.S. District judge Jeremy Fogel issued an injunction barring future federal incursions on the WAMM site. For more than a year while the order was in effect, WAMM effectively operated America's only federally permitted medical marijuana garden. When the order was rescinded in 2005, protesting WAMM members marched or pushed forth in wheelchairs, carrying marijuana plants in a loop along Santa Cruz's Pacific Avenue to city hall. As the legal fight continued, their mountain garden lay barren for years. Members grew at home or on small plots, still sharing the medicine at the Tuesday meetings. Then, on October, 19, 2009, in the midst of final negotiations to settle the WAMM lawsuit, Attorney General Eric Holder released a statement. He famously declared, "It will not be a priority to use federal resources to prosecute patients with serious illnesses or their caregivers who are complying with state laws on medical marijuana."

Holder's message was underscored in a memo the same day by Deputy Attorney General David W. Ogden. The Ogden memo declared the government would go after "illegal drug manufacturing and trafficking" and "commercial enterprises that unlawfully market and sell marijuana for profit"—but not "individuals with cancer or other serious illnesses ... or those caregivers in clear and unambiguous compliance with existing state law." The Justice Department contended that the memo's assurances made moot WAMM's lawsuit against the DEA and the government. In January 2010, the Ogden memo was attached to the settlement in the case—in which WAMM reserved its right to refile its suit if it were ever targeted again.

The Ogden memo, which made no mention of "dispensaries" or "marijuana stores," was widely greeted as a green light for state-permitted medical cannabis commerce. It accelerated the pace of cash registers ringing up transactions in a wild California marijuana market thriving in the name of nonprofit compassion. Senate Bill 420, drafted with rules as hazy as pot smoke, enabled an explosion of medical marijuana stores, staffed by well-compensated "bud tenders" and dispensary operators. In Los Angeles, a sudden glut of hundreds of new pot shops advertised special patient "donation" rates for exotically named pot strains—such as Blue Dream or Mango OG or Granddaddy Purple—bred for maximum psychoactive and pleasurable effects. As many as fifteen thousand Californians went to work in an industry that served medical marijuana users with ailments far less profound than the poignant challenges found at WAMM. In the woods of Humboldt and Mendocino Counties on California's northern coast, long-illicit marijuana growers sought legitimacy as medical cultivators and competed for a share of the legal market. A depressed urban district in Oakland flowered anew as an entrepreneurial medical marijuana center and as the heart of a celebrated political push for cannabis legalization beyond medical use. Proud Oakland officials anointed their city as the Silicon Valley of weed.

As California greeted a migration of people drawn by the Golden State's medical marijuana acceptance, developments there would create a ripple effect across America, stoking both pot liberalization and cannabis commerce in other states. Medical researchers from the University of California system conducted landmark clinical studies into the medical efficacy of marijuana, revealing benefits extending well beyond symptom relief for AIDS or cancer. Defendants in medical marijuana cases, following the WAMM media model, wove sympathetic narratives to influence legal rulings and affect the politics of pot. Ultimately, a boundless medical marijuana marketplace, with opportunistic pot doctors doling out recommendations for conditions severe or benign, fueled the cannabis green rush. The market blurred the distinction between medical marijuana and marijuana destined for recreational use. It pitched medicinal healing with the pure joy of pot. It offered soothing with seduction. A law enforcement backlash percolated. New federal challenges loomed.

Just before the eighth anniversary of the DEA raid, Valerie Corral appeared on a speaker's platform inside a circus tent behind the San Jose

Convention Center. At a massive medical cannabis trade show called HempCon, she talked about the emotional power of the Wo/Men's Alliance for Medical Marijuana, of honoring its dead, of enduring the federal raid and waging a legal battle with the DEA. Few people filled the chairs before her to listen. At a nearby booth for a stoner magazine, *Skunk,* bosomy spokesmodels—"Mary" and "Jane"—signed autographs and posed for pictures. Elsewhere, pot doctors and physician assistants greeted throngs of "patients," charging trade-show rates of fifty dollars and up for people who filled out brief questionnaires to get medical marijuana recommendations allowing them to legally use or cultivate cannabis. At a Proposition 215 patients-only sampling area, booths for retail-style marijuana dispensaries trotted out their best medicines. A line of fit-looking young people awaited admission, resembling tourists boarding a Napa Valley wine train. "I thought the WAMM consciousness would take off," Valerie Corral told her small audience. "It didn't. The dispensaries did."

Despite its transformative power for the marijuana movement, the WAMM consciousness had been rendered quaint, and obsolete, by California's fast-evolving medical marijuana industry. WAMM, and its sick and dying, engendered enduring political and social support for the use of medical cannabis. Now others reaped unanticipated rewards.

TWO

Oaksterdam

Richard Lee once found his liberation blasting down Texas highways into a roaring wind. He would brake his Suzuki Katana rice rocket to a stop at a rural airport in Pearland and, from there, unshackle himself from the limitations of earth. He climbed into his ultralight airplane. Soaring skyward over the piney woods and farmlands, snaking along the gulf shores of Galveston, he would smile at the buzzards circling and dive-bombing overhead. He would zoom beside the turkey hawks, his aerial companions, flying free.

The son of Bob and Ann Lee, Goldwater Republicans from suburban Houston who were regulars at GOP events, Richard Lee studied public relations, politics, and communications at the University of Houston. Less than a semester away from graduation, he dropped out, rejecting convention for adventure. A wiry, athletic man who could climb anything, Lee signed on as a roadie and "truss monkey" for concert-stage-lighting companies. He traveled the country, scaling scaffolding 50 to 150 feet high and navigating moving truss systems to illuminate venues for Aerosmith, Dwight Yoakum, LL Cool J, and Public Enemy. "It was like running away and joining the circus," he recalled. "It was *the life*."

But in a New Jersey warehouse, while working on lighting fixtures for an Aerosmith show, Lee's agility failed him. He was on a catwalk just fifteen feet high when he tumbled and crashed onto the concrete floor, landing on his back. His lower spine was crushed against his tool pouch. He was conscious. Lee figured he could gather himself, shake off the embarrassment of his fluke fall, and walk away. And then he couldn't. His spinal cord was irreparably damaged. From his waist down, nothing moved.

The man who lived for the freedom of the road, for the sensation of flight, for breathing deep in the sky, found himself on a path of pain and despair.

He journeyed along a darker road—"the suicide highway," Lee called it. He confided to his father he would kill himself if he ever found the nerve. He never did. Instead, he found escape, and relief, in marijuana. Lee read up on the medicinal effects of pot as he sought help for his pain, muscle spasms, and inability to sleep. Eventually he moved into a two-bedroom Houston cottage retrofitted with a wheelchair ramp. He converted a room to growing marijuana. His parents struggled to accept that their son was cultivating a plant they considered demon weed. "We grew up in a time when drugs were bad. We knew nothing about marijuana," Bob Lee recalled. Their views changed when they saw him regain his will to live and—from a wheelchair—recapture his free spirit.

In 1992, Lee opened a hemp clothing store in a wood-frame house in Houston's eclectic Montrose district. With a sense of whimsy, he called the place Legal Marijuana—the Hemp Store. It was a year before Mike and Valerie Corral founded the Wo/Men's Alliance for Medical Marijuana in Santa Cruz and several years after the AIDS crisis in San Francisco and a pot-dealing Vietnam veteran named Dennis Peron fueled the modern medical marijuana movement in California. By the quirk of a fateful fall, Richard Lee was destined for this cannabis revolution and the marijuana migration out west. Still, it all seemed distant from Texas, where at his Montrose hemp store Lee cheerfully answered the phone with the words "Legal Marijuana!" and parked a van emblazoned with the phrase outside the store, teasing police.

The cops checked him out and moved on. They later moved on a second time, abandoning him in an infuriating way when he needed help. Lee and a friend were carjacked outside a fast-food restaurant, forced out of their vehicle with pistols at their heads. He was left sprawled on the ground without his wheelchair. Police took fifty minutes to arrive and take a report. Then they told Lee to find his own way home.

Lee later recast the story with a political message. The cops weren't there for him because they were too busy busting potheads and waging a fruitless war on drugs instead of serving citizens and hunting down dangerous predators. The upstart hemp products salesman began wheeling into trade shows and delivering speeches about the history of hemp and marijuana and the failures of prohibition. He was uplifted by how audiences tuned into his message. "People said, 'Yeah, this guy isn't just a stoner after all,'" he mused. His hemp store became a local nerve center for marijuana activism. He recruited customers to turn out at political events, including a rally by the

National Organization for the Reform of Marijuana Laws outside the Houston office of the Drug Enforcement Administration. While Lee supported fully legalizing marijuana for adult use regardless of medical need, the NORML rally slammed the government for ignoring the medicinal benefits of cannabis and refusing to reclassify the drug to allow its legal use by sick people.

As he publicly railed about the reefer madness of the cops and the government, the owner of Legal Marijuana went into the illegal marijuana business. At a Houston warehouse down the street from a hydroponics store where Lee used to buy lighting and growing supplies for his home garden, he converted a rented space to grow marijuana for sale. Taking cues from the NORML event, Lee cast his pot-dealing in the rhetoric of curative cannabis. He discreetly put the word out to customers at Legal Marijuana that if they showed him some medical record of ruptured discs or illnesses or nausea, he could fix them up with what they needed. For a couple of years he earned more than enough selling weed to keep the hemp store—and its political activism—afloat and pay for trips to Amsterdam, where he bought exotic cannabis seeds and sneaked them back to Texas in his luggage.

Only occasionally did Lee stop and wonder about the risks he was taking. Cops once went to his house after a frustrated burglar, thwarted in an attempt to break in and steal his marijuana plants, called police to say a dope dealer lived there. Despite the potent smell of cannabis, the officers who came to the house didn't deem it worth their time to go inside. Another time, Lee and a companion accidentally cut open a pipe while installing a hose bib for his warehouse cultivation room. They raced to a twenty-four-hour Kmart to buy a welding kit to fix the pipe to avoid flooding the place and bursting the dam on his illicit pot operation. Lee came to realize he had a new kind of death wish. He missed the thrill of a racing motorcycle, of swooping ultralight flights, of dangling from the scaffolding at rock concerts. The danger of getting caught and thrown into prison as a drug dealer was his elixir now. "This was my suicide mission," he concluded. "Every year, I was trying to get busted."

In mid-1993, Lee went to Denver for a marijuana legalization rally. He was passing out cannabis literature and leaflets for his Legal Marijuana store when a lanky young man from South Dakota, Jeff Jones, stopped by and struck up a brief conversation with the guy in the wheelchair. "Here, take this!" Lee said brusquely, handing Jones a copy of the *Hemp Times,* which the South Dakota man later read cover to cover.

The two men parted ways, unaware they would meet again and join in a historic partnership for the California marijuana movement in a city that would become a beacon for people drawn to the cannabis crusade.

. . .

Jeff Jones, ever polite and conservative in appearance, seemed to fit in with neither a marijuana rally nor any activist crusade. But like Lee, he had had a life-changing journey. He lost his father, Wayne Jones, to cancer at the age of fourteen. He was at his side as his father, the owner of a Rapid City, South Dakota, bus company, writhed and retched from chemotherapy, unable to keep down the food his son tried to spoon-feed him. Wayne Jones never tried marijuana for his stomach sickness as he shrank from 200 pounds to 125. He found religion before he passed away. Jeff Jones became the man of the house as a teen, and he later turned to cannabis as therapy for his grief and as a gateway to reflection. He went on to read about Mary Jane Rathbun, the hospital volunteer known as "Brownie Mary" who doled out pot brownies to AIDS and cancer patients in San Francisco. He found inspiration in Dennis Peron, who—after his lover was beaten in a police raid—pushed a successful 1991 local ballot measure urging California to legalize marijuana.

As Peron started providing pot to AIDS sufferers from his apartment in San Francisco's Castro district, Jones was becoming a cannabis scholar in Rapid City. He read a September 6, 1988, ruling by the Drug Enforcement Administration's chief administrative law judge, Francis L. Young, who declared marijuana didn't meet the criteria for designation as a federally classified Schedule I drug with no accepted medical use. Young's determination that natural cannabis was "one of the safest therapeutically active substances known to man"—a finding later rejected by the DEA administrator—stoked Jones's fury. He thought about his father's ugly death from cancer. "It pissed me off," he said. "I felt a really deep-rooted anger."

In 1993, South Dakota's Democratic U.S. senator Tom Daschle came to speak at the University of South Dakota, where Jones was studying life sciences and biology. The young man from Rapid City, who was rejected by his high school debate team because his voice was too quiet, loudly challenged Daschle to explain why the United States banned cultivation of nonpsychoactive cannabis plants used in hemp products. "Because it's marijuana," the senator said, turning away. "You're not answering my question," Jones barked. Daschle faced him, answering more directly: "It's because it's being held back by people who don't like marijuana." That only pushed Jones harder in a direction he knew he was headed.

Jones had been in touch with a marijuana legalization group in California called the Cannabis Action Network, and now he followed up. He got a promise of temporary housing in the San Francisco Bay Area, where he entered a cultural realm far different from Rapid City's. He strolled the abundant head and hemp shops of Haight-Ashbury, and he passed out medicinal brownies on Berkeley's Telegraph Avenue. After Peron founded a marijuana dispensary, the San Francisco Cannabis Buyers Club, and began leading the 1996 campaign to pass the Proposition 215 initiative, Jones opened the Oakland Cannabis Buyers Cooperative amid shuttered storefronts on Broadway in downtown Oakland. Jones didn't have a car, so he began delivering pot by bicycle to customers with medical conditions. He bought most of his weed on the street, but urged medical pot users to grow their own and sell any excess back to the Buyers Cooperative.

The modest Oakland cannabis outlet, operating out of a third-floor office, was a stark contrast to Peron's flourishing San Francisco dispensary, a must-see pot emporium that offered three pot bars in a five-story building on Market Street. Peron called it his "five-story felony." Peron's marijuana model was too flamboyant for the man from Rapid City, and after the two men met, Peron sized up the young Jones as too clean-cut and too much of a conformist for marijuana activism. But Jones sought a different appeal. He wanted to create a medical cannabis club "that could be outsourced to Kansas." Hardly a bustling bonanza of bongs and buds, the Oakland Cannabis Buyers Cooperative seemed more like a walk-in hospice. Jones's top financial officer, Jim McClellan, had AIDS and would die of the disease in 2001. Sixty percent of the dispensary's patients were HIV-positive. Ten percent had cancer. Jones felt as if he kept seeing his father coming in the door.

From Houston, Lee watched the unfolding events in California with fascination. Turning pot growing into a personal art as he used his seeds from Amsterdam to produce exotic strains of *Cannabis sativa, Cannabis indica*, and hybrids of the two marijuana plant species, Lee yearned for the action of America's frontline challenge to the federal war on drugs. He envisioned himself becoming a premiere cannabis grower for Peron. But it was the understated Jones who got to him first.

In 1997, months after California voters approved Proposition 215 and the Compassionate Use Act legalizing marijuana for medical use, Richard Lee landed in the Bay Area and checked in at an Oakland hotel. Mutual acquaintances called Jeff Jones. They told him there was a guy in town who grew some monster stuff. Jones went to Lee's hotel. He would realize only later that the visitor was the man he'd met in Denver. Lee shared a small stash of his Shiva Skunk, a pungent pot strain bred from *Cannabis indica* plants. "We were blown away by the quality and by his enthusiasm," Jones said. Soon they were going through his prized collection of seeds and plotting their shared future.

Lee settled in a live/work space in an Oakland warehouse and started growing for the Oakland Cannabis Buyers Cooperative. His Shiva Skunk was quickly dubbed the "house special." It became so popular that Jones put a limit on how much people could buy. Lee loved telling people about strains he'd perfected. "I ought to be teaching this stuff," he said, as he chided Jones and other Cannabis Buyers Cooperative workers for their lack of precision in trimming leaves from marijuana buds. Jones saw Lee as a leader and an advocate, "outspoken to the point where it scared me." He kept his star grower under wraps, figuring the last thing the cannabis cooperative needed was for cops or criminals to find out about Lee's new Oakland horticulture haven.

By 1998, the Oakland Cannabis Buyers Cooperative was providing marijuana to twenty-two hundred registered medical users and drawing the attention of California's attorney general and Republican gubernatorial candidate Dan Lungren. The state attorney general was not a fan of Proposition 215 and especially not of clubs distributing cannabis. Lungren had shut down Peron's San Francisco Cannabis Buyers Club months before the initiative's 1996 passage, and his continued threats against medical pot distributors helped prompt the closure of another San Francisco establishment, CHAMPS (Cannabis Helping Alleviate Medical Problems), on January 1, 1998. Lungren also indicated that he had no problem working with federal drug agents who were targeting medical marijuana. Agitated by the attorney general's actions, Jeff Jones called Lungren's senior assistant attorney general, John Gordnier. He told him Lungren was wasting his time because the Oakland Cannabis Buyers Cooperative wasn't closing.

On January 9, 1998, Jones and an Oakland City Council member, Nate Miley, scheduled a noon press conference to blast the misplaced priorities of the state attorney general. They had a sound bite ready: "If Dan Lungren wants to fight real crime in Oakland, he needs to come to East Oakland and fight crime in the streets." But the event was preempted. That morning, United States marshals served Jones with a civil summons. The U.S. government sued the Oakland Cannabis Buyers Cooperative, charging that its cultivation and dispensing of marijuana violated federal law.

The city of Oakland boldly took up Jones's cause. The city council declared a public health emergency entailing "thousands of seriously ill persons" who "endure great pain and suffering and . . . may die as a result of the closure of the cooperative." It voted to establish a City of Oakland marijuana distribution program and designate the Oakland Cannabis Buyers Cooperative as the city's agent in administering the program. Oakland thus became the first city in America to declare distributing cannabis for medical use as an official function. Undeterred, U.S. district judge Charles Breyer authorized federal marshals to shut down the cannabis cooperative in October 1998. Jones voluntarily closed it while filing legal appeals asserting it had a protected right to dispense marijuana. The city submitted a friend-of-the-court brief to the U.S. Ninth Circuit Court of Appeals, arguing that the federal actions violated "the city's independent duty to protect the health and safety of its citizens."

Jones then opened the Patient I.D. Center under a contract with the city and, later, with the State of California. In a store where he also sold marijuana vaporizers, bongs, pot literature, and hemp products, Jones handled paperwork to enable people with physicians' recommendations to get state-approved medical marijuana patient identification cards backed up by a computerized verification system. The I.D. Center eventually processed twenty thousand applications a year for pot cards, effectively making California's medical marijuana law a functioning human reality. Jones began taking calls from cops who were busting people with weed. He helped many avoid arrest by verifying that their purchases were legal under state law, though often only after officers ripped out their marijuana plants or destroyed their medicine.

For Jones, the success of the Patient I.D. Center offered him some sense of triumph as he brought to court a landmark medical marijuana case he knew he wasn't destined to win. In 1999, Jones's lawyer, Robert Raich, excitedly called to tell him the U.S. Ninth Circuit Court of Appeals had just sided with the Oakland Cannabis Buyers Cooperative by upholding the medical necessity of marijuana for many patients. "The OCBC presented evidence that there is a class of people with serious medical conditions for whom the use of cannabis is necessary in order to treat or alleviate those conditions or their symptoms," the Ninth Circuit Court ruled, concluding, "The government, by contrast, has yet to identify any interest it may have in blocking the distribution of cannabis to those with medical needs."

The medical marijuana community celebrated. Jones fretted. He peppered Raich over the legal foundations. He didn't think the ruling provided the sweeping states' rights declaration that might stand before the U.S. Supreme Court. He was right. In 2001, in *United States v. Oakland Cannabis Buyers Cooperative and Jeffrey Jones,* Justice Clarence Thomas wrote the majority decision upholding the authority of Congress's 1970 Controlled Substances Act. Noting that the act declared marijuana "has no currently accepted medical use" and "a high potential for abuse," Thomas wrote that the Ninth Circuit Court was wrong in "considering relevant the evidence that some people have 'serious medical conditions for whom the use of cannabis is necessary.'" The nation's highest court concluded, "Medical necessity is not a defense to manufacturing and distributing marijuana."

The politics and culture of Oakland issued a decidedly different ruling. In 2004, Oakland voters overwhelmingly approved Measure Z, ordering police to assign marijuana, including "private adult cannabis offenses" of "distribution, sale, cultivation and possession," as "the City's lowest law enforcement priority." The city blossomed with "Measure Z clubs," where people openly smoked and shared cannabis. The local ordinance also directed city staff to regulate a legal medical marijuana industry. Seemingly emboldened by the unsuccessful U.S. Supreme Court challenge, Oakland set out to push both the state and the national envelope when it came to marijuana. The city embraced its role as an activist center for access to medical marijuana—and as the cradle for its commercialization. It became a destination for aspiring protagonists in the marijuana movement.

Lee went on to open an Oakland medical marijuana dispensary he named SR-71 after a Lockheed Corporation reconnaissance plane. He dubbed it the highest-flying coffee shop. He sold one-dollar cups of coffee and nonmedicinal pastries in a café out front and, in a small booth in back, charged forty dollars for an eighth of an ounce of premium California cannabis. Lockheed didn't see the humor in Lee using the name of its prized plane to sell pot. It ordered him to quit. Lee renamed the place Coffee Shop Blue Sky. Later, in forming a one-man corporation for an expanding medical marijuana network, the aviation buff lampooned the defense contractor again. He called it S. K. Seymour, parodying Lockheed's research and development mascot, Seymour Skunk.

Lee's enterprises expanded to include a marijuana nursery, a media company he dubbed O.D. Media, and a second coffee shop, the Bulldog, which stopped dispensing marijuana in 2004 but for many years maintained a popular Measure Z smoking room fragrant with cannabis scents. By 2010, his Oakland network employed sixty people and generated $5 million in annual revenues, with Lee taking fifty thousand dollars in annual salary. His centerpiece came in 2007. Inspired by a marijuana school he visited in Amsterdam, Lee, the man who had stopped just short of finishing his degree at the University of Houston, became the founder and president of Oaksterdam University. Oaksterdam's green CAN-NA-BIS crest parodied the crimson VE-RI-TAS seal of Harvard. And his school-of-pot offered a true higher education: courses in marijuana law, business, advocacy, cultivation, and production, from cannabis cooking to hash making. Oaksterdam trained fifteen thousand budding scholars to take advantage of opportunities in a legal marijuana industry and, for a time, ran satellite campuses in Los Angeles, Sebastopol (north of San Francisco) and Flint, Michigan. Lee, the university president, savored his role as a "horticulture professor" and lecturer on "cannabis in society."

"There is the reality and there is the law," he told students. "The two are miles apart. Only history will tell which will catch up with which. If I bet on it, I think the law will catch up with reality." He would soon place a major wager that he was right.

Lee's coffeehouses, modeled after cozy marijuana shops in Amsterdam, and his school of weed transformed Oakland's depressed Broadway street and nearby avenues with a Bohemian gentrification. Nearly everyone in the district came to know the cannabis entrepreneur in the wheelchair. Lee resurrected the music career of aging Oakland jazz musician and medical pot patient Vince Wallace, setting him up with regular music gigs at his establishments. He befriended retired Oakland A's hero Mike Norris, donating money to the urban baseball academy of the former pitcher who battled drug addiction and was partially crippled from surgeries for injuries in his playing days. Oaksterdam University helped fund the restoration of the 1927 downtown Fox Theater. And visitors descending on downtown to attend Lee's classes or buy his school-of-pot clothing and souvenirs invigorated the area widely known as Oaksterdam. There, Lee was ever-present. He scooted between his school and businesses, propelling his wheelchair forward with his hands in signature fingerless gloves, stopping frequently to talk to tourists or merchants or pluck litter off the sidewalks. He earned his moniker: the Mayor of Oaksterdam.

· · ·

When it came to dispensing marijuana, there was soon no bigger player in Oakland than Steve DeAngelo. While Lee's pot establishments offered intimacy and funkiness, DeAngelo created a decidedly different model—professional, high-volume holistic weed care. Five years after arriving from Washington, D.C., in 2001, DeAngelo, ever dapper in his signature fedoras, hipster haberdashery, and long pigtails, became the founding executive director of Harborside Health Center. He was the media and marketing face for what he billed as the world's largest medical marijuana dispensary. DeAngelo saw the medicinal marijuana industry on a grand scale. He embraced a nomenclature that defined medical marijuana as more than a remedy for nausea from cancer or for severe chronic pain. He saw it, and promoted it, as a "wellness" drug for daily living.

DeAngelo rejected one city-sanctioned location for a marijuana dispensary—a twenty-foot-by-eighty-foot former massage parlor—for an audacious alternative, a seven-thousand-square-foot warehouse outside of downtown, between the Interstate 880 freeway and Oakland's industrialized waterfront. He constructed windows and a natural-light waiting room in the drab-olive building, added ferns and broadleaf plants, and stationed trained, patient-friendly attendants along expansive dispensary counters between a pastel blue backdrop and the glistening glass cases offering vast, exquisite selections of cannabis.

In addition to more than five dozen designer marijuana strains, Harborside offered medicinal elixirs, creams, lotions, and baked edibles—chewy chocolate cannabis creations topped with hash frostings. Harborside, marketing its dispensary as a nonprofit wellness center, also had a naturopathic primary care doctor, an acupuncturist, a chiropractor, and life coaches offering sessions in yoga, stress management, and "universal life force energy." By 2010, Harborside had amassed a clientele of more than fifty thousand registered medical marijuana patients. It greeted more than eight hundred medical marijuana consumers a day, annually handling more than $20 million in pot transactions and paying more than $2.3 million in state sales taxes and city dispensary fees. By 2012, having opened a second dispensary in San Jose, Harborside would attract more than a hundred thousand people to sign up as members, receive patient services, and purchase its herbal medicine.

In 2008, Harborside partnered with an Oakland laboratory, Steep Hill Lab, for what it called California's first product-safety protocol for marijuana. Steep Hill tested cannabis samples to weed out batches tainted by molds or pesticides. Lab tests for potency also enabled Harborside to label its cannabis with results for tetrahydrocannabinol (THC), the psychoactive substance in marijuana. Harborside's popular Mango OG, one of its highest-potency strains, packed a medicinal mindful ranging from 14 percent THC to 22 percent. Its OG Kush products ranged from a moderate 8 percent THC to a mighty 24 percent. And DeAngelo's medical-marijuana patient cultivators also grew an OG Kush/True Blueberry hybrid cannabis strain that bred out the THC in favor of another cannabis constituent—cannabidiol, or CBD. The CBD strains offered analgesic, less euphoric properties, stirring a niche market for pot that promised relief without getting you stoned. With the panache of a pharmaceutical rep, DeAngelo hit the road to national cannabis conferences. He touted "wellness, not intoxication" as he helped bring medical marijuana to the masses.

DeAngelo, who graduated summa cum laude in American studies from the University of Maryland and enrolled for a time in law school, had started out as an old-school advocate for marijuana. Many years before emerging as the new-generation medicinal cannabis executive, he had joined the movement as a Youth International Party devotee who, in the 1970s, chained himself to the White House fence in Fourth of July smoke-ins demanding marijuana liberation. He went on to operate a Washington, D.C., hangout—called the Beat Club—in a three-story townhouse that included a music and dance club, an Ethiopian restaurant, and a rooftop garden where pot smoking was encouraged. He later rented a ten-bedroom party house—dubbed "the nuthouse"—that became a party haven for pot activists and cannabis-savoring intellectuals. One day, DeAngelo welcomed a happily wild-eyed man named Jack Herer, a San Fernando Valley head-shop owner who hyped legal pot on Los Angeles' Venice Beach boardwalk and pushed grassroots marijuana initiatives in California. Herer waved a tattered copy of his book—*The Emperor Wears No Clothes*—which would become a manifesto for the marijuana movement. It extolled America's long history of using cannabis plants to produce hemp fabrics, plastics, foods, and fuel while alleging a conspiracy by the likes of William Randolph Hearst and DuPont Chemical behind hemp and marijuana prohibition that effectively began with passage of the onerous Marijuana Stamp Act in 1937. The two men sat down and sparked up a joint. DeAngelo read the material. He turned to Herer. "This changes everything," he said. "They have to make it legal."

DeAngelo joined Herer on a national hemp tour. He produced two records—*Hempilation 1* and *Hempilation 2*—that compiled procannabis songs by performers such as Dr. Dre, the Black Crows, and Cypress Hill to promote hemp and legal marijuana. From 1990 to 2000, he ran an import company, Ecolution, that sold products—from blue jeans to cosmetics—

manufactured from hemp legally grown overseas. In 1998, DeAngelo supported the campaign for Initiative 59, a Washington, D.C., measure that won overwhelming voter support to legalize medical marijuana in the nation's capital. Congress barred the district from implementing the results under an amendment by Congressman Bob Barr to a 1999 appropriations bill. Betrayed in the nation's capital, DeAngelo answered the cannabis call of California.

He founded Harborside with Dave Wedding Dress, a San Francisco Bay Area peace activist who legally changed his name to match the flowing white gowns he wore at antinuclear protests. The man known around Harborside as "Dress" served as the dispensary's "holistic care director." And while Harborside cast itself in corporate clothes as an HMO for cannabis, DeAngelo and Dress instilled an activist creed. Harborside rewarded patients who volunteered for marijuana advocacy work with free samples of weed—up to a gram a week. Its medical marijuana consumers wrote letters of support to "prisoners of war"—inmates incarcerated for pot. DeAngelo also saw himself as a leader in bringing regulations and legitimacy to medical marijuana dispensaries that had long braved raids and were still seen as a nuisance by many California cities and counties. In that cause, he found a natural partner in Richard Lee.

The pair worked together on an Oakland ballot measure that promised the city new revenues through America's first local tax on marijuana. In June 2009, with the hearty backing of medical marijuana outlets and cannabis advocates, Oakland voters overwhelmingly approved Measure F to allow the city to collect a special 1.8 percent tax on gross receipts of the city's four pot clubs. The sudden prospect of new tax revenues inspired Oakland officials to explore an expanding marijuana economy. The long-struggling city came to see itself as the progressive center for California cannabis commercialization. Over the next year, Oakland welcomed a cavernous hydroponics store that reveled in media attention as the Walmart for marijuana cultivation supplies. The city council later set in motion controversial plans to license four commercial warehouses—vast urban factory farms that could produce pot for a thriving California medical market and, potentially, for future legalization of marijuana beyond medical use.

Richard Lee, in particular, saw the passage of Measure F as a "reverse tax revolt" and a springboard for historic acceptance of marijuana. He advanced a new political mantra—"No taxation without legalization." He began organizing, and bankrolling, a statewide ballot measure to legalize pot for any Californian twenty-one or older who wanted to smoke marijuana.

DeAngelo may have had his epiphany over a shared joint with Jack Herer that legalization was near. But he steadfastly told Lee that this wasn't the time.

Outside of pot-friendly Oakland, many cities and counties in California still banned medical marijuana dispensaries, and newly opening pot stores were making residents and officials uncomfortable in places that allowed them. DeAngelo contended that the medical marijuana industry needed to establish professional standards and broader public support. He argued that 2010—a nonpresidential election year—wouldn't attract young voters who could turn the tide on marijuana legalization. DeAngelo thought legalizing pot purely as an adult recreational pleasure was too much of a political leap.

Lee was stunned as California leaders for the national Marijuana Policy Project and the National Organization for the Reform of Marijuana Laws also told him to stand down. Dale Gieringer, NORML's state director, argued that a legalization initiative could make efforts to pass pro-marijuana legislation even more difficult at the capitol in Sacramento. Gieringer, an activist-sage with a PhD from Stanford, put it to Lee in blunt terms. "If you lose," he told the president of Oaksterdam University, "you're a *loser.*"

The movement naysayers only made Lee more determined. He also thought too many people entering the medical marijuana trade had such a good thing going they simply didn't want to change. He sensed that not everyone coming to buy marijuana had a serious medical need. "Let's just do this," he thought, "instead of having people pretend to be sick." Lee's cannabis college and medical marijuana enterprises had made him rich but also uncomfortable. He wondered how much he alone deserved his earnings. And he thought if he didn't empty his bank accounts, it was only a matter of time before the Internal Revenue Service would come after him and do it for him. So he put his cash on the line for the cause. The libertarian son of Goldwater Republicans started hiring Democratic political professionals to help him legalize nonmedical cannabis in California.

Lee also found an instant ally in Jeff Jones. The years since his epic 2001 Supreme Court battle had only added to Jones's sense of moral outrage over the government's stand against marijuana. In 2002, the same year that DEA agents raided and destroyed the WAMM garden in Santa Cruz, the former Oakland Cannabis Buyers Cooperative operator went to Sacramento to support Brian Epis of Chico, another target of a federal marijuana raid. At the outset of his trial, Epis gave Jones a stack of fliers. They depicted the marijuana grower in the upper Central Valley college town as being persecuted by the government for legally providing marijuana to patients under California law. "There is an injustice happening here," Jones shouted as he distributed the fliers outside the federal courthouse, including to prospective jurors and the prosecutor. The furious trial judge, Frank C. Damrell Jr., abruptly dismissed the forty-two-person jury pool. In 2003, U.S. magistrate Peter A. Nowinski ordered Jones thrown in prison for three months for disrupting the trial, declaring, "He is virtually thumbing his nose at the system." Nowinski reversed himself a week later, noting Jones's lack of criminal record, and gave him three years' probation and a $3,925 fine to repay the cost of bringing a new jury pool to hear the Epis case. Epis was convicted and given ten years in prison, a mandatory punishment under federal sentencing rules. Jones was convinced his giving fliers to prospective jurors cemented the court's lack of leniency. Epis's sentence, reaffirmed in 2010 (and later reduced by two and a half years in 2012), stoked Jones's grief. Continued episodes of marijuana patients being harassed by police kindled his anger.

Like Lee, Jones saw the medical marijuana establishment as entrenched, complacent, and unwilling to advance the fight. As his former champion cultivator pushed the measure to allow California adults to possess, share, or transport up to an ounce of marijuana and grow twenty-five square feet of plants regardless of medical need, Jones eagerly signed on as cosponsor of what would become known as Proposition 19.

Oaksterdam University became the nerve center for the California marijuana legalization drive as Lee contributed $1.3 million to signature gathering to qualify the initiative for the November 2010 ballot, and another three hundred thousand dollars for the campaign through his cannabis business network. After the measure qualified, DeAngelo came around and endorsed it. NORML and the Marijuana Policy Project also belatedly backed the Proposition 19 campaign, along with the Drug Policy Alliance, a national group funded by philanthropist George Soros that promoted alternatives to the drug war. Yet many old-time California pot activists, including Peron and other architects of Proposition 215, saw Richard Lee as a loose cannon in the movement. And Proposition 19 stirred deep schisms within the California medical marijuana community.

But among people who backed the initiative and its prospects of wider marijuana legalization, Lee became a galvanizing hero. Supporters mobbed him as he wheeled into a medical marijuana trade show at the Cow Palace south of San Francisco, preppy in his Oaksterdam University polo shirt. They asked to have their pictures taken with him. Lee was hoisted in his wheelchair onto a speakers' stage. He was hailed by Ed Rosenthal, the California cannabis author, growing guru, esteemed Oaksterdam University professor, former federal marijuana defendant, and fiery orator for the movement. "He said what Oakland needs and California needs is legal pot. And he did something about it," Rosenthal bellowed. "This guy took his hard-earned money and, an eighth of an ounce by an eighth of an ounce, changed history." Long after his debilitating fall, Richard Lee, the former ultralight pilot, was soaring again.

THREE

Kush Rush

Stephen Gasparas sensed the inevitability of his life's journey as soon as he started growing marijuana in the closet of his boyhood home in suburban Chicago. He felt it even after his infuriated mother yanked out his growing lights and skunk-smelling plants. He tried to suppress it as he got older, at least in between the multiple times he got busted for possession or intent to sell and his mom had to bail him out of trouble. He experimented with respectability. He opened a flooring business. For years, he installed carpets, hardwoods, and laminates and met payroll, ever fighting the urge. And then, it came to him one day as he riffed on his guitar and savored the herb: it was his time. There was a world of cannabis to explore. He was going to see it, experience it, and immerse himself in its offerings. The herb, and its spirit, would guide him.

So Gasparas hiked to the base of the Himalayas in India and traversed roads lined with fields of budding Hindu Kush marijuana. He traveled America to gatherings of the Rainbow Family and communed with nature in the company of the traveling tribe born a year after San Francisco's Summer of Love. He once awoke at a Rainbow encampment in Michigan to find miniature cannabis plants sprouting from the earth around his van. He swore it was neither a vision nor a hallucination. He just knew: "I'm on my path."

It led him to the far northeastern corner of California, where, over cannabis tokes in the deep woods of the Modoc National Forest, elders of the Rainbow Family nudged him toward his destiny. The old hippies from Haight-Ashbury had scattered long before. Many had migrated to California's upper northern coast. There, in the Emerald Triangle of Humboldt, Mendocino, and Trinity Counties, they had moved off the grid and back to the land, raising organic crops and refining the art of growing marijuana. The tricounty region was named for its redwood forests. But Emerald Triangle came to mean only one thing: home of the finest and most readily available pot in California.

In Humboldt County, in particular, hundreds of millions of marijuana dollars flowed into rural towns from a largely illicit growing culture. Marijuana stimulated local spending, boosting businesses that fed, clothed, and equipped the weed farmers. It drove the economy. Weed salvaged the hopes of a region where, over decades, the logging and fishing industries had diminished as mills shuttered and the depletion of fish populations left ever fewer salmon returning to spawn. Long after the hippies and homesteaders made a pilgrimage to the chilly northern coast, medical marijuana and a proliferation of pot dispensaries elsewhere in California ignited a new migration to the Emerald Triangle.

As Oakland emerged as a migratory nexus for cannabis activists and a laboratory for marijuana liberalization and commercialization, the state's north coast glittered as an emerald beacon for people simply wanting to grow and enjoy marijuana—and seek livelihoods through cannabis—in the permissive seclusion of the redwoods or small towns. Exploiting liberal Humboldt County rules allowing anyone with a medical marijuana recommendation to cultivate one hundred square feet of pot, the newcomers converted neighborhood homes to fragrant indoor grow houses or staked out plots for outdoor pot fields. Nudge-and-wink gardening supply centers, purportedly for organic vegetables, proliferated. They stocked shelves with grow lights and plant fertilizers called Big Bud, Bud Candy, and Voodoo Juice. In a region that had long supplied the marijuana black market of California and beyond, medical marijuana lured in newcomers inspired by new opportunities and a sense of legal cover. The influx would stir a cannabis cultural clash in pot country—and turmoil over the Emerald Triangle's place in a changing California marijuana economy.

In this environment, the Rainbow elders sensed there was an opening for new-generation seekers such as Gasparas. After he briefly settled in Oregon, one of the leaders of his toking circle from the Modoc forest spoke to Gasparas by phone and redirected him in a guiding voice: "Humboldt, that's the place you ought to be."

In 2004, Gasparas stopped at a doctor's office in Crescent City, just south of the Oregon border. He cited congestion and back pain—the latter from a bicycle motocross accident as a youth—to get a physician's recommendation for medical marijuana. He settled into a house near the Humboldt town of

Eureka. Inspired by his travels to India, he perfected a cannabis strain called Purple Hindu Kush. He sold it to a local dispensary and soon celebrated his reviews. "People said my stuff was the first to get them stoned in a long time," the suburban Chicago transplant boasted. Picking up side jobs as a carpet cleaner, he connected with college kids while shampooing carpets in weed-scented housing complexes near Arcata's Humboldt State University. He swapped his potent buds for marijuana seedlings the kids were growing in their rooms. He took their baby Purple Urkles and Grape Skunks to a cabin between Eureka and Arcata that he and a partner outfitted with growing beds and blazing lamps. He perfected bending and topping off the plants to make them bountiful with flowers, proclaiming he could produce up to a pound and three-quarters of dried buds per lamp. "The spirit," he proclaimed, "talked to me as I was going."

In Gasparas's explorative, meditative journey from suburban Chicago to India to Humboldt, the spirit also led him to the conclusion that being a pot outlaw wasn't his dharma. He loved his newfound lawfulness as a medical cultivator under California's Proposition 215. He loved being part of the great pot migration. Downtown Arcata, with its art deco theater, gingerbread-adorned storefronts, roustabout bars, and a plaza topped by giant palms, was a bustling depot for the north coast marijuana economy.

Arcata had a diverse legacy as a destination. After World War II, it flour-ished with thirty lumber mills and an influx of workers processing north coast timber. In 1990, a year after the college town passed a resolution pro-claiming itself a nuclear-weapons-free zone, Arcata and neighboring north coast communities became activist outposts for the Redwood Summer. Environmental protesters streamed into the region, by then well established as the mecca for nature-loving—and cannabis-savoring—back-to-the-landers. Demonstrators blocked logging trucks in Humboldt and Mendocino Counties, demanding an end to corporate clear-cutting in California's north-ern Headwaters Forest that threatened wildlife habitats and imperiled stream systems for endangered coho salmon.

Now a boundless sense of new marijuana freedoms lured people in again. Itinerant bud trimmers, from spike-haired skateboarders to dreadlocked hikers emerging from the woods around Arcata, streamed in for jobs scissor-cutting unwanted leaves from marijuana flowers to prep them for dispensa-ries or the underground market after the fall outdoor harvest, or throughout the year for indoor yields. Gasparas delighted in Goths, gutter punks, and hippies coming together in a marijuana melting pot.

In 2007, Gasparas opened a dispensary, called the iCenter, later the Sai Center, in downtown Arcata. He added to his marijuana offerings, bartering to buy product from local growers, many of them recast and newly certified as medical marijuana patients. They stepped out of the shadows of the north coast Redwood Curtain, from an illicit, ever suspicious culture that had long since evolved from the hippie nirvana of the Haight-Ashbury transplants. Growers came into the iCenter with turkey oven bags filled with weed. Many recoiled when Gasparas asked them to provide seller's permits or fill out Internal Revenue Service 1099 tax forms as transparent cannabis venders. Some offered to drop the price a thousand dollars a pound, even two thousand, if they didn't have to sign anything. Gasparas turned away those uncomfortable with the business protocols of medical marijuana and the dispensary market. But he made one key concession to his weed-growing venders. He wrote no checks. He paid them only in cash.

· · ·

In the Emerald Triangle, where marijuana growers cultivated a legacy of earthy outdoor pot strains produced beneath the sun and the stars, years of state and federal drug raids had changed both the community and the art of growing. The raids drove many cultivators indoors. In the forests, diesel fuel leaked from generators in half-buried shipping containers rigged with grow lamps for marijuana. In the Humboldt towns of Arcata and Eureka, or the Mendocino hamlets of Ukiah and Willits, newcomers embracing indoor pot dangerously wired bedrooms, garages, and often whole houses with rows of thousand-watt lights. The sweet stench of weed, much of it produced by new arrivals with little emotional connection to the region or its heritage, washed over neighborhoods. By 2008, when Arcata passed an ordinance restricting indoor marijuana to fifty square feet and a maximum of twelve hundred total watts of lighting, nearly one in every seven homes was presumed to be growing pot. The same year, the sheriff's department had to call in an environmental cleanup crew for diesel and oil spills after authorities raided a rural southern Humboldt property with four buildings outfitted with cultivation rooms, hundreds of growing lamps for nearly fifty-five hundred plants, and not a single room fit for human habitation. A 2007 study by Humboldt State's Schatz Energy Research Center estimated that indoor marijuana growing accounted for 10 percent of electricity use in the county of 135,000 residents, enough to power thirteen thousand homes. Between 1996, when

Californians passed the medical marijuana law, and 2010, per capita electricity use in Mendocino County spiked by three times the state average. In Humboldt, it went up by sixfold.

The Emerald Triangle was no longer the haven of Lelehnia Du Bois's childhood memories. Her mother, Carole Du Bois, was a naturalist who settled her daughters in a wooded sanctuary in Trinity County in the 1970s. She immersed them in growing pesticide-free corn, beans, peas, tomatoes, and peppers. Lelehnia was with her mother and a younger sister on a mountainous highway when a tumbling boulder crashed onto the road. Her mother swerved the car to avoid it, and their vehicle flipped into a riverbed. Lelehnia crawled up a rocky slope to the road to summon help. Her younger sister died; her mother suffered a broken back. They stayed in Trinity County, grieving, recovering, and embracing nature and their neighbors. Her mother smoked a nightly joint in the tub to quell her pain, and Lelehnia became familiar with the neighbors' marijuana gardens. By the age of nine, she was helping trim the buds at harvest time. She grew up loving the autumn and the celebratory community passage when neighbors would get together for potluck dinners to mark the end of another outdoor growing season and hail the potent, plentiful crop.

Lelehnia moved on to Southern California, became a model, worked in the retail fashion industry, and ran a restaurant and a school of dance. She didn't envision a future in pot. But in 1994, Lelehnia moved back to the Emerald Triangle after her mother, by then living in Humboldt, fell ill. Lelehnia studied nursing at Redwood College in Eureka and took a job in a senior-care facility while working toward her RN degree. In 1999, she caught a falling patient and suffered ruptured disks in her back. Suddenly, she was a patient herself, winding up on disability and, for an extended time, in a wheelchair. She got a medical marijuana recommendation and reembraced the region's cannabis arts, only this time bathed in the yellow light of an indoor growing space built next to the living room of her small Eureka apartment. Her Sweet God strain soothed her spine and brought in extra income on top of her disability checks. She supplied marijuana, homemade cannabis tinctures, and baked goods to a Eureka dispensary called the Hummingbird Healing Center. Week by week, there seemed to be new neighbors. They churned the electrical circuits, producing a cumulative mountain of weed.

In 2009, an Arts & Entertainment Network documentary depicted Arcata in *Pot City, U.S.A.*, while MSNBC's *Marijuana Inc.* chronicled the cannabis crush in the Emerald Triangle. People coming in didn't care to grasp that the marijuana market, even in California, and especially on its north coast, was already glutted. At the Humboldt Collective dispensary in Arcata, known as the THC, Tony Turner, a public school counselor who went into the marijuana business after retirement, greeted a continual procession of out-of-state dreamers. One day, Michelle Cotter, an Arizona woman who had studied alternative medicine and the healing powers of nature at the Southwest College of Naturopathic Medicine, stopped by. Cotter had never even smoked pot. But she came to the THC with friend Jaye Richards, a former Arizona property manager who had experience growing corn and soy beans on a family farm in Illinois. They had just gotten their California recommendations for medical marijuana, their tickets, they hoped, to a new lifestyle and livelihood. They looked over Turner's jars of Pot Pourri and Bud Crumble, bought a few marijuana caramels and peppered him for advice on growing. "Best to look for a place in the countryside," Turner suggested. "And get a security system." He smiled in bemusement as the women moved on, happily exploring their California cannabis adventure. Turner wondered where it would end. Just because Humboldt was pot country and marijuana was legal for medicinal use didn't mean that so many people were fit to grow medical weed or that there was a market waiting.

But with new residents burning brilliant plant lights and paying soaring electric bills and ballooning rents, Du Bois sensed a darker edge. There was competitiveness between growers, distrust, and a loss of neighborliness. Envious residents who couldn't access the dispensary market threatened to report more successful ones to the feds. Many simply winked at the idea of medical marijuana as they packed up product and shipped it out of state for maximum returns. The explosion of indoor growers hardly reminded Du Bois of Trinity County in the 1970s. "There is no honor system," she thought. "The integrity has gotten lost." The entire culture was changing.

The newcomers weren't born into this region. They had never awakened before the fall outdoor harvest to the roar of narcotics officers' wind-whipping helicopters scouring the mountains in the Campaign Against Marijuana Planting. They had never initiated emergency calls from pot-growing neighbor to pot-growing neighbor to warn that the feds or state authorities were coming. They hadn't faced the excitement or fear of selling to buyers from across California, and America, who might show up flashing stacks of bills one day and brandishing guns the next.

In southern Humboldt County, native son Joey Burger started growing pot at fourteen. He matured in the trade. He appreciated the covenants of a place where displaced loggers made their living planting marijuana and chipped in to buy fire engines or pay for paramedic training for the local volunteer fire district. By age twenty-eight, with premature flecks of gray in his hair, Burger was a community-conscious businessman who honored the pot-growing traditions but worked to bring his neighbors into the future. Burger ran an agricultural products showroom, Trim Scene Solutions, in the town of Redway. He marketed crop trimmers, drying racks, bagging machines, and scales. He posted online photos and demonstration videos for harvest equipment, including his signature Twister machine that could do the work of more than two dozen bud trimmers. His demo videos depicted processing hops for beer—not buds for bongs. But he saw his machines, with their whirring hum, as the sirens of an emerging, legitimate marijuana industry.

Burger shunned the black market to supply licensed medical marijuana dispensaries in Sacramento and other cities. He grew a meticulously tended marijuana grove, with his outdoor plants towering up to fifteen feet high before the November harvest and his buds landing among featured "top shelf" strains at dispensaries. In 2010, he worked to form the Humboldt Growers Association. The group cosponsored a fund-raiser to help pay off the campaign debt of Humboldt County district attorney Paul Gallegos. It hired a longtime county supervisor, Bonnie Neely, as a lobbyist. And it pushed a plan for the county to issue permits to medical marijuana growers with proof of providing for the dispensary market. Burger wanted to bring Humboldt County, particularly its outdoor growers, into the light of a sanctioned economy. That meant government oversight, documented sales and paper-work, and transparent relationships with cannabis stores. But many of his brethren saw county permits and oversight as intruding on a right of nature. They were too accustomed to the old ways to go legit. Burger tried to con-vince them they needed to adapt to survive. But his call was far from eagerly received.

Humboldt County was both paranoid about pot and hooked on mari-juana dollars gained largely from illicit cultivation and distribution. As much as local officials tried to tout the region's Humboldt Creamery, its grass-fed beef, or rich oyster beds, everyone knew what kept the county afloat. A study by a local banker, Jennifer Budwig, calculated that, judging from authorities' 2010 marijuana plant seizures, local marijuana growers raked in $1 billion in gross annual revenues. Of that, $415 million was spent in area businesses, accounting for one-fourth of the economy in the county of 135,000 residents.

Budwig characterized her study as a conservative analysis based on an estimate that law enforcement was eradicating one-fourth of the marijuana crop. If the cops were getting only 10 percent, Budwig calculated, Humboldt's gross annual marijuana revenues would be as high as $2.6 billion. To the south, the *Ukiah Daily Journal* and *Willits News* used her methodology to calculate that marijuana stoked the economy in Mendocino County with $675 million in direct local spending. In the county of 87,000 people and charming small towns tucked between golden hills and an enchanting coast, the estimate was more than double Mendocino's combined income from tourism, timber, wine grapes and other farming, cattle ranching, and commercial fishing.

It all made Mendocino County sheriff Tom Allman yearn for the time when the local marijuana industry indeed consisted of a bunch of pot-growing hippies. Allman was raised in southern Humboldt, son of a second-grade-teacher mother and a liquor-salesman father. The former student body president at South Fork High School in Miranda, just north of the town of Garberville, had been friends with youths drawn into the weed culture. Back then, pot was still a whisper. People didn't flaunt it. Now he was seeing young people driving loaded seventy-thousand-dollar pickup trucks, paid for in cash, and plunking down money on big-acreage lots. In 2001, voters in Mendocino approved Measure G, allowing anyone with a medical marijuana recommendation to grow twenty-five plants. Within a few years, Allman started encountering people in their twenties telling him they were growing for their personal medical needs as they tended massive outdoor gardens producing up to 7 pounds of weed per plant. The sheriff fumed as some guy would tell him he needed 175 pounds of pot for his bum shoulder. "Bullshit," Allman would answer. He got used to taking "that red bullshit flag" out of his pocket and rhetorically throwing it down.

With purported medical pot growers exploiting Mendocino's permissive twenty-five-plant-per-patient limit by compiling photocopied lists of sometimes hundreds of medical-marijuana patients to justify thousands of plants on some properties, a fed-up county supervisor, John McCowen, championed a new initiative to overturn liberal local growing rules. Approved by voters in 2008, Measure B put Mendocino County back on the state standard, employed in most California counties. That standard allowed a maximum of six mature plants per marijuana patient unless local governments approved higher levels. But Mendocino's new limits didn't stop the influx. By 2012, Allman was spending 30 percent of the sheriff's department's more than $23 million annual budget on marijuana cases. Pot growers took over private timberland and national forests. They fouled the environment, clear-cutting trees, diverting streams, and dumping fuel and pesticides.

Many people in Mendocino and elsewhere wanted to blame the worst of it on the Mexicans. For years, a California task force of federal and state drug agents and county sheriffs had eradicated millions of plants grown on public lands and in secluded California back country from the Central Valley to the Sierra Nevada and the coastal ranges. Many of the pot fields, often set up to supply cross-country drug trafficking by Mexican nationals, were tilled by illegal immigrants. They lived in encampments stocked by armed drug bosses with seasonal supplies of tortillas and beans, plus good-luck figurines of Jesus Malverde, a turn-of-the-century bandit from the Mexican state of Sinaloa who was revered as the patron saint for narcotics traffickers. In 2011, Allman spearheaded Operation Full Court Press, working with the Drug Enforcement Administration and sheriffs from Trinity, Tehama, Glenn, Colusa, and Lake Counties. The massive deployment destroyed 460,000 marijuana plants in the vast Mendocino National Forest. Officers seized over fifteen hundred pounds of processed pot and more than two dozen guns. One hundred fifty-two people were arrested. Thirteen percent were undocumented immigrants believed to be part of Mexican drug networks. Allman found the overwhelming remainder to be Caucasians from other states or elsewhere in California who simply figured there was no better place than the Mendocino forest to furtively grow their weed.

.   .   .

North coast marijuana growers melded in with seemingly legitimate forms of commerce. Living near the Mad River in the Humboldt County town of Blue Lake, David Winkle, a man in his fifties, appeared to be selling bait and tackle through a business he advertised on the Internet as Blue Lake Fishing Products. In a 2011 criminal complaint filed in the United States District Court in Rochester, U.S. drug agents depicted Winkle as a marijuana supplier known by drug dealers in New York as "Papa Winky." The complaint alleged Winkle shipped off pallets marked as "fish" and containing fishing tackle and thirty to eighty pounds of marijuana per delivery. New York dealers allegedly sent back cash payments of up to sixty thousand dollars through the U.S. Postal Service, and, upon receipt, Papa Winky texted his best wishes: "All is good, everyone accounted for, good luck selling."

Elsewhere in Humboldt, Jordan Pyhtila and Jessie Jeffries started out trafficking pot as teenagers in 1999 and went on to become land developers for the underground marijuana economy. The two young men, from Garberville and Rio Dell, used marijuana proceeds to fund their J & J Earthmoving construction company. They bought properties in several towns to launch other marijuana growers, taking a share of profits as they supplied plant clones and fertilizer and paid the pot laborers. By the time Humboldt deputies and U.S. drug agents raided them in 2007, Pyhtila and Jeffries were working with the Humboldt city of Rio Dell to develop a hundred-acre, sixty-house subdivision with five-hundred-thousand-dollar environmentally sustainable homes in a pristine setting near the Eel River. "Tragically, the conduct that brought him before the court was largely the product of a misguided youth growing up in a community that has a permissive attitude toward marijuana cultivation," Pyhtila's attorney, Ann Moorman, wrote the U.S. District Court before Pyhtila, twenty-nine, and Jeffries, twenty-eight, accepted plea deals in 2009 for six years each in federal prison.

Allman found the audacity of some growers astonishing. In 2008, the sheriff was called out as his officers, along with state and federal drug agents, raided a sprawling marijuana complex in Island Mountain in northern Mendocino. A suspect tried to leap off a ridge with a motorized hang glider and fifty thousand dollars in cash before aborting an escape that surely would have been fit for the movies. Officers found numerous greenhouses draped in black plastic, a light-deprivation technique to fool plants into premature budding to produce multiple yields. There were nearly sixty-eight hundred plants and eight hundred pounds of dried and trimmed marijuana buds.

"Holy shit, eight hundred pounds," the sheriff said, unable to suppress his grin has he greeted the chief grower following his abandoned flight. "What are you going to do with eight hundred pounds?"

"I don't know," the grower responded. "I guess my gardening plan was better than my business plan."

In five years, Allman had five unsolved homicides at or near marijuana gardens, including the killing of a man in a home invasion and a double murder near the rural Mendocino town of Covelo. In Humboldt in 2010, a local marijuana farmer, Mikal Xylon Wilde, was arrested on charges of shooting and killing one of his gardeners and seriously wounding another in a pay dispute. With the support of District Attorney Gallegos, U.S. prosecutors in San Francisco took the extraordinary step of filing a federal count of murder during the commission of a narcotics crime. Gallegos commended the government for its "commitment to the safety and security of the people of Humboldt County."

Otherwise, Gallegos, who prosecuted one thousand marijuana cases, strongly believed that marijuana enforcement needed to be triaged. He knew Humboldt County grew up on pot. He didn't like the idea of criminalizing people, from ranchers to small business owners, "who are otherwise good, law-abiding citizens." So Gallegos published prosecution guidelines declaring he would bring charges only in cases involving more than three pounds of processed marijuana or exceeding one hundred square feet of grow space or ninety-nine plants. While the Humboldt district attorney pledged to target big traffickers, he also railed about the failures of marijuana prohibition. He publicly endorsed legalizing pot beyond medical use.

To Allman, marijuana was the great social experiment and, in Mendocino County, it was failing. The sheriff was fed up with environmental destruction by illicit cultivators trespassing on private property or invading public lands for commercial-scale cultivation. He was also exasperated with deputies having to waste hours figuring out if somebody with twenty plants was operating legally or not under California medical marijuana laws. He wanted to free his officers to go after the worst offenders, people who imperiled the security and quality of life in his county. To do that, Allman set out to build relationships with marijuana growers willing to openly work with the cops.

In Mendocino, there were few pot growers more open than Matt Cohen, a philosophy major from the University of Colorado who dropped out to become an advocate for medical marijuana in California. Cohen had established his credentials in the movement in Oakland, where he bought groceries and grew free pot for Angel Raich, a medical cannabis user severely ill with a brain tumor and seizures. Cohen was one of two "John Doe" caregivers in an unsuccessful case Raich brought to the United States Supreme Court challenging the federal government's authority to prosecute medical marijuana in California. In Mendocino County, Cohen formed Northstone Organics. He signed up registered medical marijuana patients from the San Francisco Bay Area and other regions for what he billed as a legal California nonprofit collective and delivery service. It promised "premium, sun-grown medical cannabis—delivered discreetly to your door."

Thirty-two years old, lean, with a ponytail, Cohen made himself known to Allman and became a familiar presence before the Mendocino County Board of Supervisors, which in 2010 started work on a plan to regulate medical growers. Allman stayed out of the direct negotiations because pot people tended to get nervous when he showed up. Cohen, a newcomer, embraced Mendocino's marijuana traditions. He formed a local trade association called MendoGrown, promoting environmentally sustainable cannabis. Amid the oak woodlands of Mendocino's Redwood Valley, visitors found Cohen's outdoor marijuana farm just beyond a gate marked with the sign "Member, Mendocino County Farm Bureau." Cohen might have gotten a physician's recommendation to use medical marijuana for back pain, sleeplessness, and general anxiety, but he was comfortable with the media, poised with politicians, and effective in helping to draw anxious marijuana growers out of the woods to reach an unprecedented accord with the county.

In April 2010, the Mendocino County Board of Supervisors approved local Ordinance 9.31. It established California's first-ever licensing program for medical cultivators and imposed fees in an unprecedented compliance program for pot growing. Ordinance 9.31 set a limit of twenty-five marijuana plants per Mendocino parcel no matter how many growers lived or operated there. But it allowed up to ninety-nine plants for people on more than ten acres who provided verification of supplying licensed marijuana dispensaries or medical users who had physician recommendations. Cohen was one of just seventeen growers who signed up for the ninety-nine-plant regimen the first year. He used his newly minted county permit to promote Northstone Organics as "the one & only licensed, farm direct delivery service in California." The second year, ninety-four growers signed up for the program, in which the sheriff charged $50 per plant to affix numbered zip ties verifying the plant count. Other licensing fees paid for garden inspections by a Mendocino sergeant and independent monitors. Under Ordinance 9.31, medical growers with twenty-five plants or fewer who wanted guarantees of local certification and protection from arrest could get zip ties attached to plants for $25 each. Through 2011, forty thousand marijuana plants in Mendocino were tagged under the county compliance program. Ordinance 9.31 generated $630,000 in income for the sheriff's department. It allowed Allman to stave off budget cuts and reduce planned county deputy layoffs, from eleven layoffs to five.

Throughout the process, Allman developed a deep trust in Matt Cohen, a model grower under the program. After two of Cohen's delivery drivers were busted with marijuana while traveling through neighboring Sonoma County, Allman's sergeant in charge of 9.31 program-compliance inspections and a Mendocino County supervisor showed up in court to testify to the integrity of Cohen and Northstone Organics. The prosecutor in Sonoma was furious. Agents from the U.S. Drug Enforcement Administration office in San Francisco took notice.

. . .

With the advent of locally regulated medical-marijuana-growing, a brave new world of weed dawned in Mendocino County. On U.S. 101, the Redwood Highway, north of the town of Laytonville and just beyond the billboard depicting a hovering alien spacecraft, longtime marijuana grower Tim Blake had lived through the past and now preferred the future. Blake ran Area 101, a 150-acre retreat with a whole foods kitchen serving dishes free of gluten and refined sugars and a dispensary—the Mendocino Farmers Collective—featuring only outdoor, organic cannabis.

Blake had once served five and a half months in the county jail in Santa Cruz on pot charges. In Mendocino, he had once thrived as a black market cultivator. Years after going legit, he admitted he used to run U-Haul deliveries of pot into California's Central Valley. Back then, the helicopter flyovers and surging raids by DEA agents had the reverse effect of enriching pot growers who didn't get caught. The raids helped stabilize the price of weed in the Emerald Triangle at five thousand dollars a pound. But the stress of living as a marijuana outlaw became overwhelming for Blake. After a series of life-changing events, he quit the illegal trade, went from "being a kingpin to a no pin," and became a champion for legal, ecologically pure marijuana.

Before the DEA copters finally spooked him out for good, Blake had once gone to retrieve barrels of weed for a friend who was going to jail. The pot had mold in it called aspergillus, which can breed in improperly dried marijuana. It made Blake sick. He could barely stomach a piece of toast in the morning before falling back asleep "so the mold could eat the food." He also endured multiple battles with cancer. He rubbed cannabis oil into his skin to heal cancer-related sores. He reflected on his odyssey. He worked on a memoir he called "Dancing with the Feds: The Spiritual Adventures and Mishaps of the Marijuana Man." Eventually, licensed as a medical marijuana cultivator under Mendocino Ordinance 9.31, Blake set out to be the champion in restoring a "mystical place of clean cannabis."

Starting in 2003, Blake's Area 101 hosted the Emerald Cup, his celebration of the Emerald Triangle's outdoor marijuana traditions. With live music, joint-rolling contests, and "Guess the Old-School Strains" contests, the Emerald Cup became Mendocino's state fair of cannabis. For three weeks beforehand, Blake and other selected judges sampled the region's finest out-door-grown marijuana. They graded the texture of the buds, discerning the tastes, aromas, and medicinal effects. In 2010, an anonymous Mendocino grower's Sour Best Shit Ever—a cross-breed of Old School Laotian and Sage strains—won the coveted prize of best marijuana cultivar of the year. A twenty-four-year-old grower known as T-Beezle, the son of a former timber worker, took home top prize—and a signature edition bong—in the canna-bis-concentrate category for his Pure Blueberry Hash. Inevitably, the winners also earned something else—the ability to sell their organic products as pre-mium selections in California medical marijuana dispensaries.

At the Emerald Cup, amid its happily stoned throng, Blake disseminated a political, environmental, and marketing message. To Blake, the growth of the medical cannabis market and the proliferation of indoor growing were perilous for Mendocino outdoor cultivators. Their once legendary Northern Lights and Super Skunk marijuana strains had trouble competing with indoor OG Kushes and Purple Urkles, amped with maximum psychoactive THC in climate-controlled growing rooms. To Blake, indoor growing, with its heavy electrical use and carbon footprint, was wrongheaded. He called on outdoor growers to honor their art, to thrive, to protect the planet. For too long, cultivators had planted in the shade to avoid detection by DEA helicop-ters. Now it was time to bring pot out of the shadows, to let its potency thrive during nine months of outdoor growing under the Mendocino sun. It was time to compete. "We have to get out of the denial," Blake argued at a public forum. "We are a cannabis place. There is no fishing or logging. We have to take our birthright and embrace the future, or it's going to bury us."

But by 2010, there was a new threat, a marijuana legalization effort backed by Richard Lee and Jeff Jones in Oakland. The push to pass Proposition 19, and the inspired efforts in Oakland to authorize warehouse marijuana farms for the medical cannabis market—and eventual legalization for adult recrea-tional use—sent shivers through the Emerald Triangle. People feared an emerging Oakland legal cannabis cartel. Throughout the Emerald Triangle, growers increased their yields, pushing more products onto the market in fear of Proposition 19. Pot prices, already affected by the proliferation of medical cultivation across California, dropped below thirty-five hundred dollars a pound for indoor-grown marijuana and twenty-five hundred dollars for out-door and continued falling. People feared a meltdown, with the black market for weed collapsing and the price per pound flatlining in the blinding light of transparent capitalism. Some Humboldt County residents replaced their anti-DEA bumper stickers—"U.S. Out of Humboldt"—with a new one: "Save Humboldt County—Keep Pot Illegal."

Even Gasparas, the cannabis adventurer from suburban Chicago, worried over the changing marijuana economy and prospects of broader legalization. Gasparas had etched the history of his journey into his forearm with an abstract, tribal-patterned tattoo depicting a woman giving birth to a tree of life that leafed with cannabis. The medical marijuana economy in California, and his dispensary in Arcata, had crowned his passage. Gasparas was part of the cannabis establishment now. He lived north of town in an upscale subdivision with a panoramic view of the Pacific Ocean. His once disapproving mom worked in his dispensary. Suddenly, he worried about being pushed out of business by Proposition 19. Gasparas crunched the numbers. He didn't see himself surviving in a market extending beyond medicinal use. He didn't understand the need for change. With medical marijuana, he insisted, "it's already legal."

FOUR

Reefer Research

Dr. Donald Abrams knew what he was in for. He knew his partner, Mark Henry, was going to die. Two years before he met the security officer from the Maui-Intercontinental Hotel, Abrams had been treating more patients with AIDS than any other physician in San Francisco. His experiences told him Henry's deterioration from the disease would be rapid and excruciating. Yet that knowledge didn't stop him from developing a relationship with Henry after the security officer sought him out at a lecture in Hawaii in 1986. It didn't stop them from drawing close, from vacationing together, from laughing together, from reflecting together, or from smoking pot together.

Abrams was a Stanford University–educated hematologist and oncologist drawn by life-affecting events into the research and treatment of AIDS and HIV. It started for him after an unexplainable progression of young gay men with swollen glands began showing up at the Kaiser Foundation Hospital in San Francisco in 1979. Dr. Lee Wilkinson, the hospital's chief hematologist, summoned Abrams, a twenty-nine-year-old openly gay medical resident. "Hey, Duck," Wilkinson said, invoking the Disney character nickname he had bestowed on the promising young doctor. "Can you take a look at this?"

Abrams ordered lab tests on the men's lymph nodes, seeking a cause for the symptoms. The results offered nothing from which to draw conclusions. So Abrams found himself cautioning the men on unhealthy lifestyles. "Stop having so many sexual partners," he lectured. "Stop taking drugs. Move out of the fast lane."

At the urging of Wilkinson, his mentor, Abrams moved on to the hematology and oncology training program at the University of California, San Francisco. There, he started encountering more young gay men with new, more severe symptoms. By 1981, doctors at the university were seeing the first cases of Kaposi's sarcoma, a haunting, systemic affliction that left them splotched with lesions. Abrams began focusing on a strange "gay cancer" that would become known as acquired immune deficiency syndrome. He noticed many of the men had swollen glands. "How long have you had those?" Abrams asked. About two years, they told him, suggesting a troubling progression of the symptoms Abrams had noted in 1979.

Abrams applied for a grant to study lymphadenopathy syndrome, hoping to find clues about the first symptoms of illnesses leading to diagnoses of AIDS. As a research fellow treating the first-known AIDS patients in San Francisco, Abrams examined two hundred gay men with swollen glands who had yet to develop Kaposi's sarcoma or pneumocystis, the ravaging pneumonia that would signal their rapid decline. He took lymph node specimens to the UC San Francisco laboratory of Dr. Harold Varmus, a Nobel prize–winning researcher for work on cancer-causing genes. They began studying what would be identified as a retrovirus that attacked cells and altered the body's DNA and its ability to fend off disease.

In 1983, Abrams moved to San Francisco General Hospital, where oncologist Dr. Paul Volberding and infectious disease specialist Dr. Connie Wofsy established the world's first AIDS inpatient ward, Ward 5B, with Abrams as their protégé. For a time, the trio knew every AIDS patient in San Francisco. That year, a French researcher, Dr. Luc Montagnier, would be widely credited with discovering the virus that led to AIDS. Abrams later became one of three researchers to name it the human immunodeficiency virus, or HIV. Soon the rate of HIV diagnoses and the number of AIDS patients were skyrocketing. All too soon, Abrams recalled, "we didn't know everybody anymore." San Francisco became a death camp for men wasting away, disfigured, stigmatized with a gay disease. Over twenty years, nineteen thousand city residents would perish from AIDS.

Still Abrams let himself fall in love with Mark Henry after Henry sought him out. His lectures in Maui had been initiated after Henry's previous partner became the first person on the island to die of the disease. When the two men met, Henry had just had an episode of AIDS-related pneumonia. Abrams knew nearly everyone with the disease died within twelve months after a pneumocystis outbreak. Since early in his life, Abrams had had an ingrained fear of losing people he loved, going back to when he lost three grandparents as a small child and his "probably neurotic Jewish mother" took to raising him with a decided anxiety about death. Yet remarkably, Abrams's upbringing had inspired his work in oncology and his desire to treat—and learn from—cancer patients in the transition from living to dying. And after he met Henry, Abrams realized there must be something in his makeup "that allowed me to go, eyes wide open, into a relationship with a man who was going to die."

By 1986, physicians were prescribing a new antiviral drug for the treatment of AIDS. But Abrams believed the toxicity of azidothymidine, or AZT, outweighed its therapeutic benefits. Mark Henry didn't take the drug. Yet Abrams watched his partner survive through 1986, then 1987, then 1988 and into 1989, when he entered hospice care. Throughout the three years before he reached death's door, Henry smoked marijuana. Abrams, who as an undergrad at Brown University preferred pot to booze, joined him. Ultimately, the weed made the doctor feel paranoid, too in touch with his deepening sadness over his lover's pending death. So Abrams curtailed his use, but Henry did not. He went on to outlive fellow AIDS patients in one support group, then a second, then a third. When he died, Henry had survived three times longer after pneumocystis than the average for AIDS patients.

Abrams didn't know for sure if there was a medical benefit to the marijuana Henry used. The doctor also had no inkling when Henry passed away that, years later, he would become California's most renowned researcher on medical marijuana, and that clinical trials in the Golden State would challenge the federal government and medical research orthodoxy by helping establish the medical efficacy of pot. But one thing that struck Abrams at the time was that Henry had outlived most every other AIDS patient—and he used cannabis "every freakin' day."

. . .

By 1990, anguish over the unsolved epidemic of AIDS and HIV was exploding into rage in San Francisco. That year the city hosted the International Conference on AIDS, only to have the event disrupted by activists from ACT UP, the AIDS Coalition To Unleash Power. Wearing "Silence = Death" shirts, they blew piercing whistles, threw chairs, and directed shouts of "Shame!" at conference participants, including Donald Abrams and other AIDS doctors and researchers. According to the activists, people were dying because of a conspiracy of government obstruction, because of a heartless ban on immigration to the United States for people with AIDS and HIV, because of a lack of funding for AIDS treatments, and from the continued failure of researchers to find a cure.

By then, another movement was attaching itself to the cause of AIDS and gay rights—marijuana. That same year, narcotics officers raided the apartment of Dennis Peron, targeting the pot dealer who supplied weed to sick people in the gay community. Police roughed up Peron's lover, lesion-wracked and skeletal-thin AIDS sufferer Jonathan West. An enraged Peron would later describe an officer putting a boot on West's neck and taunting him: "Know what AIDS means? Asshole in Deep Shit." In 1991, Peron marshaled his fury to win 80 percent voter support for San Francisco's Measure P, an advisory measure calling on the state to legalize marijuana as medicine. It launched his political march toward passing the California medical marijuana initiative, Proposition 215, five years later. Peron also found an ally in Mary Jane Rathbun, an eccentric Irish Catholic septuagenarian with a passion for baking and for pot. She partnered with him to set up the San Francisco Cannabis Buyers Club, which went on to provide marijuana to thousands of gay men with AIDS. They would later cowrite a book, *Brownie Mary's Marijuana Cookbook and Dennis Peron's Recipe for Social Change*.

The people wanting in on that change would include the likes of Richard Lee and Steve DeAngelo, lured by Proposition 215 and the progressive pot politics and medical cannabis opportunities in Oakland. They would include suburban Chicago seeker Stephen Gasparas and other new marijuana migrants drawn to the north coast Emerald Triangle. But as the AIDS epidemic extended into the early 1990s, with antiretroviral treatments still evolving, the social movement around marijuana remained focused on pot as a still-forbidden alternative that could relieve suffering and perhaps instill hope for better days. So in the years before California voters legalized marijuana for medical use, profoundly ill people risked seeking fellowship and comfort in places such as the Santa Cruz garden of the Wo/Men's Alliance for Medical Marijuana; many others turned to cannabis to soothe their nausea, loss of appetite, and pain and maybe extend their lives in the frightened landscape of San Francisco.

It was at San Francisco General Hospital where Donald Abrams and fellow AIDS doctors got to know Mary Rathbun as "Brownie Mary." It was there where her presence would ultimately serve to inspire social change through the clinical research of marijuana. For years, Brownie Mary was an ever-present volunteer in an outpatient clinic in a converted pediatrics ward on the sixth floor of the hospital's building number 80. "Ward 86" became America's most famous AIDS clinic. There, Rathbun shuttled sick young men she dubbed her "kids" from the clinic to radiology. She also brought them fresh-baked goods infused with marijuana, becoming a media darling for her compassion for people destined to perish from the disease. Abrams and other doctors in Ward 86, most of them products of the sixties who had smoked a joint or more in college, welcomed Mary's presence. They didn't worry much about her medicinal brownies. They just appreciated that pot offered some relief despite patients' overwhelming medical challenges.

In 1992, Abrams arrived in Amsterdam for another International AIDS Conference. He flipped on the television in his hotel room. CNN International was broadcasting a breaking story from the San Francisco Bay Area: Brownie Mary had been arrested with two and a half pounds of weed, raided by police as she was crafting her confections at a friend's home in Sonoma County. Soon the City of San Francisco, which under the voter-approved Measure P now officially considered marijuana as a legitimate source of symptom relief for AIDS, cancer, and other illnesses, staged a "Brownie Mary Day." The star of the show let loose with a stream of profanity unfit for airtime. "If the narcs think I'm going to stop baking pot brownies for my kids with AIDS, they can go fuck themselves in Macy's window!" Brownie Mary let it be known. The Sonoma County district attorney later dropped the charges.

Brownie Mary's message—even scrubbed of profanity—elevated AIDS and pot as an international story, not only affecting Abrams as he watched in Amsterdam but also reaching a frustrated medical marijuana research advocate named Rick Doblin in North Carolina. Doblin, a graduate of New College of Florida, was preparing to resume his doctorate studies in public policy at Harvard after completing his Harvard master's degree with a thesis on medical marijuana. Doblin had founded a group called the Multidisciplinary Association for Psychedelic Studies, which advocated research on alternative medicines, including marijuana and the drug known as Ecstasy.

Doblin had no medical degree. But for two years he had shopped around a research protocol for studying marijuana's effectiveness in reversing the nausea and loss of appetite that led to wasting syndrome and starved AIDS patients into hollow-eyed human forms. After Doblin saw Brownie Mary on television, he wrote a letter "to whom it may concern" at the AIDS program at San Francisco General Hospital. The letter, urging someone there to take on the research project, was routed to Donald Abrams. The doctor followed up, and Doblin made an instant impression. Doblin insisted that groundbreaking marijuana research "should come from Brownie Mary's institution." Abrams was bemused by the thought of becoming the Brownie Mary Research Institute. But he was inspired by the study idea. Doblin's idea made him think of Henry. It reminded him of how pot had seemed to keep his lover alive and functioning for so long.

By 1992, Abrams was working with San Francisco's Community Consortium, a group of physicians setting up community-based clinical trials to explore treatments with AIDS and HIV patients. Despite being intrigued, Abrams was skeptical of Doblin's plan to investigate the medicinal effectiveness of marijuana brownies. He didn't see a way to standardize cannabis doses in brownies, particularly over a multiweek clinical research trial. But Doblin insisted that some kind of study of marijuana's effect on wasting syndrome needed to happen. Doblin contacted the Food and Drug Administration about supporting a clinical trial and got a positive response. He arranged with a Dutch medical marijuana firm to grow cannabis for the research.

The same year, the prescription drug Marinol, containing a synthetically produced version of marijuana's psychoactive delta 9-tetrahydrocannabinol (THC) constituent, had been approved for treatment of people with HIV wasting syndrome. But patients of Community Consortium physicians reported that swallowing Marinol left them zoned out for hours. Many reported they preferred smoking pot because they could regulate their dose through the number and spacing of hits from a joint. The Community Consortium's board decided to back a study to assess separate groups of wasting patients—who either smoked marijuana or took Marinol—for changes in HIV immune system levels, body weight, and body composition. Research review boards from UC San Francisco and the State of California signed off on the study. Soon multiple government entities appeared determined to stop it from happening.

The Drug Enforcement Administration refused to allow the marijuana for the study, then being cultivated in Amsterdam, to be imported into the United States unless the Dutch government would send the DEA a letter saying it was okay for the company to export it. The Dutch government wouldn't send the letter unless the DEA said it was okay to import it. So the Food and Drug Administration told Abrams to get in touch with the National Institute on Drug Abuse, which had access to government-grown marijuana, cultivated since 1970 under a closely supervised program at the University of Mississippi. Since 1976, the five-acre government pot farm had produced monthly tins of three hundred marijuana cigarettes, which were sent to about a dozen patients in the little-known Compassionate Investigational New Drug program of the FDA. The program was created after a lawsuit by glaucoma patient Robert Randall, who sued the government after a raid on his pot garden in 1975. A U.S. District Court in Washington ruled Randall's use of marijuana was a medical necessity—pot helped keep him from going blind—and ordered the government to provide Randall with the drug. A dozen more people were later added to the Compassionate IND program. Otherwise, getting weed out of Uncle Sam's pot garden was all but impossible—especially so for medical research that might show the benefits of cannabis.

The fact that Donald Abrams was working on the front lines of the AIDS epidemic, in which people were starving and dying with wasting syndrome, wasn't enough to force the hand of the National Institute on Drug Abuse or its director, Alan I. Leshner. NIDA rejected Abrams's plan for a community-based, outpatient study. The agency contended the study protocol didn't provide adequate supervision of patients' diets. It also suggested that research subjects with AIDS wasting syndrome might deal the government's pot to their friends.

Leshner told Abrams he needed to go to the National Institutes of Health to have his study peer reviewed. Abrams reworked the study as a supervised, inpatient clinical trial at San Francisco General Hospital, in which subjects admitted for two fifteen-day evaluation periods would smoke marijuana or placebo joints with the psychoactive THC removed. The National Institutes of Health reviewed the study but effectively killed it, because the agency didn't bother to attach a research score, an action critical to ranking the trial for potential government funding. Two peer reviewers questioned why researchers wanted to test a "toxic" substance such as pot. Another suggested that wasting patients rediscovering their appetites might develop high cholesterol, clogged arteries, and reduced suppression of tumor cells. Abrams was incredulous. People with wasting syndrome didn't live remotely long enough for any of that to occur. These people obviously don't see the same patients I do, he thought.

In 1995, Leshner wrote Abrams, formally notifying him that the study idea was flawed and not worth the government's resources. Rick Doblin and fellow board members of the Multidisciplinary Association for Psychedelic Studies went to the National Conference on Marijuana Use, Prevention, Treatment and Research in Washington, D.C. In a silent protest, they unfurled banners charging that NIDA was blocking critical medical marijuana studies. Abrams, a clinician perpetually calm and cerebral with a wry humor, went off on Leshner in a furious missive.

"To receive the first communication from your office nine months after we sent the initial submission is offensive and insulting," Abrams wrote. His letter rose in intensity as he challenged the NIDA director's purported concern for wasting patients. "Finally, the sincerity in which you share my 'hope that new treatments will be found swiftly' feels so hypocritical that it makes me cringe," Abrams wrote. He went on: "You and your institution had an opportunity to do a service to the community of people living with AIDS. You and your institution failed. In the words of the AIDS activist community: SHAME!"

By November 1996, when California voters passed Proposition 215, the prospects for research still remained uncertain at best. Three months earlier, the National Institutes of Health had joined in rejecting Abrams's wasting syndrome study. Yet there was new hope in San Francisco and its gay community. Improved protease inhibitor drugs and other new antiretroviral medications were ending the death sentence of AIDS. Far fewer people were afflicted with wasting syndrome. And, though it made no reference to medical research, California's historic medical marijuana vote seemed to cry out for studies on pot's effectiveness in conditions such as AIDS/HIV, cancer, anorexia, spasticity, and pain.

In January 1997, after attending President Bill Clinton's inauguration for his second term, Abrams got an audience at the National Institute on Drug Abuse in Bethesda, Maryland, with Alan Leshner. Abrams wanted to know what it would take for the government to support cannabis studies. Their meeting was both cordial and revealing.

"You know, I have better things to do than to continue to write grants to study marijuana," Abrams began. He argued to Leshner that people were still going to smoke pot if studies showed it was harmful. He also suggested it was unlikely that more people would use marijuana if it was proven beneficial and safe.

"That's where you may be wrong," Leshner answered.

It was a year before the United States government would file civil actions to close Jeff Jones's Oakland Cannabis Buyers Cooperative, declaring that the facility, which purported to offer medicinal comfort for sufferers of AIDS, cancer, and other serious illnesses, was drug trafficking under federal law. And the director of the National Institute on Drug Abuse told Abrams that proving pot's medical efficacy could be problematic. Leshner suggested that it might challenge the government to rethink marijuana's legal status as a prohibited Schedule I drug deemed to have no medical benefits and a high potential for abuse. He informed him that NIDA's congressional mandate was to study substances of abuse or addiction. Leshner said the agency wasn't intent on blocking all medical cannabis studies, particularly those with favorable peer review. But he made it clear that research protocols designed to establish marijuana's medical benefits were unlikely to get agency backing or funding.

"We are the National Institute *on* Drug Abuse, not *for* drug abuse," Abrams reported Leshner told him. The director denied using the phrase.

After Proposition 215's passage, Abrams attended meetings with the San Francisco Department of Public Health in 1997 to discuss how to make the law operational for people who needed cannabis. At one meeting, he met an ACT UP member worried about the recent death of an AIDS patient who had been taking Ecstasy. The drug had blocked the liver's metabolism of protease inhibitor drugs, heightening the patient's vulnerability to the disease. By then, an estimated eleven thousand gay men in San Francisco were using marijuana for AIDS or HIV. The ACT UP activist wanted to know whether pot, too, could interfere with lifesaving antiretroviral drugs. Abrams had an epiphany. He could study the risk of pot for patients on protease inhibitors. He wrote up a research protocol for a clinical trial on the potential interaction between marijuana and the AIDS-fighting medications, arguing the connection "is worrisome since many HIV-infected patients continue to smoke marijuana as an appetite stimulant or to decrease nausea."

On April Fools Day in 1997, Abrams attended a planning conference for the Office of AIDS Research in Washington, D.C. During a morning break, a colleague told Abrams there was a man from the National Institute on Drug Abuse who wanted to talk with him. Abrams found himself discussing his research aspirations with Dr. Jag Khalsa, a program officer with NIDA's Center on AIDS and Other Medical Consequences. Khalsa told Abrams he funded studies on health and medical effects of substances of abuse. He said a study into whether marijuana interfered with protease inhibitor drugs might fit the bill.

"Send it to me," he said of Abrams's research plan.

"Do you know who I am?" Abrams asked, convinced this must be an April Fools joke.

"I know who you are," Khalsa replied. "Send it to me."

In August 1997, after a peer review by specialists whom Abrams had suggested—in clinical pharmacology, immunology, virology, endocrinology, and HIV medicine—NIDA and other government agencies signed off on the project. With $1 million in funding awarded for the research, Abrams accepted delivery from NIDA of fourteen hundred government-rolled joints from the University of Mississippi, plus a research supply of the synthetic THC drug Marinol from the pharmaceutical manufacturer Roxane Laboratories, of Columbus, Ohio. The pot was stored at San Francisco General Hospital in a locked freezer equipped with a burglar alarm.

On May 12, 1998, the first patients were enrolled for the study. In total, 67 confirmed HIV patients—89 percent men—who used protease inhibitors were selected for the study from 603 research volunteers. Five dropped out within two weeks. For twenty-one days, the others were kept in the hospital without visitors. One group smoked three marijuana joints daily that had been prepped in a humidifier and which contained 3.95 percent THC. Another group smoked cannabis-fragrant placebo joints with the THC removed. A third group took oral applications of Marinol. The sixteen-member research team led by Abrams monitored the weight, cell counts, and viral health of the patients.

The study concluded that use of cannabinoids, the natural THC in pot or synthetic THC in Marinol, neither increased the viral load of individuals with HIV infection nor interfered with their protease inhibitor drugs. Anecdotally, the researchers noted that patients given Marinol were more lethargic and spent more time in bed, while those smoking pot were more active. The research, Abrams wrote, failed to demonstrate "clinically significant interactions with cannabinoids that would warrant dose adjustments of protease inhibitors." He delivered the conclusion that marijuana was a safe medicine for people with HIV. It didn't interfere with anti-AIDS drugs. And there was something more. Patients using marijuana and Marinol saw increased production of healthy cells, with marginally higher levels for the pot smokers. People in the marijuana group also put on an average of 7.7 pounds in twenty-one days, compared to 7 pounds for the Marinol group and 2.9 pounds for the placebo group. Though there were no wasting patients in the study, the clinical trial signaled that pot could boost the immune system for people with HIV and AIDS.

Despite the results, no leading medical research journal was eager to publish a medical marijuana study. Abrams was rejected by the prestigious medical journal *Lancet,* by the *New England Journal of Medicine,* and by the *Journal of the American Medical Association.* Ultimately, after an initial denial, the *Annals of Internal Medicine of the American College of Physicians* interviewed Abrams on his study. In 2003, it published his research. Clinical evidence of the efficacy of cannabis with HIV patients was now part of accepted medical literature. In the study and with the media, Abrams was politic about the conclusions. He wrote that the findings meant "placebo-controlled studies of the efficacy of smoked marijuana could be considered in the future." He called for more research.

After the death of Mark Henry, Abrams had found a new life partner in Clint Werner, with whom he began a relationship in 1994 and later married. Years after Abrams's clinical trial on cannabis and patients with HIV infection, Werner revealed the doctor's internal sense of triumph. What Abrams mostly refrained from broadcasting, Werner, a natural-foods chef devoted to the dietary prevention of disease, all but shouted out. "The clinical trial was a Trojan horse, finally allowing researchers to get the data they had been seeking for years," Werner wrote in his book *Marijuana Gateway to Health*. Abrams's "true purpose" in the study, Werner wrote, "had been to ascertain whether marijuana helped improve the appetite of AIDS patients—and it did." Abrams's husband concluded with a flourish: "Science had spoken. THC really did cause the munchies."

. . .

After Donald Abrams's breakthrough clinical trial, state assemblyman John Vasconcellos sought to make medical cannabis research a fully funded priority of the state. Vasconcellos championed legislation calling for creation of a California "Center for Medicinal Cannabis Research." Its mission would be to provide answers—affirmative, negative, or both—to the question "Does marijuana have therapeutic value?"

Vasconcellos set out to develop the concept in consultation with some of the top medical and research professionals in the University of California system. One of them was Dr. Igor Grant, a renowned neuropsychiatrist at the University of California, San Diego. Grant directed the UC San Diego HIV neurobehavioral program, which used brain imaging and neuropsychological studies to research the effects of HIV and AIDS on the brain. Grant also had a long-standing interest in the impacts of alcohol and drug abuse, going back to when, as a young faculty member at the University of Pennsylvania in the 1970s, he analyzed literature on whether long-term marijuana use could cause brain dysfunction. Grant looked at rodent studies suggesting that high-dose exposure to THC in young rats could produce learning and performance deficits. He extrapolated the data to humans. To achieve the same effect, Grant would later conclude, a 154-pound man or woman would have to smoke 420 joints day.

Grant believed the discovery, in the early 1990s, of receptors in the brain that reacted to marijuana had opened the door to new medical research for pot. Researchers looking at the effects of THC named the first of these molecular neurotransmitters anandamide, using the Sanskrit word for bliss. They discovered that THC would bind itself to these receptors, found on the surface of cells throughout the central nervous system. The receptors were later named cannabinoid receptors, after the cannabis plant. Natural compounds produced by the body and acted upon by marijuana were named endocannabinoids. For Grant, identifying a molecular signaling system for pot—a system that worked much like the different receptors in the body that reacted to opiate drugs such as morphine or codeine—meant researchers could look at pot's potential for treating conditions such as multiple sclerosis, glaucoma, gastrointestinal disorders, cancer, and chronic pain.

Such research on pot was not possible in California unless Vasconcellos could get a marijuana research bill through the legislature. Vasconcellos, a self-described "old-time liberal," found an unexpected ally during the 1998 election season in a law-and-order conservative, Dan Lungren, who was then attorney general. Lungren, who had been an ardent opponent of Proposition 215, ran for governor in 1998. He drew a Republican primary challenge from Dennis Peron, whose cannabis club had been targeted by the attorney general. With no shot at winning, Peron served as an antagonist to remind people that Lungren opposed the will of voters on medical marijuana. Looking to find middle ground on pot for the November general-election race against Democrat Gray Davis, Lungren endorsed research on the medical use of cannabis. Vasconcellos saw a political opportunity. He reached out to the attorney general. Their staffs began drafting legislation for unprecedented medical marijuana studies.

Lungren was gone from office, defeated in the governor's election, and Vasconcellos had moved to the state senate when the pot legislation—Senate Bill 847—reached the floor in 1999. Lungren's endorsement helped pry loose crucial Republican votes. Vasconcellos needed twenty-seven votes—a two-thirds majority of the forty-member senate—to pass the appropriation. With no votes to spare, Vasconcellos offered procedural cover to three Republican senators—Jim Brulte, Tim Leslie, and Pete Knight—who were skittish about being the twenty-seventh vote on a pro-marijuana bill. The GOP trio agreed to shout "aye" in unison so that no individual got the blame as California lawmakers voted to spend $8.7 million in state tax dollars to study weed.

The Center for Medicinal Cannabis Research was created in 2000 and headquartered at UC San Diego, with Dr. Igor Grant as its director. Research proposals began streaming in by 2001. Over the next decade, the center would approve and oversee fifteen California clinical studies, including seven trials directly testing pot's effect on research subjects. The center established an exhaustive peer review process and used the legislative clout of the most populous state in the nation to win research approval from multiple federal agencies. Grant, who didn't conduct any research himself, saw to it that the center handled all research applications and that his clinicians didn't have to fight the government to do cannabis work. Meanwhile, Grant demanded rigorous, modern trials that could be published in medical research literature. He figured there was no point in wasting California tax money on studies "that wouldn't see the light of day."

One of those applying for a research grant, Dr. Barth Wilsey, a pain management physician at the University of California, Davis, sought funding for a study on whether cannabis provided relief for people with neuropathic pain from spinal cord injuries, diabetes, strokes, and other conditions causing life-disrupting discomfort from nerve damage or injury. Earlier in his career, Wilsey was a fellow in pain management at UC San Francisco, seeing patients in a small clinic in the city. People coming in would tell him they turned to marijuana when nothing else seemed to work. Wilsey, a licensed acupuncturist, was interested in alternative therapies. As a pain doctor, he figured that 40 to 60 percent of his patients didn't get adequate relief from prescriptions he wrote. He saw cannabis as an alternative worth exploring.

Dr. Mark Wallace, an anesthesiologist and pain specialist at UC San Diego proposed a study in which healthy subjects would smoke marijuana and researchers would study the analgesic effects of cannabis after injecting capsaicin, the hot ingredient in chili peppers, into their skin. Dr. Jody Corey-Bloom, director of the UC San Diego Multiple Sclerosis Center, set out to see if marijuana could relieve spasticity in MS patients whose use of pharmaceuticals often failed to alleviate their suffering. Donald Abrams and Dr. Ron Ellis, a UC San Diego neurologist, worked to see if pot could quell tingling and shooting pains that would start in the feet of AIDS and HIV patients and move to their fingers and hands, disrupting their ability to sleep, to exercise, and, often, to cope.

In separate, overlapping studies between 2002 and 2006, patients with neuropathic pain from HIV smoked pot under the supervision of Abrams's nine-member research team at UC San Francisco's General Clinical Research Center and Ellis's eight-member team at the UC San Diego Medical Center. In San Francisco, fifty-five patients, mostly men with HIV infection for fourteen years, smoked three marijuana cigarettes or placebo joints a day in five-day trials. In surveys for chronic pain during the trials, cannabis was found to reduce the subjects' pain by an average of 34 percent—double the rate of the marijuana placebo. Tests in which brushes were stroked against the subjects' skin showed pot could quell shooting pain sensations in HIV patients, for whom things as benign as pulling a bedsheet over their toes could trigger lightning bolts of agony. Yet in tests involving applying heat to HIV patients' shoulders, Abrams's team failed to show similar benefits of marijuana in cases of acute pain such as might be experienced after an injury or surgery.

In San Diego, research subjects were given placebo joints or three potency levels of marijuana. Ellis's team monitored twenty-eight HIV subjects as they toked on marijuana or the pot placebos over two-week periods, with a two-week break with no marijuana use allowed between each new research stage. Notably, Ellis also had all subjects continue taking their pharmaceutical pain medications during the study. He found they still got a boost from cannabis, with the pot group reporting pain relief at two and a half times the frequency of the placebo group. Ellis also measured impairment. He tested people's ability to connect random letters and numbers on a page, and he had them operate a driving machine, in which they were to avoid simulated traffic obstacles and follow lights and signs. In both tests, patients scored worse after smoking cannabis than before.

One of Ellis's original thirty-four enrolled research subjects had to be excused when he developed an intractable cough from smoking pot. Another subject, who had never before used marijuana, gave researchers a scare. After smoking his first joint, he started staring into space. He stopped responding to questions. The man was in a catatonic state, "attending to what was going on in his head," Ellis observed. Doctors and nurses watching from outside the study room rushed in. They checked his vitals. His heartbeat was normal. He was fine. He came to in a couple of hours with no memory of what happened. He was dropped from the study.

Afterward, University of California researchers enrolled only research subjects who had previously smoked cannabis. They also required drug testing to ensure that subjects were weed-free for thirty days before any clinical research. In every trial, subjects reported a degree of impairment. Pot, even at low, government-grade doses, got them high.

Dr. Corey-Bloom reported that MS patients given cannabis showed modest cognitive impairment. However, her study on thirty patients also demonstrated that smoking marijuana could reduce painful, often disabling symptoms of spasticity. At UC Davis, Dr. Wilsey found something he wasn't counting on. In outpatient sessions of three to twenty-one days, Wilsey and his seven-member team monitored thirty-two patients with nerve injuries as they smoked marijuana with 7 percent or 3.5 percent THC or toked on THC-free placebo joints in a university research center at the Veterans Administration Hospital in Sacramento County. Subjects in both marijuana groups found significant relief from chronic pain. What surprised Wilsey is that they got the same relief with the lower cannabis dose as with the higher dose, only with less impairment. That set Wilsey on a new quest. He sought to find out if patients with painful neuropathy could get relief from marijuana that had further-reduced levels of THC—and without getting stoned.

By the end of Wilsey's first study, Abrams had demonstrated the effectiveness of a healthier marijuana delivery system in another trial. Abrams brought fourteen healthy research volunteers to UC San Francisco and monitored them as they smoked joints or inhaled cannabis from a German-made Volcano Vaporizer, a smokeless delivery device that heated marijuana without lighting it. The heat released cannabis particles into a plastic bag, from which the subjects would breathe medicinal vapors. Abrams found that people using the vaporizer took in significantly reduced levels of carbon monoxide. THC detected in the blood after six hours was the same for people smoking joints and for those consuming cannabis by vaporizing, but vaporizing produced much higher THC levels for the first hour. Abrams's study showed that the vaporizer delivered medicinal effects more efficiently. More important for political acceptance of cannabis research, the vaporizer also could deliver low-tar marijuana.

So for his second study in 2011, Wilsey used the Volcano and pot from the University of Mississippi with 3.5 percent THC, with 1.3 percent THC, and with the THC removed. People such as Gene Murphy, a fifty-seven-year-old former nuclear plant worker with multiple sclerosis, took measured, timed hits from the vaporizer; subjects were given a different dose each week over three separate weeks. For years, Murphy had lived with such a roller coaster of discomfort that, at times, it seemed as if he could step on broken glass and feel nothing. At other times, it felt as if he could land his foot on a single grain of rice and writhe on the ground in pain.

Other than on a few occasions, Murphy hadn't smoked marijuana since he was a young man. His primary care doctor initially forbade him to participate in the marijuana study, then relented after talking with Wilsey and getting Murphy's agreement to continue taking his Vicodin. For Murphy, the government marijuana in the UC Davis study didn't rekindle fond memories. He found Uncle Sam's pot harsh and hardly pleasurable. He quipped to researchers, "Can't you get something better out of Humboldt County?" But Murphy noticed at one point that, with whatever it was he was ingesting, he was feeling less pain.

Wilsey, Murphy, and other research subjects were partners on a journey. Wilsey believed he and his research subjects were "traveling together" to find out if pot patients could find "a suitable dose that doesn't impair people—or impairs them minimally."

Six months after the study, while Wilsey analyzed the data to determine whether a miniscule THC dose could trigger relief, Murphy went to see a Sacramento doctor to get his first medical marijuana recommendation. He found himself getting annoyed at some of the others in the waiting room, the younger, seemingly fitter people who bounded in to see the physician. In contrast, Murphy painfully swiveled out of his chair as his brain told his legs to move and his legs said they would get around to it. But after he got his physician-approved medical cannabis card, he waited weeks before venturing inside a dispensary. There he bought some exotic-named pot he'd never heard of and, once back home, took an introductory hit "to make sure I wasn't going to be a zombie in the next five minutes." Murphy still found Vicodin better for his bad back, but pot addressed the unnerving shooting pains the pharmaceutical didn't seem to touch.

At UC San Diego, the results of Dr. Wallace's study using the ingredient in hot chili powder produced compelling evidence of cannabis's effectiveness with pain while stirring questions about marijuana dosing. Wallace had healthy research subjects smoke marijuana joints with 2, 4, and 8 percent THC, then injected capsaicin into one of each subject's forearms five minutes afterward, and into the other forearm forty-five minutes afterward. When the subjects were injected after five minutes, pot had no significant effect in reducing the capsaicin-induced pain. When injected after forty-five minutes, subjects taking the 2 percent THC dose reported little or no pain reduction. But people smoking 4 percent THC reported significant relief. And people smoking cannabis with 8 percent THC found their pain actually increased. For Wallace, the results were significant. They showed "a therapeutic window" for analgesic relief from marijuana.

The trial left Wallace wanting more research. He knew the dangers faced by pain patients taking opiates—toxic and highly addictive drugs, such as Oxycontin or morphine, that could cause overdose or death. He knew people didn't die from pot overdose, because "with cannabis, there is no lethal dose." But his clinical trial revealed exposure levels where marijuana was both effective and not. On the open market, the constituents and strength of pot varied widely. And there was little dosing information for cannabis buds.

In the last of his four cannabis trials, which had started when he triumphed over government resistance in affirming that marijuana was safe for HIV patients taking protease inhibitors, Donald Abrams got the National Institute on Drug Abuse to fund a study to find out if cannabis could be a suitable cotherapy for use with patients taking opiate drugs. Twenty-one people taking morphine or oxycodone for severe, chronic pain began an additional treatment—inhaling marijuana from a vaporizer. Abrams and his team monitored their blood levels. Morphine in the blood fell insignificantly among patients taking that drug. For people taking oxycodone, the drug levels were unchanged. In both groups, patients' pain dropped markedly. Pot didn't interfere with the conventional meds; it seemed to make them more effective. In his analysis published in 2011, Abrams concluded cannabis was a useful companion drug that also could help people taking toxic, highly addictive opiates reduce their medication levels and side effects.

When it came to medicine and research, Abrams found pot was his "gateway drug." It led him to study other alternative therapies, including whether *Pleurotus ostreatus*—oyster mushrooms—could reduce cholesterol in HIV patients whose lipid levels jumped with antiretroviral treatments. The oyster mushrooms didn't produce measurable benefits, although Abrams's study noted that "there were no adverse experiences reported other than patients' distaste for the preparation." Pot lured Abrams to expand into the study and practice of integrative medicine, focusing on alternative therapies and holistic health methods. As he treated cancer patients as the chief of oncology and hematology at San Francisco General, he also met many patients at UC San Francisco's Osher Center for Integrative Medicine. There, he counseled them on nutrition, fitness training, massage, meditation, yoga, tai chi, and herbs, including cannabis.

Abrams found that, for some people, he could recommend pot in place of a half dozen different prescriptions. It worked for chemotherapy patients who didn't like taking ondansetron for their nausea and vomiting, or didn't care for Vicodin for pain or Ambien for sleeping, or wanted alternative medications for anorexia, anxiety, or depression. Abrams recommended pot for a woman terminally ill with cancer so she could stomach family meals with loved ones before her time came. He counseled Troy Larson, a cancer-stricken commercial lighting salesman referred by another oncologist. Larson had lost sixty-five pounds during cancer treatments that would bring the disease to remission. To keep Larson's strength up, Abrams ran him through health-boosting options, including acupuncture for his discomfort and a diet short on red meat and processed food and long on fruits and vegetables. He also told him cannabis could be another tool. Larson liked how Abrams didn't push it but merely put pot on the menu of available health and medical choices. He waited months before using the recommendation Abrams wrote. And then Larson especially liked it when his weight and strength recovered, when he was able to resume attending his children's soccer games and resume his life.

In February 2010, Dr. Igor Grant and the University of California system researchers who had conducted clinical trials on cannabis with more than three hundred subjects gathered at the state capitol to present their preliminary findings. Their answer to the state-mandated question—Does marijuana have therapeutic value?—was yes. "As a result of this program of systematic research, we now have reasonable evidence that cannabis is a promising treatment," Grant announced. At the time, he refrained from pointing out that the results flew in the face of the U.S. government's classification of marijuana as a Schedule I drug with no accepted medical use. In 2012, with the California clinical trials completed and the last studies being published, Grant let it be known that the Schedule I classification "is completely at odds with existing science" and "seems intellectually dishonest."

Every clinical study by the Center for Medicinal Cannabis Research showed potential medical benefits from cannabis. Yet the California trials didn't include anywhere close to sufficient numbers of patients to meet Food and Drug Administration standards for evaluating marijuana's potential as a prescription medication. National drug abuse and addiction surveys said marijuana—though it presented less perceived danger than other substances—could be addictive, with 9 percent of users developing an unhealthy pot dependency. And Grant cautioned that a significant body of medical literature raised legitimate concerns over pot's danger for people susceptible to schizophrenia or other psychotic illnesses and over its potential harms for teenagers, whose brains were still developing. The government pot used in the studies also wasn't even close to the bottom-shelf intensity of designer weed strains sold at many California medical marijuana dispensaries, meaning researchers didn't test what was actually on the market. They also didn't have the option of looking at new niche marijuana strains bred with low-THC and high concentrations of cannabidiol, or CBD, a cannabis constituent believed to deliver analgesic benefits without impairment.

Grant and his research teams characterized marijuana as a promising, secondary therapy that offered relief for people for whom other treatments failed. Grant saw the work as a clarion call for more research, not necessarily a ticket for Californians to smoke pot or for the burgeoning of a medical marijuana industry. But outside the University of California system research laboratories, newly minted medical-cannabis physicians seized on an old herb to promote new-generation medicine. They opened medical pot clinics as profitable new ventures. The new pot docs doled out hundreds of thousands of medical recommendations to people wanting to use marijuana legally. They became the essential conduits for the medical marijuana economy.

FIVE

The Pot Docs

Before he fell "victim to this drug war," before he emerged as the antiprohibition physician and seized his role as a doctor to override government intolerance of marijuana and enable people to use it as medicine, Dr. David Allen was a star surgeon in Pascagoula, Mississippi. He used to feel the hush of reverence as he strode the hallways of Singing River Hospital. He was a cardiothoracic surgeon who commanded the operating room. He directed his team in lifesaving procedures such as harvesting the greater saphenous vein from a man's leg and using it to bypass blocked coronary arteries. He performed Singing River Hospital's first beating-heart bypass in another operation, earning a profile in the *Sun Herald* newspaper in southern Mississippi for his medical heroics in extending the life of seventy-four-year-old Ora Mae Wilson of Ocean Springs. His more than two decades as a heart surgeon earned him a million-dollar ranch estate called the "Blue Hole." The fifty acres included a lake and ponds rimmed with longleaf pines and brimming with bass and blue gill and crappie.

But in 2009, Dr. Allen retired as a heart surgeon and moved to California to become a marijuana doctor. He opened a clinic in Sacramento. He hung the framed news clipping about his beating-heart surgery, his awards, and his medical degree from the University of Texas at San Antonio next to office murals depicting Bob Marley, Snoop Dogg, and Barack Obama—the latter with a paraphrased remark from the 2008 presidential candidate suggesting he would end federal raids on state-permitted medical marijuana.

Dr. Allen had smoked marijuana since he was seventeen. He had used it to overcome the stress of exams as a medical student. He didn't consume it on days when he performed open-heart surgeries in Mississippi. But the nights before, when he weighed the pressures of the operating room, of directing the surgical team, of holding a patient's life in his hands, of knowing that any mistake could devastate a family and destroy his career, he lit up a joint to drive the anxiety away. Yet he couldn't alleviate his sense that his livelihood as a heart surgeon was threatened. Allen saw cardiologists in hospital emergency rooms as performing "wallet biopsies," diagnoses of insurance coverage and patients' ability to pay. He saw more patients with heart lesions getting stents put in instead of undergoing more extensive open-heart surgeries. The surgeon's star was diminishing. Allen was performing only a fraction of the heart procedures he used to. And just as he hated insurance companies and hospital politics, he was fascinated by emerging medical literature on the endocannabinoid system and the body's interactions with pot. He was also inspired by profitable opportunities in cannabis medicine in California.

At his Sacramento clinic, Allen posted a sign at the door with a medical cross, a marijuana leaf, and the proclamation "By legal democratic vote, cannabis is medicine." For $150 per patient, he wrote recommendations that could allow Californians to use marijuana and to purchase it at medical cannabis dispensaries or grow it. A steady stream of paying clients sought out the former heart doc with dusty blond hair tied in a ponytail. Construction worker Brent Bomia, who had crushed his vertebrae after crashing to the ground on a house-framing job and undergone back surgery, found the new doctor in town to be his lifesaver for pain that prescription drugs didn't sufficiently alleviate. He saw Allen as a community "stepping-stone" supporting pot's place as accepted therapy. Others coming in told Allen that marijuana worked for soothing their migraines or menstrual cramps or asthma. "How can you deny these patients?" Allen exclaimed. One beleaguered man seeking a medicinal recommendation told Allen he had used pot for forty-five years. He had a blood disease, chronic pain, and stress and insisted cannabis had never failed him, that it had weaned him off of his methadone addiction and—before that—helped with his heroin addiction.

"Would you say you drink less because you use cannabis?" Allen asked.

"Oh yeah," the man said. "I used to drink a half a pint of whiskey a night."

"It's the antidrug, isn't it?" the doctor remarked as he wrote out the recommendation.

Inspired by his new career in marijuana medicine, the transplanted Mississippi heart surgeon announced widely and often that "cannabis is a miracle drug." He declared it "safer than table salt." But for Allen, it was also a substance that would bring him heartache, loss of liberty, and near ruin.

Back in Mississippi, word of the Pascagoula heart doc cashing in as a pot doc in California reached the Narcotics Task Force of Jackson County. The local drug officers staged a raid on Allen's "Blue Hole" estate. They arrested his sister and confiscated eight hundred dollars' worth of marijuana and a thousand dollars' worth of hash from Allen's brother-in-law. They charged the doctor with trafficking marijuana for sale and had him extradited from California, shackled for days in the rear seating area of a private van carrying other suspects from state to state. Mississippi drug officers took his million dollar property, erecting a No Trespassing sign and declaring the Blue Hole "seized for illegal drug activity by the Narcotics Task Force of Jackson County."

Allen's status as a legal marijuana doctor in California was an inherent curse in his home state. "In the state of Mississippi, whether you think it's for medical use or not, it's against the law," Jackson County Narcotics Task force Lt. Commander Curtis Spiers told Allen's new hometown newspaper, *The Sacramento Bee*. After Allen posted bail and returned to California, drug officers in Mississippi weren't at all impressed with online videos the physician and supporters put up, depicting the Mississippi narcs as "professional thieves" and "terrorists" out to steal the good doctor's land. And when Allen made the mistake of going back to Mississippi to visit his sister and brother-in-law, authorities in Jackson County charged him with witness tampering and bribery for offering to buy his sister a two-hundred-dollar cell phone and pay for the couple's travel to California. The Mississippi drug cops locked him up without bail for fourteen months, awaiting trial on marijuana counts that could get him sixty years in prison. Jailed, traumatized, Allen reflected on his brief existence as a California cannabis physician. If he got out, Dr. Allen promised himself, he would do more than just write medical recommendations. He would use marijuana medicine to act on "a mission from God to end prohibition and stop the war on God's plant."

By the time the cell door closed on Dr. David Allen in Mississippi, pot medicine in California was big business. Scores of physicians were lined up to take his place. Marijuana's status as a federally prohibited drug still prevented them from writing formal prescriptions for pot. Weed wasn't to be found at any legal pharmacy. And a large majority of the California medical establishment wanted nothing to do with marijuana medicine. But doctors willing, or eager, to write patients "recommendations" to use marijuana as therapy found they could reap a fortune. Their endorsements of the medical use of cannabis helped the seriously ill to regain weight and equilibrium, to find soothing, palliative relief for symptoms. Doctors recommending cannabis also provided people—the sick, less sick, and not-so-sick—safe passage around state marijuana laws. Physicians' recommendations became the entry ticket to shelves of exotic marijuana strains and edibles at often loosely regulated medical cannabis dispensaries flowering in California cities. Marijuana doctors and pot clubs were to have no direct ties or business relationships. The Medical Board of California—and federal law—strictly forbade physicians from providing marijuana or even instructing patients on where to get it. Yet cannabis doctors left leaflets and stacks of business cards at the dispensaries. Well after the passage of Proposition 215, an unofficial nexus of pot docs and pot clubs ignited California's exploding cannabis commerce.

Little of that had seemed fathomable when California had legalized medical use of marijuana. Leading up to the 1996 initiative, U.S. drug czar Barry McCaffrey, director of the Clinton administration's Office of National Drug Control Policy, announced that the government wasn't going to stand idly as doctors recommended marijuana. "This is not medicine," the retired army general declared. "This is a cruel hoax that sounds more like something out of a Cheech and Chong show." Days before the vote, he warned that any California doctors recommending marijuana would face federal prosecution. After Prop 215's passage, the Office of National Drug Control Policy declared that physician endorsement of medical marijuana use "is not consistent with the 'public interest,'" citing a key catchphrase in the federal Controlled Substances Act. It said physicians even discussing marijuana with patients could be targeted by the Drug Enforcement Administration. The feds then clarified their threat: doctors writing recommendations for pot would lose their DEA licenses to prescribe medicine.

Medical marijuana advocates, who after Proposition 215's passage were having trouble finding physicians to write marijuana recommendations, went searching for a figurehead for a legal challenge against McCaffrey and the federal government. They approached Dr. Marcus Conant, a respected professor at University of California, San Francisco Medical Center, and the director of the Conant Medical Group, one of the largest private AIDS practices in the United States. Conant hadn't written a formal medical recommendation for pot. But many times, he had advised his emaciated patients of what hundreds of AIDS and HIV sufferers had told him—that smoking a joint might help. Conant was furious over McCaffrey's threats against doctors. Yet he told the Drug Policy Alliance, the Marijuana Policy Project, and the ACLU that "I've got more things to do than fight the government" as part of their lawsuit. Joe Robinson, administrator for Conant's practice, implored him to recognize that every cause—from race relations to the plight of AIDS patients—needed a champion. He urged Conant to sign on. Robinson also jokingly reminded the AIDS doctor that his sister and her husband had a house he could flee to in France should his challenging the U.S. government go terribly wrong.

In 1997, days before Dr. Donald Abrams got his meeting with the director of the National Institute on Drug Abuse to advocate medical cannabis research, Dr. Marcus Conant became the lead plaintiff in *Conant v. McCaffrey*. In the lawsuit, physicians treating patients with AIDS, cancer, infectious diseases, wasting syndrome, breast cancer, and debilitating seizures sued McCaffrey's Office of National Drug Control Policy, the DEA, Attorney General Janet Reno, and Health and Human Services Secretary Donna Shalala.

The plaintiffs in the lawsuit included Dr. Arnold Leff, the former official in Richard Nixon's White House Office of Drug Abuse Prevention who went on to treat AIDS patients in Santa Cruz, including members of the Wo/Men's Alliance for Medical Marijuana. Leff, who was afraid to venture anywhere near the WAMM garden, and who said he was wary of discussing cannabis with patients for fear that the government would go after his medical license, filed a declaration saying marijuana was medically appropriate to combat nausea from AIDS. He was joined in the suit by several medical cannabis patients, including Valerie Corral. She declared that it was marijuana—not the fog of prescription medicines, including Mysoline, Dilantin, phenobarbital, Percodan, and Valium—that had saved her from the horror and agony of protracted grand mal seizures after traumatic head injuries in her car accident.

It was up to Dr. Marcus Conant to spearhead the fight. In a pretrial deposition, the lead plaintiff found himself questioned by a stern federal attorney who asked how he had voted on Proposition 215. Conant refused to say. The government lawyer dropped the question, and then asked if Conant had suggested pot to his patients as a medical therapy. The doctor's attorneys hustled him into a hallway, where they advised him not to answer. The parties resumed. Conant replied, "Yes." He started thinking he might need that house in France after all.

The government charged Conant with aiding and abetting a drug crime. But the courts rendered it moot with decisive rulings supporting the rights of physicians concerning medical marijuana. "Physicians have a legitimate need to discuss and recommend to their patients all medically accepted forms of treatment," wrote U.S. district judge William Alsup in a ruling on behalf of Conant in 2000. He went on: "If such recommendations could not be communicated, then the physician-patient relationship would be seriously impaired." After the case was appealed, redubbed *Conant v. Walters* (for the new Bush administration drug czar, John P. Walters), Chief Judge Mary M. Schroder of the U.S. Ninth Circuit Court of Appeals wrote in 2002 that "core First Amendment values" protected doctors from government attempts to "punish" them. The Ninth Circuit Court ruled doctors could recommend marijuana as long as they didn't help people obtain the pot. When the U.S. Supreme Court declined to grant the government's request for a certiorari on October 4, 2003, recommending marijuana became certified as a physician's right.

In the ensuing years, Conant wrote out only a handful of recommendations for marijuana use. Despite the legal victory, many other California doctors remained wary about pot—save for one particularly determined and outspoken Berkeley psychiatrist. Dr. Tod H. Mikuriya became celebrated as the grandfather of marijuana medicine and "doctor of last resort" for cannabis. In 1967, Mikuriya had been a consulting research psychiatrist at the Center for Narcotics and Drug Abuse Studies at the National Institute of Mental Health. He quit after several months, charging that the government, fearful of marijuana use by anti-Vietnam protestors and the counterculture, had suppressed evidence of its medical benefits. "Marijuana was seen as something dangerous that was being adopted by subversive organizations," Mikuriya recounted in 2006. "I ended up coming to California and ended up defecting." He published *Marijuana: Medical Papers, 1839–1972*, an anthology of premarijuana-prohibition medical literature. And he backed a California pot legalization measure, which was routed by voters in 1972. He also embraced the slogan "Back to the future!" as he began recommending marijuana to patients six years before Proposition 215. He was credited with adding to that initiative the phrase "or any other illness for which marijuana provides relief," which vastly expanded legal use of marijuana in California.

Over fourteen years, Mikuriya issued more than nine thousand marijuana recommendations. He drafted a list of more than 250 symptoms for which he said marijuana could provide relief. The list, from autism to whiplash, included color blindness, constipation, dyslexia, eczema, genital herpes, hiccups, irritable bowel syndrome, menopausal syndrome, restless legs syndrome, sinusitis, sleep apnea, and stuttering. He also suggested pot could be used for schizophrenia, mania, and other psychiatric conditions. To the Medical Board of California, which investigated Mikuriya for seven years, fined him seventy-five thousand dollars, and put him on probation in lieu of revoking his license, Mikuriya acted in "an extreme departure from the standard of care." The board cited him in sixteen cases for failing to perform adequate examinations or obtain medical records for pot-seeking patients reporting symptoms ranging from pain to panic attacks. The cannabis community celebrated Mikuriya as a courageous pioneer unjustly targeted and framed by undercover cops and smeared by the medical board. After his death in 2007, Mikuriya's list of symptoms addressed by marijuana was adopted by scores of medical cannabis clinics.

From 1996 to 2010, the Medical Board of California investigated eighty-one complaints against doctors who recommended marijuana, revoking licenses of ten physicians but issuing stays in each case, permitting sanctioned doctors to continue practicing under probationary status. The board's general charge was that many pot docs conducted either insufficient medical exams or no exams at all. It alleged that many failed to detect overt drug-seeking behaviors of people simply wanting a piece of paper so they could smoke weed legally.

In 2004, the medical board targeted a Mikuriya disciple, Dr. Marion Fry. She was a breast cancer survivor whose heart-wrenching story of radical surgery, suffering, and recovery through cannabis rallied the medical marijuana community. Fry ran one of California's early cannabis medicine clinics, greeting thousands of people in a small town in the Sierra Nevada foothills outside of Sacramento. The medical board charged her with "gross negligence" for alleged actions including recommending marijuana to a paranoid schizophrenic who believed "he was the second coming of Jesus Christ, Bill Gates was after him, and he had a camera in his head." After a complaint from the man's family, the board claimed Fry ignored warnings from the Merced County Department of Mental Health that pot exacerbated his condition. Fry noted in her medical report that the man did "not like psych meds." She contended that he offered her paperwork for a bipolar condition and an "atypical mood disorder," that he made "good eye contact" and had a job and appointments for therapy. The medical board wasn't satisfied. In 2008, it put Fry on three years' probation after granting a stay on revoking her license. Well before then, U.S. authorities targeted Fry and her attorney husband, Dale Schafer, in a federal marijuana prosecution that would cast her as a tragic heroine for the medical cannabis movement.

The Medical Board of California itself came under fire as physicians complained that its investigations of marijuana doctors and lack of guidelines for cannabis scared away reputable practitioners. In 2004, the board, officially declaring its "commitment to physicians who recommend medical marijuana," said it wouldn't target doctors who followed policies that included conducting "good faith" examinations of patients, getting medical histories, developing treatment plans, and arranging periodic reviews to discuss with patients marijuana's efficacy or side effects.

One of the board's harshest critics, Dr. Frank Lucido, was a Berkeley family practice doctor and a peacenik. Lucido was approached by cannabis advocates who urged him to incorporate marijuana recommendations into his practice after he showed his activist mettle by getting arrested in antinuke protests at the Nevada Test Site. Lucido saw the new medical-board marijuana guidelines as a joke, bereft of real protocols to help physicians working with patients seeking an alternative medicine. So Lucido penned his own guidelines— "Implementation of the Compassionate Use Act in a Family Medical Practice"—for a cannabis medical journal. He demanded that people seeking a marijuana recommendation demonstrate that they took their conditions seriously enough to have seen their primary care doctors. "I don't want to be the only physician who is aware of your illness," Lucido wrote. He would call family members to ask how some patients responded to marijuana. He turned away patients—or restricted them to medical marijuana recommendations of three months or less—if their medical records or treatment programs were lacking.

"When did you last see your doctor?" Lucido would ask people who came in.

"Well, I don't believe in Western medicine," some would reply.

That wouldn't do, Lucido told them. He implored his patients to demonstrate, with proper records, evidence of a medical condition in case they were ever called into court. He also cautioned other physicians to reject people who said they just wanted to enjoy marijuana or relax. Figure those people are cops, he warned. When one strangely obstinate man came in saying he was missing a toe—and thus needed pot—Lucido was suspicious. After the man removed his sock to show that indeed a digit was missing, the doctor asked, "So what's the problem there?"

"Can't you see?" the man replied.

"Do you have pain?"

"No," the man said. "It's just driving me crazy."

"Is there a mental disorder?"

"No."

Lucido thought the man wanted him to make up a diagnosis to justify a cannabis recommendation—something that could get Lucido busted by the medical board. The patient became belligerent. Lucido refunded his money, ordered him to leave, and called the cops.

The Berkeley doctor wasn't on speed dial for many pot card seekers. He charged $250 for a one-year marijuana recommendation and required a thirty-to-forty-five-minute consultation, including a problem-specific physical exam. One day, a twenty-five-year-old man came in seeking a cannabis recommendation for asthma, anxiety, and insomnia. Lucido felt the man's thyroid and noticed a nodule. "You need to have that looked at," he said. He wrote a three-month recommendation and said he would extend it only if the man brought in proof that he got his thyroid checked. The patient followed through. Doctors found cancer that had spread from the patient's thyroid to his lungs.

Given Lucido's credibility, cannabis advocates sought him out again to be the doctor of record in another court challenge to the federal government over medical marijuana, and Lucido became the physician for Angel Raich. She was the wife of Robert Raich, a lawyer in the earlier Oakland Cannabis Buyers Cooperative case that ended with the U.S. Supreme Court ruling rejecting a medical necessity defense for marijuana. Angel Raich had an inoperable brain tumor, seizures, and fibromyalgia. Lucido wrote a court declaration: "Her body reacts with violent side effects to almost all pharmaceutical medications. Angel will suffer imminent harm without access to cannabis. Chronic severe pain constitutes harm. Nausea and anorexia resulting in weight loss, risking malnutrition, cachexia, starvation, and death, constitute harm. Untreated seizures constitute harm. . . . Angel needs to medicate every two waking hours."

The Raich case, which would reach the Supreme Court, invoked a state's-rights defense for medical marijuana under the Commerce Clause of the Constitution. Lucido thus joined the legal and political crusade for medical cannabis. He also became a vehement critic of "paper mill" clinics that sprang up in California, churning out thousands of recommendations for pot with little or no medical review. He saw what was developing—a California carnival in the name of medical marijuana.

•   •   •

On Los Angeles' Ocean Front Walk along Venice Beach, amid the metal-clanging workout yard of Muscle Beach and the sidewalk conga troupes, sand sculptors, and tarot card readers, the commerce of doling out medical cannabis recommendations found its grandest stage. "Hash bar, patients welcome!" shouted a sidewalk barker outside one of three offices of the Medical Kush Doctor. The clinic operated directly next door to the Medical Kush Beach Club dispensary, where the proprietor, dubbed "Sean Kush," appeared in a video toking on foot-long fatties with Tommy Chong from the famed stoner movies. Up Ocean Front Walk, inside a landmark wood-plank Victorian, the Blu House, another Medical Kush Doctor clinic shared a roof with the Kush Clubhouse dispensary. "Get legal today!" a barker there shouted, summoning beachgoers who could meet the pot doc in one door and get a hookup for weed in the next.

Anyone who missed out on the flourishing Venice Beach medical cannabis show could watch it all on "Hash Bar TV," an online network advertised on L.A. billboards. In the segments, after the opening logo of a cartoonish TV on a bed of marijuana buds, Sean Kush, real name Sean Cardillo, appeared, tattooed with a skeleton with fire-red eyes and piercing fangs. He was supercharged in pitching the possibilities of medical pot in one of his Hash Bar TV spots that introduced viewers to a grandfatherly Medical Kush Doctor physician, Dr. William Stuart Weil, and in explaining the ease of getting a marijuana recommendation.

"So, I'm the champ from the Hash Bar Olympics," a young woman said excitedly, bounding in to greet the clinic's medical receptionist in the Hash Bar TV segment. "I've got to get ready for the Hash Cup. So I need my renewal. How does that work?"

"Basically, you're still going to fill out the paperwork," the receptionist for Dr. Weil replied. "We'll take you in to the doctor again, and you're good."

In the Venice boardwalk medical office, Dr. Weil explained different plant species of marijuana: "a tall thin plant," sativa, "that is a stimulant, an upper," and indica, "a short fat little bush" that's "a depressant" and body relaxant. "Marijuana is of course natural. And when you wake up you're usually very refreshed," Dr. Weil said. "It doesn't have any hangover at all." He added, "It's great stuff."

The host, Sean Kush, entered as Dr. Weil went on about pot's reduced cancer danger when compared to cigarettes, and the doctor also suggested that marijuana had the potential to stunt the growth of cancer cells. "Did you hear that?" the host exclaimed, adding a boast that he personally smoked twenty to thirty joints a day. "The more you smoke the less cancer you get. Straight from the doc!"

"Hash Bar TV. Medical Kush Doctor. Dr. Weil," Sean Kush said. "The best doctor on the whole fucking planet!" He simulated toking on a joint and blew a kiss.

On this teeming beach boardwalk in Venice, the notion of marijuana as medicine blurred with that of pot for pleasure. For all the relief that cannabis provided the seriously and gravely ill, the boardwalk delivered a message that medical marijuana and recreational use were indistinguishable in popular culture.

In 2010, police and California medical board investigators raided the Medical Kush Doctor clinics. In 2012, the board filed accusations in order to revoke the state medical licenses and surgical certificates of Weil and two other Medical Kush Doctor physicians. The board's complaint alleged the medical corporation was illegally run by nonphysicians—the same company that ran the Medical Kush Beach Club and Kush Clubhouse hash bars. It charged that the company running the dispensaries also took a financial cut from every marijuana recommendation the doctors wrote. A year later, Dr. Weil, the kindly physician from the Hash Bar TV promotion, was formally reprimanded by the medical board but retained his right to practice medicine. The Los Angeles District Attorney's Office charged Sean Cardillo, the chief officer, and an associate with thirteen criminal counts, including illegal marijuana sales and distribution and filing false tax returns. As Cardillo awaited trial in 2013, a state appeals court allowed prosecutors to reinstate another charge against him: practicing medicine without a license.

Even groups fighting for marijuana legalization took issue with some doctors and cannabis medicine clinics. The California chapter of the National Organization for the Reform of Marijuana Laws announced it was excluding from its online medical cannabis physician listings any doctors with suspended licenses, as well as medical clinics owned by nondoctors. It also posted an advisory—"Warning: Beware [of] bogus clinics!"—about a small number of physicians charging extra fees for a "cultivation license" purportedly allowing patients to grow anywhere from twenty-five to ninety-nine plants for personal use in treating their medical conditions. "There is no such thing as a 'cultivation license' under California law," NORML asserted, warning that cops were unlikely to respect it.

Yet wannabe marijuana growers traveled hundreds of miles to see Dr. Milan Hopkins in his storefront clinic on Main Street in Upper Lake, a tiny town near the shores of Clear Lake in Northern California's Lake County. They came to see Hopkins for the standard medical cannabis recommendation he wrote. For $250 for six months or $100 for a renewal, Hopkins wrote recommendations declaring that every one of his patients, regardless of condition, "may need to grow 99 mature plants and possess 19 pounds of processed cannabis for their yearly medical needs." Few doctors in California even mentioned quantities of marijuana. But Hopkins, a gray-haired navy veteran and lead guitarist in a rock band called the Freak Show—after a local free clinic he used to operate—asserted he was fed up with anti-marijuana prosecutors hauling him into court to testify to how much pot some sick person they had busted actually needed.

Hopkins's California medical license was put on probationary status twice by the medical board, in 1979 and 1998, when Hopkins was charged with issuing excessive prescriptions for painkillers. He surrendered his DEA prescription license in favor of recommending cannabis—"an herb with a will to heal," he called it—and for a time also offered beauty-enhancing laser surgery. Hopkins started out recommending twenty-five marijuana plants and five pounds of pot, based on the twenty-five-plant cultivation rule in nearby Mendocino County. He upped his numbers after a state Supreme Court ruling overturned state growing limits, the policy in most counties, of six mature plants per patient. Patients came to him from places where police still regarded growers with more than six plants as marijuana traffickers. One of Dr. Hopkins's twenty-five-plant, five-pound cannabis recommendations failed to protect a disabled former oil-rig scuba diver who packed three pounds of pot from his marijuana garden in his luggage, which was searched at Sacramento International Airport. Matt Zugsberger promptly presented his recommendation from Dr. Hopkins to airport security officers. It didn't spare him from a conviction for illegal marijuana transportation.

Hopkins made no apologies for his blanket recommendations promising a bounty of marijuana. "My politics are left and my attitude is fuck the cops," he explained. Dr. Hopkins embraced his resentment of the "patriarchal authority" of people wanting to trample on cannabis and the rights of medical users. He saw himself as their foil and was willing to take their flak while running his business. "Yeah, it's worth it to me," he said. "I'm making a lot of money on it."

Seemingly no one in marijuana medicine made more money, nor marketed the practice of cannabis care to the masses better, than MediCann. Founded by Dr. Jean Talleyrand, who formerly had a private practice in San Francisco's Mission District, MediCann became California's largest medical marijuana physicians' network, with clinics in twenty-one California cities. It also displayed its advertising genius in making light of stoner stereotypes to sell marijuana medicine as an increasingly mainstream option. On billboards along California thoroughfares, in magazine ads, and on abundant fliers papering marijuana dispensaries, MediCann depicted productive people as "typical stoners." Medical marijuana patient Karen, one of the ads said, was "a typical stoner" who used cannabis for insomnia and had just been made full professor. "Typical stoner" Josh, another ad claimed, was diagnosed with HIV, but—with the help of marijuana—was keeping up his tennis game, law school studies, and community volunteerism. "Typical stoner" Dan, a thirty-five-year-old investment broker, suffered from clinical anxiety but came to work "rested and relaxed" thanks to cannabis. "Typical stoner" Andy, happily fixing a sink, was back on the job as a plumber thanks to back pain–relieving medical marijuana. "Typical stoner" Mary, a retired teacher looking fit while working out with a barbell, was enjoying her grandchildren, free of arthritis pain after getting a MediCann recommendation. Using stock photos and a message that medical cannabis patients were average Californians contributing to society, MediCann grossed more than $20 million as it doled out recommendations—most for $150—to more than 230,000 individuals between 2004 and 2011.

By 2011, a California NORML survey estimated that California doctors had issued recommendations to between 750,000 and 1.1 million individual medical marijuana users. As the market grew, the price of recommendations went into free fall. And yet doctors still made money. One California medical network—Med/Rx'C—which charged $50 for recommendations in Sacramento—advertised online for new pot docs, proclaiming, "You can earn up to $16,000 per month!" On Los Angeles' Melrose Avenue, across the street from three marijuana dispensaries, the Doc420 offices of Dr. Sona Patel filled with people drawn by her $30 and $40 pot recommendations, "no qualify no pay" guarantees, and her sizzling cannabis magazine ads, in which she ripped open her American eagle T-shirt, drawing readers' eyes to her red, white, and blue bikini and high-heeled pumps. At the Kush Expo Medical Marijuana Show in Anaheim, a team in lime-green medical smocks adorned with pot leaves lured conventioneers in for similarly priced quickie medical marijuana cards from the Green Doctor, a new cannabis clinic born on the boardwalk at Venice Beach and employing some of the same physicians as the Medical Kush Doctor.

. . .

The new pot docs won no love from the symbol of the state medical establishment, the California Medical Association, a private professional body representing thirty-five thousand California doctors. In 2010, an association committee headed by Dr. Donald Lyman, former deputy director of the California Department of Public Health, began assessing the role of the cannabis doctor in California. Lyman was disturbed by what he was seeing. He visited a dispensary and noticed marijuana lollipops labeled "two doses." He wondered just what a dose was. In Lyman's eyes, marijuana doctors and dispensaries alike often "have no idea what's in this stuff." He believed that as many as four in five people seeking medical marijuana recommendations were pursuing pot for pleasure, not medicinal healing. Lyman endorsed the doctor-patient relationships that enabled people with serious conditions to benefit from cannabis—but not simply to make marijuana legal. In 2011, the California Medical Association threw up its hands in a bold declaration. Calling federal cannabis prohibition "a failed public health policy," it said marijuana should be regulated, taxed, and dispensed like alcohol or cigarettes, effectively removing many doctors from the equation. "The public movement towards legalization of medical cannabis has inappropriately placed physicians in the role of gatekeeper for public access to this botanical," the association declared.

Awaiting trial in Mississippi, Dr. David Allen only dreamed of freeing himself from jail and returning to California to be that very gatekeeper helping people find a safe path to cannabis. He penned a letter from the George County Regional Correctional Facility in Lucedale, Mississippi: "I am a prisoner of war. . . . The reasons for this war are not clear, nor are the reasons based on scientific fact. . . . The true motives are hidden agendas." He pored over his Bible. He underlined a passage in Genesis 1:29, "And God said, Behold I have given you every herb bearing seed," and another in Romans 14:3 that Allen saw as speaking to the drug warriors: "Let not him which eateth not judge him that eateth."

Before Allen's trial in Jackson County, Mississippi, Circuit Judge Robert Krebs threw out the prosecutor's added charges of witness tampering and bribing a witness, which had resulted from the doctor's meeting with his sister and brother-in-law. But as Dr. Allen went before a jury, media accounts reported he allegedly ran a sophisticated cultivation room at his Blue Hole estate that could produce an annual pot yield worth a half million dollars. That narrative fell apart in court. Though narcotics officers had seized a couple of grow lamps and a prosecutor summoned a jailhouse informant to testify that Allen told him he grew marijuana, neither any plants nor direct evidence of cultivation was found on the property. Curtis Spiers, the narcotics lieutenant commander, admitted on the witness stand that a photo of a room filled with marijuana plants he gave to a Mississippi television station came from another case and had nothing to do with Allen. The judge, without disclosing which way the jury was leaning, declared a mistrial after jurors deadlocked eleven to one and seven to five on charges of transporting and manufacturing a controlled substance. In January 2012, the district attorney, Tony Lawrence, dropped the charges. "A jury comprised of 12 citizens from Jackson County did not find evidence to convict David Allen," Lawrence said, saying a retrial was ill-advised "in light of the fact that there was no actual grown marijuana found on the property and no new evidence exists."

Allen got his land back in Mississippi and his life back in California. His hair now gray and cut short, his face noticeably drawn, he reopened his medical cannabis practice in a low-rent suite outside of downtown Sacramento, where he posted a sign on the door for Dr. David Allen, cardiothoracic surgeon. He charged $60 per annual recommendation, down from $150. He wrote patient guidelines, advising cancer sufferers to use Phoenix Tears cannabis oil and suggesting that those at risk of heart disease or stroke eat doses of Cannatonic or Harlequin or ATF (Alaskan Thunder Fuck), marijuana stains with high levels of nonpsychoactive cannabidiol. Dr. Allen also advised patients on jury nullification in marijuana cases. "When unjust laws threaten honest men, the jury has a right to vote not guilty," he wrote in his medical instructions. "Get on a jury and free a cannabis patient."

Free from his prohibitionist hell in Mississippi, safely back in California in his modest clinic and his small role in the blooming medical marijuana economy, Dr. David Allen was proud to be a gatekeeper for legal cannabis.

SIX

L.A. Excess

Inland from Venice Beach and the boardwalk barkers for medicinal Kush care, Yamileth "Yami" Bolanos, a fiery voice for cannabis patients, found occasional solitude on a blue settee beneath the arching palm leaves of the Pure Life Alternative Wellness Center. It was her sanctuary when she wasn't busy haranguing the Los Angeles City Council for allowing America's second-largest metropolis to become overrun by marijuana stores and then blaming reputable operators for the unregulated mess.

In her dispensary on bustling La Cienega Boulevard in west L.A., Yami would eagerly await the regular visits of a special patient. Carlos Kruschewsky was a Brazilian immigrant and a quadriplegic after a skateboarding accident suffered while he was a college student in Santa Cruz. Kruschewsky would enter, navigating his wheelchair with a lever beneath his chin, bringing his resilient spirit.

Kruschewsky could only raise one arm a few inches off his lap. But he could work a computer mouse by tilting his neck and reflecting a laser light off a metal dot on his forehead. He was even a regular at a local dance studio, where he would spin his motorized chair to rock, salsa, and samba. "I don't want to sit around all day pitying myself," Kruschewsky would tell Yami. "That's my job—being happy."

Kruschewsky couldn't do his job—living on his terms—when his shoulders would spasm and seize up, stiffening his neck. So Bolanos helped him. In her palm-shaded "vapor room," she inflated a plastic bag with hot marijuana gusts from a stainless steel machine. She held the bag to his mouth, administering the medicine, letting Carlos breathe in, rest, and breathe in again until his spasms went away. He would let her know. "I can feel it," he would say. "It's life changing."

"This isn't some damn party room," Yami announced, over and over. But in the eyes of the Los Angeles City Council, it may as well have been. By early 2010, the city of Los Angeles declared itself overdosed with pot shops. Los Angeles, the refrain went, had *more marijuana dispensaries than Starbucks.* Soon that couldn't capture the extent of it all. Neon marijuana leaves from cannabis stores lit the night on eclectic Melrose Avenue, where a potpourri of pot shops sprouted amid actors' halls, comedy clubs, and ethnic districts from Colombian to Thai to Slavic. Cannabis magazines brimmed with ads for new marijuana stores that spanned the sprawling metropolis. A buxom pot nurse, holding a red stethoscope to her breast, summoned patients to the California Organic Collective in Canoga Park. Compassionate Caregivers invited patrons to "medicate" during its 3-to-7-p.m. "happy hour" near downtown. Rap music star and pop culture icon Snoop Dogg smoked a joint in an ad that touted "free bong hits" at KushMart in Hollywood.

For years, Yami Bolanos, who had opened one of the city's early dispensaries in 2005, yelled at Los Angeles officials to regulate the emerging local cannabis industry. The city council in 2007 passed a feckless moratorium against new marijuana clubs, hoping to buy time to set some rules. That only brought lawsuits and hundreds of new dispensaries. So in 2010, the city council tried again. It set a cap of 70 marijuana stores and grandfathered in another 116, meaning as many as 800 would have to close. The new ordinance said Los Angeles police could freely audit dispensary books. It also banned all onsite consumption, meaning Yami no longer could help Carlos medicate in her vapor room. Bolanos was also ordered to move her dispensary—and find a new location within a week—under strict zoning rules to keep marijuana outlets away from schools, neighborhoods, even the alleys that snaked behind business districts in the planning grid that defined the city. Yami saw a conspiracy in the rules to close nearly all medical cannabis outlets in Los Angeles.

Ever since she had survived cervical cancer and a hysterectomy at age twenty-four, Bolanos had tried to stay in control of her life and shape the environment around her. She adopted and reared a daughter. She was the bookkeeper and fund-raising chairwoman for her daughter's softball league in La Habra, in Orange County. It was on the softball field where Yami—at forty-one—became overwhelmed with dizziness, started vomiting, and noticed she was bleeding. She was taken away in an ambulance. She later underwent liver transplant surgery at Stanford University. For four years, she was in and out of bed. She got nauseous from just seeing the mangos she used to love in Costa Rica. She got rashes just from touching an avocado. Eventually, using cannabis drove away the sick feeling that had long hollowed out her insides. It comforted her, boosting her spirits the way her mother used to when she would rub the bottoms of Yami's feet when she got cramps as a teenager.

After her recovery, Bolanos retained little of her mother's bedside manner when it came to some healthy-looking young people who ventured into her dispensary. When an eighteen-year-old, fresh out of high school and clutching a crisp doctor's recommendation for marijuana, told her he needed pot to help him sleep, Yami looked him over. "Go run around a track several times," she replied, running him off. "That will make you tired." By 2010, the former fund-raiser for girls' softball was president of the Greater Los Angeles Collective Association, GLACA, representing about forty-five of the city's oldest and generally most reputable dispensaries. And it was the city that was giving her fits. *You let this happen,* she repeatedly lectured the city council. She charged that the city's own ineptitude had allowed L.A.'s dispensary explosion, and that now, honorable cannabis clubs and patients who needed medical marijuana stood to suffer under a restrictive new ordinance. And when the city suggested Bolanos might not meet the requirements to stay in business as a dispensary that had existed before the 2007 moratorium—because she had added a new manager—Yami erupted. "What country do we live in?" she asked. "Who the hell do you think was running my store when I had to be here three days a week *schooling* you?"

. . .

The more that L.A. sought to rein in its pot trade, the more the city seemed to get schooled as dispensaries and medical marijuana advocates sued and the city's cannabis market only continued to surge. San Francisco and Oakland, two cities unwaveringly welcoming to cannabis, had early on passed regulations that limited the number of dispensaries to twenty-seven in San Francisco and just four in Oakland. As many as two hundred California cities and counties successfully barred marijuana stores. Yet the availability of cut-rate physicians' recommendations for medical marijuana, and the relative ease of getting them, ignited soaring cannabis commerce elsewhere. Some two hundred dispensaries would sprout in San Diego and more than a hundred in San Jose. Despite a county ban, nearly one hundred marijuana stores flowered in Sacramento County, and the capital city of Sacramento authorized another thirty-eight. Scores more pot shops opened in many smaller cities, from Bakersfield to Redding, on the distant reaches of California's Central Valley.

There was no greater marijuana market exuberance than in Los Angeles. The L.A. boom continued even as the city's top prosecutors threatened dispensaries' right to exist. Los Angeles County district attorney Steve Cooley and the city attorney, Carmen A. Trutanich, notably declared marijuana stores were not only unwelcome in L.A. but illegal under California law.

Cooley and Trutanich rejected California medical marijuana guidelines, which had been drafted by Attorney General Jerry Brown in 2008. In interpreting the state's 2004 law, created by Senate Bill 420, for distributing medical marijuana, Brown had said storefront dispensaries weren't recognized under the law but could legally operate as nonprofit groups of medical marijuana patients accepting reimbursement for costs of providing marijuana. The district attorney and city attorney saw the stores as profiteering shams. They argued that dispensaries couldn't so much as ring up a single cash-register sale under the law. In 2009, Cooley appeared at a conference of the California Narcotic Officers' Association featuring sessions on "eradication of medical marijuana dispensaries in the city of Los Angeles and Los Angeles County." He told the city council that if it couldn't do something about proliferating pot stores, he would. Running for attorney general in 2010, Cooley declared that "communities throughout the nation are waiting to see how we handle storefronts illegally pushing pot."

But it was the pugnacious city attorney, Trutanich, who came to personify L.A.'s campaign against its cannabis clubs. Trutanich filed nuisance and narcotics abatement suits to close medical marijuana stores and pressured the city council to enact tough regulations. Ultimately, he used a notorious allegation concerning toxic pot buds to argue that L.A. dispensaries were a menace to human health. In 2009, undercover Los Angeles police officers bought marijuana at an Eagle Rock dispensary called Hemp Factory V in a case Trutanich held up as shattering the myth of dispensaries collectively, benevolently cultivating marijuana for sick people. In early 2010, a Superior Court judge, James C. Chalfant, ordered the dispensary closed. He ruled that officers' cumulative cash purchases of cannabis, including Blue Cheese and Hawaiian Haze, Bubba OG and Head Band Kush, revealed Hemp Factory V as little more than "a retail sales operation for marijuana"—not a legal patients' collective.

But well before the judge's declaration, Trutanich seized on laboratory tests that showed marijuana bought at the Eagle Rock pot shop had levels of a pesticide—bifenthrin—registering 170 times the "tolerable" level that guidelines by the Environmental Protection Agency set for human food or animal feed. Tests also revealed traces of five pesticides banned in the United States. Trutanich's office began warning of toxic weed. He suggested L.A. dispensaries might be dealing illegal pot smuggled in from Mexico or grown by illicit traffickers—not produced by conscientious medical cultivators. In late 2009, armed with his evidence of tainted marijuana, Trutanich brusquely got in the face of marijuana advocates as he fielded questions at city hall.

"I'm a medical marijuana patient in Los Angeles," a cancer survivor named Kathyrn Schorr began.

Trutanich jumped in. "How do you like smoking pot with pesticides?"

Schorr started to ask something about emergency room visits for pesticide-laced pot. "So let me see if I can get this right," Trutanich interrupted. "Let your children play with lead toys."

Schorr tried again. She questioned him on the toxic pot results, suggesting authorities needed to test up to ten pounds of marijuana to ascertain pesticide levels. Trutanich answered that lab tests could prove contamination from mere traces of pot. He stepped closer, raising his voice. "You're wrong! You're dead wrong!"

"Has there ever been one emergency room visit . . . one single victim of this pesticide you allege?" Schorr pressed him.

"Make sure you go home and take some pesticide and spread it on your salad. . . . If you want to ingest pesticides, that's your right," Trutanich replied.

A second woman followed Schorr to the podium.

"So you're the hard-ass enforcer?" she asked.

"I'm not the hard-ass enforcer, lady," the city attorney said. "I'm for medical marijuana. I'm not for poisoning people."

Yet Trutanich's railings against toxic buds barely got a line in the voluminous script being written by Los Angeles' thriving medical cannabis dispensaries. One of its many authors was Brian Berens. He was a former newspaper reporter from Philadelphia who had been a script editor at Warner Brothers. He worked on shows, including *Angel*, a spin-off of *Buffy the Vampire Slayer*, for the WB. It was a well-paying but inglorious existence. In Berens's view, many writers in Hollywood were treated as "peons." Producers and directors generally didn't deign to talk to them, unless it was to yell at them. Berens wanted his own show to run. And when twelve thousand members of the Writers Guild of America walked off the job in 2007 in a bitter, two-year contract fight that devastated Hollywood, Berens decided on an alternative production. He saw a growing industry—medical marijuana—that didn't appear to be going on strike anytime soon.

So Berens became the "producer, director, and the cinematographer" for the Green Oasis in west Los Angeles. After learning the trade in another marijuana club, he opened the Green Oasis a few miles from Los Angeles International Airport, in early 2009, despite a city moratorium that had disallowed new cannabis clubs after November 2007. Berens served up exotic strains of L.A. Confidential and Woody Kush, the latter a tribute to cannabis-savoring actor Woody Harrelson. On a block once known as "Thunder Alley" for its custom-car shops, Berens put a mahogany cannabis counter downstairs and opened an upstairs medication room with tables outfitted with Volcano Vaporizers and bubble bongs. The room had foosball and pool and Internet access. It was a cannabis version of a neighborhood tavern or coffeehouse. Patients consumed marijuana as they typed on laptops, checked their email, or played games of eight ball.

The Green Oasis became a working haven for Hollywood aspirants such as Megan Albertus, a graduate of Washington State University and an up-and-coming actress who found her job in a marijuana dispensary far more exciting than the cliché of waiting tables. Over a couple of years, when she wasn't appearing as a sobbing secretary on AMC's hit series *Mad Men* or competing for the affections of a firefighter, real estate broker, and college student on the NBC reality show *Momma's Boys,* Albertus was baking extrastrength pot brownies, each packed with half a gram of weed, for the Green Oasis.

Back in 1988, when Barry Kramer was an off-Broadway actor playing the dog in *The Heart of the Dog,* a *New York Times* reviewer took note, observing that "Kramer is quite good as the dog, barking and howling and biting." But as a Hollywood actor, save for some almost-famous cameos on Seinfeld and in the movie *Speed,* Kramer supported himself between auditions by working in a Melrose Avenue head shop, the Galaxy Gallery, which also hosted radio programs on pot legalization and medical marijuana. The experience led him to start one of L.A.'s first dispensaries, the California Patients Alliance. Though he opened it just down Melrose Avenue from the Improv comedy club, Kramer offered little stage presence. His cannabis outlet, with soft jazz music, sand sculptures, and the feel of a therapist's office, was in an enclosed suite with neither street signage nor a shimmering sidewalk cannabis leaf. "I didn't figure people needed to know where I was—unless they were sick," Kramer explained.

Another Hollywood product who became one of L.A.'s dispensary pioneers, and who also shunned pot promotion, was Brennan Thicke. He was a voice actor known for offering chipper expressions of the cartoon Dennis the Menace. Thicke was also a songwriter and a nightclub DJ who worked the Whiskey and Roxy on the Sunset Strip, as well as a successful Los Angeles real estate broker. And he had diabetes, sleeping problems, and neuropathic pain, for which he used cannabis. So Thicke told his father, actor Alan Thicke, who had played the psychiatrist father on the family sit-com *Growing Pains*, that he was going to open a marijuana dispensary on Lincoln Boulevard in Venice. Brennan Thicke understood his dad was worried, "like any parent is," about his son "facing jail and prosecution." But the elder Thicke respected Brennan's choice as he opened the Venice Beach Care Center. It became the first dispensary in Los Angeles to unionize its employees. And Brennan Thicke, whose younger brother, Robin, became a megahit singer and songwriter, took pride in running a medical cannabis store. He boasted he had a "connoisseur's nose" for acquiring high-quality, lab-tested marijuana products "that our patients love."

Thicke and Kramer joined with Yami Bolanos as leaders of the Greater Los Angeles Collective Association. GLACA created its own dispensary accreditation team. It sent secret shoppers into GLACA dispensaries to make sure they were accepting only original copies of patients' medical recommendations, weren't selling more than two ounces of cannabis at a time, weren't distributing to anyone under eighteen, and weren't allowing multiple patient purchases per day.

One of GLACA's early members, Brad Barnes, who attended meetings and backed professional standards for the L.A. dispensary industry, made some cannabis advocates uncomfortable. Bolanos, the former girls' softball officer, noted that Barnes ran "a tittie bar"—in fact, a lucrative San Fernando Valley adult entertainment complex. Adult movie fans knew Barnes as actor Brick Majors. Excalibur Films proclaimed him in its "porn star" profile as "a blonde-haired, blue-eyed bundle of muscle . . . considered one of the most dependable studs on the scene." As Brick Majors, Barnes, a former lifeguard and Chippendales dancer, made over 350 adult films for the likes of Adam & Eve, Sin City, Wicked Pictures, Extreme, Hustler Video, and Totally Tasteless. He was a millionaire businessman, the proprietor of an all-nude juice bar, Xposed; a booze-serving bikini bar, the Wet Spot; and a sex-toy emporium, Private Moments, which Barnes boasted drew "every church lady in the Valley" with its selection of fishnet teddies, thigh-high boots, bedroom aids, and steamy DVDS—including the best of Brick Majors. In 2006, Barnes heard about a group of people looking for a place to open a medical marijuana dispensary. He invited them to open the cannabis club on his west San Fernando Valley site, directly next door to his adult pleasure palaces. "I've got a location that won't upset anybody," he suggested.

Barnes neither smoked pot nor had an interest in starting. But he got himself a physician's recommendation for medical marijuana, citing multiple shoulder injuries as a bodybuilder. He became a patient-member of his new tenants' organization, a cannabis collective dubbed the "2 A.M. Dispensary" for its nightly closing time for serving up pricey medical marijuana selections. The 2 A.M. Dispensary charged seventy-five dollars for an eighth of an ounce of premium cannabis—up to a third more expensive than most Los Angeles dispensaries—for what Barnes touted as the best buds in the valley. The place had another lure too. Many of Barnes's exotic dancers, registered as medical marijuana patients, worked shifts in the cannabis club, dispensing marijuana medicine in bikini tops and booty shorts. The former porn star said his new tenants had "the cutest bud tenders in Los Angeles." Throughout the city, Barnes erected a hundred billboards for Xposed, marketing the place as L.A.'s hottest gentlemen's club. He added one more billboard above the Hollywood Freeway, near the Cahuenga Boulevard headquarters of Vivid Entertainment. It beckoned travelers to the 2 A.M. Dispensary in the Valley.

The first night the 2 A.M. Dispensary opened, a stream of LAPD black-and-whites zoomed into the parking lot of the strip club and drove around to the door of the cannabis club. The officers stopped and looked, then circled around and stopped and looked a second time in disbelief before leaving. Soon a retired LAPD officer with degenerative disc disease was one of the establishment's first and most loyal customers.

Barnes professed to have no business tie to the dispensary beyond taking a monthly consulting fee. He worked to ensure—just as he had with his adult entertainment license and liquor license—that the cannabis club was legally permitted by the city and in compliance with zoning laws. He read up thoroughly on California cannabis law and became known within GLACA as someone who knew what he was talking about. A police watch commander eventually told him the 2 A.M. Dispensary was the safest pot club in the city—thanks largely to the ninety-six security cameras Barnes had installed around the parking lot of his adult complex. One night, two overly confident robbers shot out the dispensary door. They came running out with bags stuffed with marijuana. Barnes's security officers swarmed and smothered them just outside the door.

The former Brick Majors considered the 2 A.M. Dispensary an alluring addition to his complex. He loved it when people would stop in for cannabis, then visit the adult novelty store, have a drink at the Wet Spot, and enjoy the company of the girls at Xposed. He didn't allow cannabis use in the other businesses, except in the dancers' dressing room at Xposed. Since many of the women were medical marijuana patients, it was okay with Barnes if they medicated before performing on stage or inviting patrons for lap dances, twenty dollars for topless, thirty dollars for nude.

. . .

Los Angeles' early efforts to regulate its medical cannabis dispensaries came as Brian Berens was risking his savings to break into the dispensary business. He finally opened Green Oasis in February 2009, fifteen months after the city adopted an interim ordinance setting a moratorium on new dispensaries in August 2007. After the city council extended the moratorium in June 2009, Berens, son of a Philadelphia lawyer, took the city to court. His lawsuit charged that the interim ordinance was arbitrary and unenforceable. In October 2009, Judge Chalfant agreed. The judge noted that all the city had done in its moratorium was complain of the cumulative harm of its growing dispensary glut while taking no concrete steps to solve the problem. "The remedy is for the city to adopt a permanent ordinance which either bans medical marijuana dispensaries completely or strictly regulates them," the judge wrote. "It has had two years to do so, and cannot rely on an ineffective ordinance to regulate that activity now."

Los Angeles city council member Dennis Zine, a former police sergeant and past vice president of the Los Angeles Police Protective League union, honestly felt he had tried to work with the city's cannabis clubs. The ex-cop visited dispensaries. He talked with people dying of cancer. He offered sympathy to people who convinced him they needed medical marijuana and protection from "that dark cloud of illegal possession." But the city was getting shown up in court and being taken for a ride on its own streets. Zine saw pot stores everywhere. He saw them charging three hundred dollars an ounce for medical marijuana, raking in wads of cash in what hardly appeared to be an exercise in "compassion." "We're not going to legalize marijuana under the guise of medical marijuana," he declared. So Zine, with Yami Bolanos and other medical cannabis operators yelling in his ears to do something, guided passage of the 2010 ordinance that was supposed to bring sanity to it all. The result was more chaos.

Yami and Brennan Thicke were among the first to file suit, signing on as plaintiffs in litigation by Americans for Safe Access, the advocacy group for medical marijuana patients. The suit charged that city requirements ordering many existing dispensaries to find new locations in commercial or industrial zones—within seven days—were onerous and unreasonable. Dozens of other dispensary suits followed, with operators charging they were getting closed without hearings and that marijuana store audits by police violated patient rights to privacy. But scores of cannabis clubs shut down, and Trutanich prepared notices warning 459 more of pending court action to close them. Then another judge's order stumped L.A.'s efforts again.

In December 2011, Los Angeles Superior Court judge Anthony J. Mohr noted that it was "laudable and necessary" that Los Angeles was trying to control dispensaries in its midst. But he also expressed concern that police continued to raid "collectives where, allegedly, no laws have been broken." He acknowledged that, in California, "what constitutes a medical marijuana collective remains a matter for debate." In granting a preliminary injunction in favor of the marijuana stores, Mohr let the city have it for a flawed ordinance that violated the rights of medical marijuana patients. Despite the city's good intentions to rein in its excessive cannabis trade, the judge said the ordinance needed to be reworked.

"The record in the actions before this court displays a serious threat to the public welfare caused by the burgeoning number of medical marijuana collectives in our community," Mohr wrote. "The city has a duty to address the problem of drug dealers and recreational users who are attempting to hijack California's medical marijuana legislation for their own benefit. Failure to do so will not only endanger the citizens as a whole, but will negatively impact the ability of legitimate patients to obtain the medical marijuana they need. But in discharging its powers and duties . . . the City must not lose sight of the fact that the People of the State of California have conferred on qualified patients the right to obtain marijuana for medical purposes. No local subdivision should be allowed to curtail that right or regulate it out of existence."

The Los Angeles City Council went back to the drawing board to rework its ordinance, eventually winning the approval of Mohr, who lifted his injunction. But the city's new plan to hold a lottery—to enforce a limit of one hundred dispensaries—drew additional legal challenges.

At the Los Angeles County District Attorney's Office, Steve Cooley turned to his director of specialized prosecutions, Joseph Esposito, to tame the tide of dispensaries. Esposito held meetings throughout the city as the district attorney's point person on medical marijuana. At first, many people at neighborhood gatherings told the district attorney's representative to leave the cannabis clubs alone. "I was treated as the bad guy," he said. After the number of dispensaries doubled and tripled, people started imploring him to do something. A spate of robberies at cash-filled marijuana stores, including the 2010 murder of a dispensary employee in Eagle Rock, added to calls for action. As the district attorney's office went after criminals preying on marijuana stores, Esposito also oversaw fifty to seventy-five prosecutions of dispensaries a year, mostly cases seeking to close them while reaching plea bargains on charges including illegal marijuana sales, tax evasion, and money laundering. Esposito looked to prosecute dispensary operators who drew community complaints, who stood out. He found a prime candidate in Jeffrey Joseph, a medical pot purveyor who, despite numerous brushes with police, refused to go away.

Jeff Joseph, a former hemp products store owner, opened a dispensary in Venice on the border of Culver City. Police there took notice almost immediately, especially after residents complained that Joseph's Organica dispensary left fliers advertising free grams of pot on cars belonging to students attending Culver City High School. Joseph, who opened his store before L.A.'s cannabis club moratorium, offered a downstairs cannabis store with a rooftop marijuana garden and lounge. In 2008, he was raided by Culver City police and Drug Enforcement Administration agents. They seized psilocybin mushrooms, more than a hundred pounds of marijuana, and $17,000 in cash. Despite the raid, Joseph reopened. He delivered speeches to the Los Angeles City Council on "due process and government for the people and by the people." He made online videos, declaring himself a model, legal medical marijuana provider. "I think California is going to be the example for the rest of the country," he said. "Medicine needs to be used organically and ethically. . . . People shouldn't have to hide their gardens. . . . So we can say, yes, this is medicine."

Authorities said income from medicine sales at Organica averaged $400,000 a month. In April 2009, a California Highway Patrol officer who stopped Joseph for a traffic violation found $92,352 in cash, a pill bottle of mushrooms, and—in a passenger's possession—cocaine. Police raided his dispensary again in August 2009 and once again in February 2010, seizing a total of more than three hundred pounds of marijuana in the three raids. Joseph ultimately pleaded no contest to marijuana sales and money laundering in September 2011 in exchange for community service and a year in county jail in lieu of four years in state prison. However, he still appealed, arguing he had operated legally under the Proposition 215 California medical marijuana law and as a licensed dispensary in Los Angeles. "Joseph presented no admissible evidence to show that any triable issue of material fact existed or that he was entitled to any defense, including any defense under the Compassionate Use Act of 1996," a state court of appeal ruled in 2012.

Soon afterward, city officials reported that Los Angeles by then had 762 marijuana dispensaries they knew of and likely scores more that they didn't. The City of Angels was winged with cannabis. But in July 2012, Trutanich won a major victory. The state's Second Appellate District Court reinstated the city's 2010 dispensary ordinance. Moreover, the court said the city could effectively impose a blanket ban on all cannabis clubs by acting on a "sunset clause" in the 2010 ordinance that allowed Los Angeles to close every medical marijuana collective of four or more cannabis patients if the city hadn't passed new rules by June 6, 2012.

Trutanich and a new ally on the city council, council member Jose Huizar from East Los Angeles, set out to put the dispensaries out of business once and for all. They brought forth an ordinance they called a "gentle ban." It sought to shutter every marijuana store in Los Angeles, to let medical-cannabis user groups composed of three people or fewer cultivate their own cannabis, and to permit hospices, home health agencies, and primary caregivers to give sick people marijuana.

Yami Bolanos showed up a day before the vote with Carlos Kruschewsky, who parked his motorized chair in a line of medical cannabis patients in wheelchairs. He held aloft a sign, "Don't ban my medicine," as patients and their dispensary operators waved signs attacking the plan as draconian and utterly unworkable for tens of thousands of Angelinos who used medical marijuana. Inside the city council chambers a day later, Huizar put together a compelling show of people who had had enough of pot shops. Yolanda Rodriguez of Boyle Heights testified to the council in Spanish that the marijuana smell from dispensaries was so pervasive it overwhelmed the sweet bread scents of the neighborhood *panaderías*. Eric Moore of East Hollywood decried the eight to ten "pot clinics" five blocks from his home. Betty Bryant of the Victoria Park Association told of dispensary customers smoking weed in their cars in her community. She beseeched the council "to bring our quality of life back."

Huizar implored his colleagues to recognize that "if we wait any longer, we will continue to chase our tail as we have for the past five years." Colleague Dennis Zine, lamenting the failed 2010 ordinance, said the medical cannabis situation in L.A. was now "a merry-go-round. It has to stop." Zine also said the city should expect a slew of lawsuits to come. The council voted unanimously to approve the "gentle ban." It then also voted thirteen to one, with Huizar objecting, to work with city staff on a potential future ordinance to permit dozens of long-standing cannabis establishments to remain. The second vote smacked of 2007 and 2010 all over again—as a potential recipe for Los Angeles' marijuana stores to ride out still another political storm.

Brian Berens, having already beaten the city in court, wasn't going to close Green Oasis. "Steve Cooley and Carmen Trutanich aren't my Daddy," he said in his lobby, next to his tax certificate as a city-licensed medical marijuana dispensary. Yami Bolanos retired after the vote to her former vapor room at the Pure Life Alternative Wellness Center. She had stopped allowing on-site consumption while continuing to provide cannabis for caregivers to administer to Carlos at his home. Yami wasn't closing either. In her eyes, the city still didn't have a clue. In her six-plus years of working and fighting with the city, Los Angeles leaders had forged a long saga of failed cannabis regulation, of passing ineffective measures, of getting whipped in court, of luring in an excess of cannabis clubs—some reputable, some disreputable, and eventually, a few criminally audacious. "The city didn't have the stomach for it then, and now, because they didn't do anything, every greedy mo-fo and their mama came to L.A.," Yami groused. For good reasons and bad, Yami didn't remotely believe it was over. L.A.'s unresolved cannabis epic was destined to continue.

SEVEN

Wafting Widely

On the pages of *West Coast Cannabis,* a Sacramento-based publication offering marijuana cooking and gardening tips and billing itself as the *Sunset Magazine* of weed, Dragonfly de la Luz penned reviews called "Getting High with Dragonfly." She informed consumers that a marijuana cultivar called Blue Dream, a strain bred mostly from the *Cannabis sativa* plant but with a gentle genetic touch of *Cannabis indica,* was "fast becoming a new favorite" at California medical marijuana dispensaries and in the state's sophisticated cannabis-savoring culture. "It completely takes over your senses," Dragonfly shared with print and online readers. "Its bluish hue with frosty sparkles makes it look like it got blasted to Earth from some intergalactic candy land. Its high crystal content delights your sense of touch, teasing your fingers with its resinous stickiness."

In a state where residents consumed 16 million ounces of weed a year, Dragonfly de la Luz floated and buzzed on a cultural wave driven by the marketing of medical marijuana as both a healing medicine and a pleasurable pursuit. In 2009, almost 3.5 million Californians, nearly one-tenth of the population, used marijuana. More than four hundred thousand Californians smoked it every day. In the summer of 2010, a survey by the Field Poll for *The Sacramento Bee* revealed that 47 percent of California voters had smoked marijuana in their lives, up from 28 percent in 1975. The number of voters having consumed pot (including 41 percent of Republicans, 47 percent of Democrats, and 53 percent of independents) exceeded the registration of any political party in the state. That stirred hopes for advocates, including Richard Lee and Jeff Jones in Oakland, who were pushing a ballot initiative to legalize marijuana beyond medical use. But it was the marketing of cannabis in California, and marijuana's seemingly easy availability from hundreds of newly opening medical dispensaries, that was truly spreading the reach of pot in the Golden State.

Generations of crop perfection, both in illicit harvests and, increasingly, in crops grown for the medical market, elevated the branding and cultural appeal of cannabis, redoubling its lure. In 2010, the *Field Guide to California Agriculture* listed marijuana—not grapes, not almonds, not oranges, not tomatoes, not rice, and certainly not broccoli—as the Golden State's largest cash crop. Evan Mills, a staff scientist at the Lawrence Berkeley National Laboratory who analyzed the carbon footprint of California's indoor cannabis production, estimated in 2011 that the indoor gardens of thousands of marijuana growers accounted for 3 percent of all electricity use in California.

Given the variety of cannabis products reaching the medical market, the Berkeley Patients Care Collective created a popular set of marijuana trading cards to explain its "sweet and exotic" offerings from *Cannabis sativa* or *Cannabis indica* or genetic hybrids bred in California from the two marijuana plant species. Elsewhere across the Golden State, to learned consumers in this world of legal medicinal use and winelike marketing, a good Grand Daddy Purple indica could well be savored as if it were a California cannabis cabernet sauvignon. A heavy sativa Sage & Sour could have the lure of an herbal chardonnay. A Blackberry Kush clear indica? Perhaps an earthy pinot noir.

The landscape of California cannabis was ripe for the arrival of a modern pot culture phenomenon, Dragonfly de la Luz. Raised in the East Coast as Stephanie Taylor, her birth name, she graduated from college in English literature and women's studies in New Mexico and moved on to British Columbia, lured by a concert by her favorite band, Radiohead, and, briefly, by the prospect of postgraduate work in feminism and social justice. She was quickly drawn into Vancouver's cannabis culture—"a pot lovers' paradise," she called it. She became a contributing writer for Canada's *Cannabis Culture* magazine and, in a life-changing move, traveled to Northern California's Mendocino County. She roamed the famous pot country as a two-hundred-dollar-a-pound bud trimmer, savoring the company of cannabis growers in Ukiah, Willits, and Laytonville. She learned to trim marijuana so well, lovingly manicuring the buds, shearing away the tiny leaves to show off the purplish hues and glistening psychoactive trichomes of pot flowers, that she proclaimed herself "a ganja stylist." The persona of Dragonfly de la Luz, roving correspondent and rising cannabis star, took flight.

Drawn to the San Francisco Bay Area, where she eventually settled, Dragonfly marveled at fragrant party gatherings of high achievers in the city, where "everybody is smoking weed and people are handing out their business cards." Soon Dragonfly de la Luz's reviews were being published in ganja-celebrating publications—*Cannabis Culture* and *Skunk, West Coast Cannabis* and *Kush,* the latter two brimming with ads for California marijuana dispensaries, cannabis physicians, leasing agents, lawyers, and products for the evolving industry. Dragonfly appreciated marijuana's legal status as medicine in California and let it be known she was glad there were medicinal benefits from smoking pot. But she didn't write "Getting High with Dragonfly" for people with glaucoma or back pain. She was the voice of the "chronnoisseur"—blending *connoisseur* with *chronic,* slang for "devoted marijuana smoker"—and a proud "professional stoner." Cannabis publishers hailed their "weedly world traveler" and "ganja princess" for her pot passions, her upbeat marijuana marauding, and her allure as a slender, ebony woman dressed in what Dragonfly called her "postapocalyptic" style: five-buckle, knee-high Goth boots and plaid skirts accompanying dark tops, wrist warmers, and her signature rippling dreadlocks tied in pigtails.

For those high-achievers she met in San Francisco or Silicon Valley, "Getting High with Dragonfly" served up Dragonfly's endorsement of Dr. Walker's Daze. It was a "rare and exotic sativa" that could allow them to approach "even the most mundane activity with happy alertness" and "have the energy and motivation to actually do what you planned." For the chronnoisseurs, Dragonfly described the strain's "distinctive haze smell accented with cacao" and its dry hit "with a certain spiciness" and "a hint of pepper." For the average working suburbanite just wanting a release and "a couch embrace" at the end of the day, Dragonfly touted Blueberry Kush, an indica that smelled of "concord grape, lavender, vanilla and sage," offered a taste "with floral overtones," and ensured the "peaceful tranquility" of "doing nothing at all."

. . .

Marijuana, legal as medicine in California, assuredly was providing relief for sick people. Yet with its vast availability for both medical and recreational use, and with its rapid evolution in popular culture, marijuana was also changing the social dynamic of the state. In 2010, the Field Poll report commissioned by *The Sacramento Bee* showed that marijuana was woven into the tapestry of California. While the poll of 962 adults offered little surprise in finding that current pot use was highest among people ages eighteen to twenty-nine and earning less than forty thousand dollars a year, it also revealed marijuana's place in multiple tiers of California society. In fact, people earning more than a hundred thousand dollars a year were more likely to be current marijuana smokers than people earning between sixty thousand and a hundred thousand or between forty thousand and sixty thousand. And Californians aged forty to forty-nine—those who grew up a decade or more too late to have cherished the hippie era or experienced San Francisco's 1967 Summer of Love—were most likely to have used marijuana in their lives.

Moreover, the poll said that roughly the same number of active marijuana consumers had used cannabis to treat a medical condition (42 percent) and for the pleasure of socializing and having fun with friends (39 percent). Less-active smokers saw pot as a party drug (56 percent), a stimulant for creativity (9 percent), or something to accompany drinking alcohol (7 percent), compared with 14 percent who viewed cannabis as a remedy for illness or health conditions and 22 percent who saw it as a relaxant or sleep aid. Notably, most poll respondents interviewed in the survey never ventured inside California's medical marijuana dispensaries. Yet inevitably, they seemed to have friends or family who patronized the establishments or, in some cases, grew their own medical cannabis—and eagerly shared it.

The rise of California's marijuana market brought cannabis curiosity back to the future, creating a secondary market and ripples of acceptance for marijuana use. For Robert Girvetz, a well-to-do retiree in the Orange County beach community of San Juan Capistrano, medical marijuana stirred nostalgia for the Caribbean cruise he'd taken as a young man, when he and friends had smoked marijuana and listened to the Beatles' *Sgt. Pepper's Lonely Hearts Club Band* as they passed through the Panama Canal. Girvetz recalled that he didn't care much for the Beatles, but he sure enjoyed the pot. So when he was seventy-eight, having long since sold his window-blind company in Pasadena, Girvetz was intrigued to learn his stepdaughter had been given a medical marijuana recommendation for a painful digestive condition. His stepdaughter later gave up using cannabis when she got pregnant, but Girvetz came to enjoy it, even though the modern-day California marijuana she occasionally brought him on visits home was way stronger than Girvetz remembered. "It was a couple of hits and woooo," he exclaimed. Girvetz didn't really like the parched throat that smoking pot gave him, so a cousin bought him a vaporizer—"a little contraption with a hose coming out of it," he marveled. Girvetz came to enjoy it so much he ditched his occasional martinis for weed.

Steve Keegan, a forty-year-old Los Angeles businessman earning a six-figure salary marketing sports and fitness products, was reintroduced to cannabis by his artist girlfriend, who had a physician's recommendation for medical marijuana. Keegan, who didn't bother seeing a doctor for cannabis himself, found he could take a hit from a joint before he went to bed and it would slow down the marketing survey data and sales presentations still spinning in his head, helping him fall asleep. The couple came to enjoy flipping through Los Angeles cannabis magazines to look over the advertised pot products and places to purchase them. Inevitably, Keegan's girlfriend would pick up some sweet variety of sativa. On weekends, they would drive to Zuma Beach, take a couple of deep hits in the car, and then savor the day in the surf and sand.

Among others interviewed by the Field Poll and *The Sacramento Bee,* Kyle Printz, a forty-four-year-old computer software engineer in Marin County, cared little for marijuana culture. He would be the last person to hang a pot leaf or Bob Marley poster in his room. But sometimes after writing computer code—"and dealing with zeros and ones" for hours—he liked to decompress with cannabis. California college student Ryan Issaco would give his friends forty-five dollars to pick up an eighth of an ounce of Train Wreck from Humboldt or Mendocino—or, if they had medical cannabis recommendations, from dispensaries closer to home in the Silicon Valley. He and his buddies kicked back with pot two or three times a week, never before exams but inevitably afterward. Most of all, Issaco came to love talking politics when he was stoned. Dawn Sanford, forty-three, a call center data entry worker in Sacramento, who preferred to relax with a tequila sunrise, also came to rely on friends with medical recommendations to bring her some marijuana when life and work made her anxious. Thirty-year-old Annette Drennan in Riverside County, who studied medical assisting and considered herself an amateur astrologist—"a bit of a cliché," she laughed—didn't care for the heavy sativas her boyfriend brought over. They gave her anxiety attacks. But when she smoked an indica, "the lighter and fluffier" the better, it made her think, "I can really feel the present."

Medical marijuana professionals such Steve DeAngelo, face of the state's largest and most celebrated medical cannabis dispensary, saw pot's emergence into California popular culture as evidence that an increasing number of people were turning to cannabis for what actually were life and health issues. DeAngelo, whose Harborside dispensaries in Oakland and San Jose promoted cannabis as a wellness drug, liked to talk about a fictional dad who was so stressed out from work he couldn't sleep, couldn't play with his kids, and seldom made love with his wife. DeAngelo would wrap up his soliloquy with the guy smoking a joint, freeing himself of stress and depression, becoming a better dad and better, more loving husband, and starting to live again. Yet DeAngelo also recognized that people without medical recommendations smoking pot, much of it obtained secondhand from legal dispensaries, was bad news for the industry. It was fodder, DeAngelo feared, for cops and prohibitionists eager for any chance to depict medical cannabis outlets serving ill patients as drug purveyors diverting weed into California communities. DeAngelo sensed the peril of legal and illegal cannabis markets existing virtually side by side. So dispensaries such as Harborside implemented anti-diversion rules to try to stop medical marijuana patients from filling shopping orders for their friends. Harborside banned cell phone use. It instructed its staff to identify people making suspicious transactions, such as buying an ounce of cannabis in twenty-eight one-gram packages or grabbing twenty-five marijuana lozenges at a time. Harborside also kept an eye out for people who seemed to come in too often and set a purchasing limit of two ounces per week per patient. Its security officers ran off anyone seen trading marijuana on or near its parking lot.

But people such as John Redman, executive director of Californians for Drug Free Youth, saw marijuana's emerging status as a maddening paradox. Redman fairly seethed over the contradictions as California's anti-tobacco campaigns succeeded in severely restricting the sale of tobacco to youths, even making the Joe Camel logo a negative cultural icon, while the appeal of pot, and smoking it, seemed only to grow among teens and young adults. Redman found it "disgusting" that, to get medical marijuana recommendations, eighteen-year-olds were going in "to some pot doc in L.A. who wears a bikini and has a really sexy body." He grimaced at how older teens were welcomed as customers in dispensaries offering free grams or joints for first-time buyers. "Tell me, where can you get free Vicodin with your first visit?" Redman asked incredulously. "How is it that we as a society cannot take a look at that?"

To Redman, medical marijuana was a recipe for drug diversion, no matter how many cell phones dispensaries were silencing. Many California high school kids were devouring pot cookies obtained directly or indirectly from dispensaries or wolfing down potent brownies some students baked at home after reading up on cannabis cooking online. In two days in February 2010, four students from three Sacramento-area high schools requested medical assistance—and two were transported by ambulance to a hospital—to recover from the dizzying effects of overindulging in marijuana brownies. Dispensaries, professional cannabis bakers, and medical marijuana advocates began publishing warnings for consumers of pot edibles—for both the young and old. The Berkeley-based Medical Cannabis Safety Council put out an advisory for medical marijuana patients who preferred eating their medicine to smoking it. It suggested starting with a quarter dose—or a bare nibble of a brownie—and then waiting an hour to "analyze the effects" before ingesting more. For some young person with the munchies, waiting an hour between brownie bites surely seemed counterintuitive.

Even some experienced marijuana smokers found themselves mesmerized by the offerings of California's medical cannabis marketplace. John Wade, a forty-three-year-old San Francisco sales rep and lighting production specialist who shared his experiences with the Field Poll and *The Sacramento Bee,* had smoked pot since he was a teenager. He quit for several years after moving to Alabama, where he found the weed offerings and quality detestable. In 2007, he returned to California, got his medical marijuana recommendation, and went into the Bay Area's dispensaries. He found the plethora of exotic offerings confounding and realized—to his surprise—that some strains knocked him too deeply back into his chair. Risking his cannabis cred, Wade settled on less-potent varieties. He found his tolerance level, and he took to smoking marijuana as part of his lifestyle. He and his buddies enjoyed firing up a joint while ascending to Sierra Nevada ski runs in gondolas they dubbed "gondoobies." He traveled with his one-hitter, a porcelain faux cigarette with a pinch of weed. He used it on the golf course, finding that a well-timed hit took the anxiety out of a drive or steadied him before a putt. One challenge for outdoor consumption came at his beloved Giants baseball games at San Francisco's AT&T Park. Ushers there were on the lookout for pot smokers. Wade found he could occasionally enjoy his one-hitter and the ballgame if he moved strategically, changing seats every few innings.

Evidently other fans of the Giants and cannabis were more accomplished at blending baseball and buds. During the 2010 World Series between the Giants and the Texas Rangers, Rangers star Josh Hamilton, a recovering alcoholic and narcotics abuser, was surprised to smell the fans' marijuana smoke drifting in from the bleacher seats. And Newy Scruggs, a sports reporter from NBC's Dallas–Fort Worth affiliate, was doing a pregame standup near the stadium's famed McCovey Cove when the scents of California came wafting over to him. "This is San Francisco, and I can tell you—right over there, there are some people smoking weed! Because it's coming this way!" Scruggs exclaimed as he opened his live report. "We are truly in San Francisco. Hey, I'm standing here, and I'm like, 'That's not cigarettes. That's weed! That's weed!'"

The coanchors back home peppered him with questions on California's pot culture.

"Is it legal there?"

"Is it a little more liberal maybe?"

They tried to redirect Newy back to baseball, asking how he was being treated as a Texas Rangers fan in San Francisco.

"People are nice here. We're not in New York, okay," Scruggs answered. "Nobody is going to spit on us. Nobody is going to tell us we're bad people. This is San Francisco. They're smoking weed over there. They don't care. They want to see their team win. But they're all half-buzzed out."

"They look like fun people," one of the anchors offered.

"Yes, they are."

. . .

California may have legalized medical marijuana in 1996 amid poignant images of AIDS and cancer patients seeking relief from suffering. But a decade later, people with AIDS or cancer accounted for only a tiny fraction of those seeking medical marijuana recommendations at MediCann, California's largest network of medical cannabis physicians. For a 2006 survey, researchers writing for the *Journal of Drug Policy Analysis* gleaned information from charts of 1,655 people who went to MediCann for doctors' recommendations for cannabis. While 3 percent of MediCann patients had AIDS or cancer, the overwhelming majority reported they were seeking marijuana for pain relief, followed—in order—by spasms, headache, anxiety, nausea, depression, cramps, panic, diarrhea, and itching. Seventy-one percent reported that pot helped them sleep; 54 percent said it helped them relax. Twenty-four percent said marijuana provided focus. Fifteen percent said it gave them energy. Half of the subjects considered marijuana to be a substitute for prescription medications. Fourteen percent said pot took the place of booze.

A quarter of the MediCann patients were college graduates, and nearly a third had gone to college. One in ten was a veteran. And while the people seeking marijuana recommendations came from all age groups (22 percent were aged thirty-five to forty-four, 19 percent were forty-five to fifty-four, and a little more than 13 percent were over fifty-five), there was a definite demographic trend—young and male. Seventy-three percent of those wanting doctor referrals to legally use marijuana were men. Eighteen percent of the MediCann patients, male and female, were eighteen to twenty-four years old, and 28 percent were twenty-five to thirty-four years old, young people seemingly living their fittest, healthiest years.

Given the demographics of medical marijuana, perhaps it was little surprise that its most exploitive marketing was aimed at young dudes and featured images of hot women. In Los Angeles, where Brad Barnes, the former porn actor known as Brick Majors, had strippers working inside the dispensary at his adult entertainment complex, other marijuana stores marketed cannabis less as a healing medicine than as an aphrodisiac. "The place where patients are high-spirited!" announced pot magazine ads for L.A.'s Grateful Meds dispensary. They depicted seminude women ripping off their clothes, apparently in excitement over the offers of free joints and marijuana brownies for new patients. The Reserve dispensary in Sacramento County featured a model in a metal-studded brassiere and Old West gun belt to hype its potent Green Ribbon, which packed 25 percent psychoactive THC, pitching the strain as if it were some supercharged malt liquor of bud. In the marketing of California medical marijuana, bikini-wearing bud girls became as common as the Budweiser girls.

Popular culture and the medical marijuana market created separate and, often, awkwardly overlapping constituencies. The suffering of seriously ill people that elevated cannabis's status as a healing medicine clashed with brazen appeals hyping pot and sexuality. At the HempCon medical marijuana trade show in San Jose, featuring cannabis culture, advocacy, and reams of consumption accessories, the event's own marketing director angrily slammed down a magazine—*Cali Chronic X*—that depicted scantily dressed models posing suggestively with smoking accessories. "I don't know why we have to mix marijuana with porn," said Shawna Webb, a communications professional who used medical cannabis for pain from a ruptured disc. She told the magazine's publisher, Jeffrey Peterson, a pot culture performer known as "the 420 comic," that California needed to get back to the values of Proposition 215, its 1996 medical marijuana initiative.

But California marijuana pop culture, at least, was more about 420 than 215. Pot's legendary numeric moniker 420 signaled a celebration of the pleasures of marijuana. Though some attributed the name to the estimated four hundred or so ingredients believed to be in the cannabis plant, the California legend of 420 originated with high school students—called the Waldos—

who met in 1971 at 4:20 P.M. daily at the statue of Louis Pasteur at San Rafael High School in the San Francisco Bay Area to set off on afternoons of pot smoking. Years later, April 20—4/20—became marijuana's Fourth of July. Annually, thousands of people lit up in celebratory smoke-ins at Porter Meadow at the University of California, Santa Cruz, or at Golden Gate Park in San Francisco. Marijuana dispensaries across California offered 4/20 specials, live music, and other commemorations.

And so Peterson, the 420 comic, pushed back at the HempCon publicist. He declared that 215, and its notion of cannabis as simply for the sick, had become prudish. When it came to fun, 420 trumped 215. One of Peterson's magazine models, Sativa Grace, real name Andrea Frye, twenty-one, suggested 420 was empowering. "Hey, I may have sex appeal," said Sativa Grace, dressed as a tawdry Alice in Wonderland, "but I can smoke all day like a guy."

Vanessa Sahagun, who grew up attending St. Mary Magdalen Elementary and St. Genevieve High School in Los Angeles' San Fernando Valley, graduated to become a savvy businesswoman capitalizing on 420 culture. By age twenty-six, she had built a marketing franchise as ChaCha VaVoom, CEO and president of the 420 Nurses. The 420 Nurses sold nursing bonnets, aprons, tight skirts, and hot pants adorned with green medical marijuana crosses, launching women into modeling careers in medical cannabis promotion. The "nurses" who purchased these products earned anywhere from ten to twenty-five dollars an hour staffing dispensaries or passing out business cards for cannabis physicians, and a hundred to a thousand dollars a day for promotional video or photo shoots for marijuana businesses and smoking accessories. ChaCha VaVoom was a cannabis culture dynamo. Her arms and shoulders stylishly tattooed in a flowery Day of the Dead motif, ChaCha took online bong hits with her fellow nurses and put out the message that "you can be beautiful with who you are, beautiful with what you smoke." Her company's slogan, "A blunt a day brings the 420 Nurses to play," lured advertisers for the 420 Nurses website and calendars. Sahagun expanded her 420 Nurses franchise to Colorado and other medical marijuana states. She stated, proudly, that she was "creating 'green jobs' for ladies."

At the Kush Expo medical cannabis show at the Anaheim Convention Center, near Disneyland, in Orange County, ChaCha and her nurses merely blended in with the sexual imagery and car-show-style spokesmodels for products from medicinal Ganja Juice and a beer-pong-style toking game called 420 Football. There was no pot use allowed in the convention hall—there was a 215-patients' medication area just outside—but excitement wafted through the room. By the Expo stage, giant posters of a naked woman—strategically covered with long blond hair and an extralong Pure Glass bong—showed off the trophy to be awarded to the winner of the Hot Kush Girl bikini contest. Besides the exquisite bong, the winner would get a thousand dollars and a studio portfolio shoot.

"These are some sexy models—half-naked!" announced the contest's host, Francesca Del Carpio, who was introduced as one of *Maxim* magazine's "top 100 hometown hotties" and as someone who loves "smoking out of the Vape," a digital, pen-sized pot vaporizer on sale at the Expo.

Francesca called out the contestants, bikini models with green numbers painted on their thighs or abdomens, to preen for the cheering audience, tout their products, and celebrate how they consumed medical marijuana.

"Chelsea . . . likes happy people and hot food—and her favorite strain is True OG," Francesca announced. "So let's hear from Chelsea herself! What's your favorite way to medicate?"

"I like a crisp, full, clean bong!" Chelsea said.

"Guys, if you're going to have a girl over, make sure you clean your bong!" Francesca responded as the crowd—mostly men—erupted.

"Now it's our freakiest first-place winner," Francesca continued, summoning the reigning champion, Dania. "Her favorite strain is OG Kush."

"I definitely like my bong hits hard!" Dania exclaimed. "So I choose the gravity bong."

Then there was Holly, whose favorite strain was Skywalker. "My favorite way to medicate," she began, pausing for effect, "I think it would be mouth to mouth."

"She loves to shotgun!" Francesca shouted.

Dania Estrada was the winner, defending her Kush Expo crown. She marched out on the catwalk, carrying the winner's Pure Glass bong, wearing an imitation pot leaf lei, waving to the crowd, and blowing kisses. The Orange County accountant/bookkeeper and promotional model, who described herself as a medical marijuana patient using cannabis to treat her migraines, went off to sign her posters for a line of admirers.

"I don't do any drugs except this," Dania offered. "And it's legal now."

. . .

To the medical cannabis movement, popular culture often seemed to be its worst enemy. Advocates such as Lanette Davies took notice—and offense.

Police were still ripping out gardens of medical marijuana cultivators and raiding dispensaries; and as far as she was concerned, politicians remained courage-challenged when it came to passing legislation to protect medical access for patients benefiting from cannabis. Davies was co-operator of the Canna Care dispensary in Sacramento with her husband, Bryan Davies, and the voice of a Christian-themed medical marijuana advocacy group, Crusaders for Patients' Rights. She didn't see women with cannabis leaves seductively placed over their breasts as helping the medical marijuana movement or its politics. And she found an ally in Dragonfly de la Luz. The ganja princess may have been a stoner icon hailing weed as a pleasurable pursuit, but she joined with Davies in condemning the sexual marketing of pot as "contributing to the degradation of women" and giving the movement—medical or otherwise—a bad name. Dragonfly, the professional stoner, and Lanette Davies, the Christian cannabis crusader, would eventually become curious political allies in a ballot fight over the future of marijuana in California that otherwise would split many medical cannabis activists from supporters of legalization for purely recreational use.

Lanette and Bryan Davies saw themselves as representing a new mainstream for medical cannabis acceptance. Their Canna Care dispensary was a devoutly religious place, stocked with far more Bibles than bongs and dispensing cannabis with a Christly message. Bryan, who sent all five of their children to parochial schools while Lanette tended to the household, lost his livelihood running a truck-washing business when his spine nearly gave out from curvature and torturous inflammation due to bone disease. A stout man with a long, flowing beard, Davies was horrified when his Kaiser doctor suggested cannabis might help his pain. When he later got the notion of a new career running "a pot club," he thought he was possessed by the devil, before becoming convinced it was the Lord who called him. So once Lanette got done telling him he was going to wind up in jail, Bryan found a place for a dispensary in a warehouse office next door to the Victory Outreach Church in Sacramento. He invited church leaders over for 6 P.M. prayer services. Bryan and Lanette Davies didn't worship the cannabis plant itself in the manner of some marijuana spiritualists. They didn't pitch pot as "God's medicine," just as a healing aid for human beings. But they posted the Ten Commandments in their dispensary, and they doled out three thousand Bibles in five years.

When a medical grower brought in a popular sativa strain called Green Crack, Bryan Davies felt the wrath of God upon him. "I am not putting up any crack," he thundered. "That name brings degradation. It lowers the morals." Told it was good medicine, Bryan and Lanette changed the name. They called the strain Blue Lady. Canna Care also went on the air with California's first known mainstream television commercial for a medical marijuana dispensary. Their spot featured their adult daughter, Brittany Davies, who, like her father, had acquired a bone disease. In the Canna Care ad, which also included a woman injured by a drunk driver in a traffic accident and featured people with diabetes, hypertension, and HIV, Brittany talked about cannabis giving her "a way to live."

One day, somewhere between his cannabis counter selections and dispensary signs—"Blessed is the Nation whose God is the Lord" and "Pray Big"—Bryan Davies comforted a cancer patient questioning his own faith for seeking out medical marijuana.

"I went to church every day," the man told Bryan in a crying voice. "I paid my tithes, and they tell me I'm going to die."

Bryan saw the devil putting his finger on the man's suffering. He wrested it away.

"You didn't ask for cancer," Davies counseled him. "You didn't ask that cannabis help you out. Obviously, it was God's will."

Godly or otherwise, there was a definite will behind medical marijuana and its emergence in the industry and culture in California. In San Francisco, a sputtering economy drove Al Shawa out of the fashion industry that had made him a wealthy retailer and provided a yearly ticket to fashion week in Paris. After his seven 20/20 clothing stores—selling eclectic, contemporary styles at California shopping malls—went under, Shaw decided to open a dispensary on a gritty block in the San Francisco Mission District. He added lights and security and ran off the sidewalk pot dealers. His Shambhala Healing Center resembled a regal jeweler's shop, with Shawa, in designer suits and turtlenecks, offering a comforting ambiance with soft music, elegant display cases, and magnifying lamps that made medicinal strains of Purple Haze or Alien Train Wreck glisten like gemstones. In Sacramento, Lino Catabran started in the waterbed business in the 1970s. He then opened a used car dealership, selling Porsches to young professionals and switching, as he got older, to selling recreational vehicles to retirees. When the recreational-vehicle business went under, Catabran turned his empty showroom into a dispensary. The place still looked like a used car center, only with specials painted on the showroom window advertising fortune-wheel spins for free edibles or joints at 4:20 P.M. Catabran called the dispensary One Love

Wellness and said he was never going back to the car business. "This is more fun," he said. "I mean, truly. There is no service department. There is no warranty department. And there are very few unhappy customers."

As thousands of Californians took to growing their own marijuana, igniting a boom in hydroponics stores and specialized products for at-home cultivators, construction workers Don Devries and Jarron Genzlinger traveled to trade shows to demonstrate their new, must-have addition for any cannabis-loving home. While on deck-building and other home improvement jobs, the two men from the Sierra Nevada town of Foresthill had encountered scores of houses that were fire traps, strewn with wires in dangerous hookups for indoor pot cultivation. So they developed a professionally wired, galvanized-steel growing room that would fit into most any garage. For just $11,500, their top model enclosure could produce ten pounds of premium pot in just sixty-five days, they promised. They called it the Pro Grow Time Machine. As marijuana became deeply rooted in the California landscape and its culture, this time machine appeared to allow no turning back.

EIGHT

Courting Compassion

Eugene Davidovich was on the air, often. "Good afternoon, I'm Gene Davidovich," the young father, former computer consulting project manager, former U.S. Navy petty officer third class, would inevitably begin. "Some of you may have heard my story out there." The twenty-nine-year-old Davidovich, a medical marijuana defendant, was facing a 2010 trial in San Diego County Superior Court that could send him to prison for six years. Medical marijuana was enmeshed in the fabric of California. But the battle for its political—and legal—acceptance was far from resolved. And the shy sailor had become an unlikely voice, courting an outpouring of public support and sympathy for his case and a larger cause.

Davidovich was getting media attention for a narrative decidedly different from the prosecutor's assertion that he was a "dishonorable" drug dealer who preyed on residents living in military housing. Eugene Davidovich learned to become his own media machine. He covered his own court case. He spoke to the camera in near daily trial updates. He posted his own stories on multiple websites he created.

Davidovich addressed online viewers beneath a fireplace mantel adorned with his navy achievement medals and embroidered hats from the USS *John S. McCain* destroyer, on which he had served two tours in the Persian Gulf, and the USS *Cowpens* guided missile cruiser, on which he was deployed in the Mediterranean Sea. And he wove his story from a bench at San Diego's Balboa Park, telling how a police drug task force had burst into his apartment at 2 A.M. in February 2009, three months after Davidovich sold marijuana for $120 to an undercover officer. The officer had acquired a phony medical marijuana recommendation and called in an order to Davidovich's medical cannabis delivery service.

In a pressed white shirt, black-and-silver tie, and conservative navy haircut, Davidovich also did online reports from in front of the San Diego County Courthouse. He predicted—despite his inner fear—that jurors would see through the crusade of San Diego County district attorney Bonnie Dumanis and the authorities' hyped sweep against purported gangs and narcotics traffickers, called Operation Green Rx. Davidovich was putting out a different story—that "Operation Green Rx was funded and executed to target medical marijuana patients, collectives and providers in San Diego." The media was picking up on his account, and questioning authorities' version.

Eugene Davidovich was shaken, confused, and humiliated when narcotics officers pulled him out of his apartment, handcuffing him in his underwear and leaving him on his front step for the neighbors to see. Police searched his apartment and, later, his car, where they found a backpack with his medical marijuana recommendation, a little over an ounce of marijuana in 3.5-gram packages, a half ounce of hash, and a book on marijuana laws.

"Did you know your husband is a damned drug dealer?" one of the officers asked Davidovich's wife. Davidovich had assured her that his medical marijuana delivery service—which he posted in listings of the San Diego chapter of the National Organization for Reform of Marijuana Laws—was legal and safe. Now he was an accused drug criminal. His marriage would fall apart. He had a seventy-thousand-dollar-a-year job with a software consulting firm in San Diego's Mission Valley he was about to lose. Still Davidovich didn't grasp what he was in for until he was taken to a police station for booking and a detective thumbed through a tabulated notebook—titled "Operation Green Rx." He flipped past the photos of dozens of suspects, people whom the former Navy petty officer had neither met nor heard of. Finally, the detective stopped at Davidovich's photo and file.

"We know what you're up to," the detective said. "We've been watching you guys."

Davidovich was brought into a San Diego courtroom for arraignment on two charges of transporting marijuana and one count of possession with intent to distribute. Authorities would later drop one of the transportation counts and add a charge of possession of concentrated cannabis. Davidovich looked about the courtroom. He saw a television camera. "Who do I tell that I don't want to be on camera?" he asked the public defender who showed up for his appearance. The judge told him the camera would stay, that the public had a right to know.

That afternoon, local stations broke the story of sweeping arrests under Operation Green Rx, in which a former San Diego sailor named Eugene Davidovich was the first suspect arraigned in a crackdown on hoodlums and drug dealers targeting San Diego–area military housing. District Attorney Dumanis would announce that authorities arrested dozens of people, recovering guns and cocaine. Dumanis shared the determined anti-cannabis-commerce stance of Carmen Trutanich, the fiery L.A. city attorney, and Los Angeles district attorney Steve Cooley and many others in local law enforcement in California. Dumanis argued that nothing in Proposition 215 or the state's Senate Bill 420, also known as the Medical Marijuana Program Act, sanctioned retail-style dispensaries or delivery services. In targeting the ex-sailor and the breadth of San Diego's marijuana dispensary industry, she broadly charged that Eugene Davidovich and his ilk were criminals hiding behind the ruse of medical marijuana. "It is a gateway drug," Dumanis added in a television appearance after his arraignment. "It does have ramifications, and people commit crimes in order to get it."

Davidovich, who had actually been picked up in an Operation Green Rx offshoot called Operation Endless Summer, got into his car after posting bail. Ashamed, he raced to tell his parents before they saw the news on television. Between waves of panic, he reflected on why he was a medical marijuana patient and how it could be that he was in this mess.

Eugene Davidovich was a personnel officer in the navy, and yet he had had some tense moments. On the *John S. McCain,* he had been summoned to man a dual chamber fifty-caliber machine gun on the bridgeway. The destroyer was on a Gulf deployment to enforce the oil-for-food program embargo against Iraq and was stopping ships off the Iraqi coast. An unidentified boat sped toward the destroyer, not responding to communications. Officers ordered the crew to lock and load. Davidovich, his adrenaline rising, prepared to fire, "to do whatever the navy needed me to do." The boat veered off, deemed as neither a threat nor a vessel circumventing the embargo. Later, off the coast of Vladivostok, on the USS *Cowpens,* Davidovich, who was fluent in Russian and Ukrainian, worked as the cryptologist translating instructions from shore as the *Cowpens* entered into port. An officer on deck gave the wrong order as the ship was backing into port, too fast, toward a pier. Davidovich shouted over the officer, in a breach of authority. He gave the correct instructions to the hull man.

Davidovich loved his tenure in the navy and was proud of his service. But after his discharge, he was besieged by panic attacks, with migraines, sweats, and throwing up. He had no idea, really, if it was trauma from his naval service—from the stress of challenging an officer or nearly opening fire on a boat in the Persian Gulf—or whether it was a totally unrelated problem with his psyche. His doctor put him on antidepressant and antianxiety drugs, and Davidovich, who had used marijuana in high school, got a cannabis recommendation. Later, Davidovich and three other medical marijuana patients pooled their resources and started growing cannabis—with the landlord's approval—in a storage space in Kearny Mesa. They listed a delivery service, called San Diego Cannabis Providers. They were behind on their rent, barely recovering from their deliveries the costs of producing medical marijuana for their own use.

One day, a man saying his name was Jamie Conlan telephoned Davidovich. "I'm a patient," he told him. "I've got a back problem. What kind of stuff do you guys carry?"

Davidovich asked for the name of the man's physician and said he would call him back after verifying his medical recommendation. It checked out. Conlan ordered an eighth of an ounce each of Bubba Kush and Sour Diesel and gave him his address. Davidovich drove to a shaded, ranch-style house in Pacific Beach. He had no idea it was military housing.

. . .

Nothing he had faced in the navy measured up to the stress of being charged—and cast—as a drug criminal in San Diego County. Davidovich reached out for support. He contacted the local office of Americans for Safe Access, an advocacy group for medical marijuana patients. Eventually, he spoke to Don Duncan, the group's California director. "You've got to fight this with a two-pronged attack," Duncan told him. "You've got to fight this in the media. You've got to fight this in court. And you need a campaign plan." Duncan suggested Davidovich start by writing his autobiography and getting out the story of who he was as a person. Davidovich began with the public comments microphone before the San Diego City Council. He said he was a man who served his country, who was following California medical marijuana laws, who was targeted in a misguided drug operation defaming legal patients and providers. Other Operation Green Rx defendants did the same, appearing before the council, some furiously dumping out vials of prescription meds they said cannabis had helped replace.

Davidovich, terrified by a television camera at his first court appearance, went to work to draw the cameras back. The software consultant, who had designed "cloud-based" platforms for purchasing orders for retailers, created a website on his criminal case, a Eugene Davidovich channel on YouTube, a Facebook page, and an online blog—called "Operation Green Rx, Navigating the Serpentine Roadmap"—that chronicled cases of medical marijuana defendants caught in the dragnet of Dumanis and the San Diego drug cops. And when one of his lawyers, Michael McCabe, got a police surveillance tape through court discovery, Davidovich rushed it onto the Web. The grainy video offered the first clear indication that maybe ex-sailor Eugene Davidovich wasn't quite the drug criminal that the police portrayed him to be.

The video showed Davidovich driving his small white sedan up to a house. There were sounds of a blaring football game on the television in the house and men inside laughing, and cursing, at the action. The tape, recorded by an undercover officer, didn't pick up Davidovich's first words in a cell phone call to the house. But later in the video, it became evident that Davidovich was asking the customer, whom he thought was Jamie Conlan, to present verification of being a legal medical marijuana patient.

"Do you think I'm going to rob you or something?" said Conlan, actually an undercover San Diego Police Department narcotics detective, Scott Henderson. "Okay, yeah, I'll be right out."

The detective, with shaggy, long blonde hair and in blue jeans and a T-shirt, emerged from the house. Davidovich, in a white dress shirt and black slacks, greeted him. The video showed Davidovich looking over the man's physician's recommendation and identification, then returning to his car, where he retrieved the medical marijuana before they entered the house. "Thanks, bro," the person purporting to be Jamie Conlan said. The footage seemed to suggest at least one of them, Davidovich, was trying to follow the law.

Before his case went to trial, Davidovich, having been asked to leave his software consulting job, took over as the San Diego director for Americans for Safe Access. He used ASA webcasts to rally supporters to the courthouse to attend the hearings of other medical marijuana defendants, including Jovan Jackson, another navy veteran facing trial in San Diego Superior Court after a 2008 raid on his Answerdam Alternative Care dispensary in Kearny Mesa, and James Stacy, a martial arts instructor facing federal charges in 2009 for a dispensary—Movement in Action—in Vista.

In June and July of 2008, undercover San Diego police officers posing as patients made small purchases at Jackson's dispensary. They later raided the marijuana store along with Drug Enforcement Administration agents, seizing 5.25 pounds of marijuana and $280. At Jackson's house, they found another pound of pot, along with fourteen tablets of Ecstasy and three Xanax pills. Yet when Jackson went on trial, in a courtroom packed with medical marijuana supporters, the prosecution's depiction of Jackson's dispensary as an illegal narcotics operation ignominiously fell apart. The jury acquitted Jackson on each marijuana possession and sales charge while convicting him on two counts—possessing Ecstasy and Xanax—that had been afterthoughts to the prosecution's case. Jurors said there was nothing to indicate Jackson was operating his dispensary in violation of California medical marijuana law. "If you're going to hold someone to the law, you have to define that law," juror Perry Wright told the *San Diego Union-Tribune*. Jovan Jackson wept with relief. Then he went on Eugene Davidovich's online show for Americans for Safe Access San Diego.

"The verdict is back and you've been found not guilty," Davidovich began. "Do you think you had a fair trial?"

"My life has been affected by this tremendously," Jackson told the host and fellow medical cannabis defendant. "I never expected it to be an easy fight. This is a good day. . . . If the politicians and rule makers don't understand that medical marijuana is law after this case, I don't know what other way we can present it to them."

As his case neared trial in March 2010, Eugene Davidovich had a well-developed message to present both inside and outside of court. He was by now familiar, the face of the medical marijuana debate in San Diego. People tuned in when Davidovich broadcast on the Web on the eve of his trial, announcing, "They offered me a plea bargain, which I did not accept," and warning, "I assume the consequences will get worse from now on."

As the trial opened, Deputy District Attorney Theresa Pham portrayed Operation Green Rx and the undercover officer who obtained a medical marijuana recommendation under false pretenses as a noble campaign—funded under a federal grant—to target drug criminals or gang members. In this case, she suggested, the crime involved a navy veteran exploiting the good intentions of California's medical marijuana law and—in an ultimate act of dishonor—dealing drugs in military housing.

"Mr. Davidovich delivered and sold to Detective Henderson 6.92 grams of medical marijuana for $120," Pham stated in her opening, pausing for effect. "Ladies and gentlemen, by the end of this trial, you will find beyond a reasonable doubt the defendant is guilty of all the charges." She asserted that the evidence made clear that "you have Mr. Davidovich taking a law, hiding behind it, using it and abusing it for his own turpitude." And the prosecutor set out to use Davidovich's own statements as ASA advocate and self-promoting, Web-mastering defendant to convict him in court.

Davidovich's attorney Michael McCabe depicted his client as "an honest and truthful man and one who at great personal loss undertook something good for the people in society who required his assistance." McCabe further noted, "As a result of that he was put on trial for an extremely minor amount of marijuana possessed for his own use."

Media members, some bailing out after the opening arguments, were able to keep up with the case through Eugene Davidovich online. In his posttrial segments, which he opened with a newscaster's "Good afternoon," Davidovich offered a summary of the events, courtroom intrigue, and links to more information. He ended with a daily mantra: "Operation Green Rx must come to an end. We will help bring it to an end."

Davidovich knew San Diego prosecutors didn't comment once a trial was in progress. He knew he had an uncontested voice in the court of public opinion. After McCabe called him to the witness stand to testify in his own defense, he posted a taped webcast. He told viewers, "That was probably the most scary and most stressful thing I've ever had to do aside from the first week of boot camp in the navy." He described Pham attempting to blister him in cross-examination and called for people to keep massing at the courthouse in his support.

"My medical conditions were taken apart," Davidovich said, detailing his "interrogation" by Pham. "I was forced to discuss in detail how I suffered, why I suffered, when I suffered, when I saw my doctors. She questioned my navy service in detail. . . . She went on to question my marriage. She went on to talk about my associations with Americans for Safe Access and NORML. She demanded to know if I was associated with these organizations in any way."

After a second day of facing the deputy district attorney's cross-examination, Davidovich concluded that Pham "tried to get me upset on the stand several times. . . . She was not successful. I retained my composure." He then delivered his closing argument to the public: "The jury is aware that the district attorney's office is conducting a political war against medical marijuana in San Diego."

Davidovich put up one more trial video. It showed him standing outside the courthouse, saying little and mostly smiling broadly as his attorneys, McCabe and Bahar Ansari, exulted in the verdict. Soon afterward, on the

Eugene Davidovich trial website, a headline roared: NOT GUILTY ON ALL COUNTS!!!

. . .

The events in and out of court in San Diego illustrated how medical marijuana defendants and advocates could outflank authorities and shape public opinion with stories framed in compassionate narratives about sick people and lives and spirits lifted by medical marijuana. It was the message powerfully delivered in 2002 when severely ill patients locked a gate to trap the DEA convoy during the drug agents' raid on the Wo/Men's Alliance for Medical Marijuana. And now, when police and district attorneys sought to weave narratives of greedy pot profiteers, advocates depicted retail-style dispensaries, cannabis delivery services, and marijuana growers as caring servants providing "safe access" for people in need. When prosecutors brought self-described medical marijuana defendants to trial, advocates spun stories of drug cops circumventing the will of California voters, who had passed Proposition 215.

In a third high-profile San Diego marijuana prosecution, medical cannabis patients wearing green ribbons packed the city's United States courthouse on behalf of James Stacy, who had woven his own narrative as an honorable man ensnared in the raids on fourteen San Diego County medical marijuana providers on a single day, September 9, 2009. Stacy faced nine federal charges after San Diego authorities referred his case to U.S. prosecutors, counting on a better result in a federal court, where all marijuana—medical or otherwise—was illegal. Stacy attempted a legal maneuver that authorities tried to deride as an Obama-made-me-do-it defense. Stacy, who ran the Movement in Action Dispensary for ten weeks in the front of his martial arts studio in the community of Vista, had pointed to comments by presidential candidate Barack Obama that he was "not going to use Justice Department resources to try to circumvent state laws" on medical marijuana. He also cited the Justice Department memo by Deputy Attorney General David Ogden, written after Stacy's arrest, that said government wasn't going to target individuals "in clear and unambiguous compliance" with medical marijuana laws—though the memo had said nothing about marijuana stores.

Lobbied by medical marijuana advocates, two California congressional members, Democrat Sam Farr and Republican Dana Rohrabacher, wrote the House Judiciary Committee to defend Stacy, "the first to face federal prosecution under the Obama administration's new policy." Their letter declared, "Medical marijuana patients remain vulnerable to federal enforcement, raids, arrest and prosecution by U.S. Attorneys. Worse still, these persons are barred from introducing evidence that demonstrates that he or she was acting in accordance with state law."

U.S. district judge Barry Ted Moskowitz rejected Stacy's request to argue to the jury that Obama administration policy signaled that medical cannabis outlets were acceptable. But federal prosecutors offered leniency: three years' probation and time served—fourteen days—on a single count of manufacturing marijuana. Stacy took the deal. He listened on January 7, 2011, as Assistant U.S. Attorney Andrew G. Schopler called him "one of the most respectful defendants that I have prosecuted" and Moskowitz, pronouncing sentence, declared that two years' probation—not three—was sufficient.

San Diego's narcotics enforcement establishment hadn't contemplated getting frustrated by a legal, political, and activist strategy of courting compassion for medical marijuana defendants, of influencing potential jurors and persuading judges to consider leniency. It was long-crafted strategy by marijuana advocates, exploited after the WAMM raid in 2002 and after the United States government earlier that year targeted a famous cannabis grower and author known as the Guru of Ganja.

On February 2002, DEA agents raided the Oakland home of Ed Rosenthal, confiscating some 100 starter plants grown by Rosenthal for the Harm Reduction Center, a San Francisco medical marijuana dispensary. Authorities also raided the dispensary, seizing 628 plants and cataloging another 405 plants bought by DEA agents. Ed Rosenthal was an icon of cannabis culture and the marijuana movement. He was author of *High Times* magazine's "Ask Ed" column, the Ann Landers of marijuana growing. He was on his way to becoming America's most renowned pot publisher with his cultivators' bible, *Ed Rosenthal's Marijuana Grower's Handbook,* and later his multivolume *Big Book of Buds,* a seductively photographed index of seemingly most every marijuana strain known to man.

Rosenthal, as a result of the famed Oakland Cannabis Buyers Cooperative case that went to the U.S. Supreme Court, contended he was also a licensed "officer of the City of Oakland." Rosenthal had grown marijuana for the pioneering club opened by Jeff Jones. He argued he was covered under Oakland's order designating the OCBC as the city's agent in administering its medical marijuana distribution program. Yet Rosenthal's arrest by U.S.

drug agents got only minor play in the *San Francisco Chronicle,* infuriating a young but seasoned activist named Steph Sherer.

Two years earlier, Sherer, then a twenty-four-year-old from San Diego participating in Washington, D.C., protests at meetings of the World Bank and the International Monetary Fund, was grabbed by the neck by a U.S. marshal who was clearing crowds away from vans carrying some of the six hundred arrested protesters to court. He flung her to the ground, tearing ligaments in her shoulder. Sherer started using medical marijuana for resulting chronic pain. She moved to the San Francisco Bay Area to be closer to dispensaries and the center of the cannabis movement. After Rosenthal's arrest, she called Don Duncan, a political junkie who had worked on the Proposition 215 campaign in between protests against U.S. military interventions in the Middle East. Duncan was cofounder of the Berkeley Patients Group dispensary but was thinking of moving on to save old-growth redwoods. Sherer convened an emergency meeting over Ed Rosenthal's arrest. "What you guys need is a media campaign that will shine a national spotlight on what is happening in California," she said.

Sherer saw an immediate media opportunity. DEA administrator Asa Hutchinson was coming to San Francisco. She organized a protest, seizing on Hutchinson's name for a temporary strategic campaign, called Americans for Safe Access, that would stand up for Ed Rosenthal and against federal assaults on medical marijuana. To Sherer, it was to be "ASA vs. Asa." Newly signed up ASA activists made placards ranging from "DEA Go Away!" to "Stop Taking My Medicine!" for their protests.

When Rosenthal went to trial in January 2003, ASA put on two simultaneous demonstrations outside the San Francisco federal courthouse. One group of protesters stood silently with duct tape over their mouths, decrying a ruling by U.S. district judge Charles R. Breyer that California's Proposition 215 law didn't apply in federal court and that providing medical marijuana would be no defense. A second group vocally approached passersby, handing out leaflets arguing that Rosenthal's arrest and prosecution was wrong and that jurors had the right to vote their conscience. Ed Rosenthal was convicted of three counts of marijuana cultivation and conspiracy involving more than one hundred plants. And then something startling happened. Days after their verdict, five members of the jury and an alternate juror called a press conference. They charged that they had been duped into convicting a man without being told he was growing for medical marijuana patients. "'I'm sorry' doesn't begin to cover it," said juror Marney Craig, who said she would have acquitted Rosenthal had she known. Juror Charles Sackett said the panel "was kept in the dark" and "I never want to see this happen again."

Rosenthal's conviction appeared to guarantee him at least five years in prison under federal sentencing guidelines. Prosecutors sought six and a half years. Yet in June 2003, Breyer declared, "This is not an ordinary drug case." He found that Rosenthal "honestly believed he was acting as a city official" of Oakland in growing marijuana "in accordance with state and local law." He said the case warranted a "substantial departure" from the sentencing guidelines. He sentenced the Guru of Ganja to time served—one day in jail—and a thousand-dollar fine.

"This is Day 1 in the crusade to bring down the marijuana laws," Rosenthal declared in a parking lot press conference, ripping the government for the unfairness of his trial, the denial of evidence he was supplying medical marijuana, and the fact that federal law "makes no distinction between medical and recreational marijuana."

In 2006, a federal appeals court threw out Rosenthal's conviction and granted a retrial. The government filed the case again, this time piling on added counts of tax evasion and money laundering. Joe Elford, a young Yale Law School graduate and the general counsel for the now established advocacy group for medical marijuana patients, Americans for Safe Access, wrote a brief seeking dismissal of the added charges as "vindictive prosecution." Elford argued that an assistant U.S. Attorney, George Bevan, was out to bury Rosenthal in retaliation for his posttrial press conference in 2003. "The government's case against Rosenthal, at most, warrants a one-day sentence and has gone on long enough," Elford wrote. "The overzealousness of the prosecutor at Rosenthal's expense should be brought to an end." Breyer agreed it was vindictive prosecution and threw out the tax and money laundering charges. After a second jury convicted Rosenthal of the same marijuana charges in 2007, this time without a posttrial revolt, Breyer declined to sentence him to any additional penalty.

By 2008, Americans for Safe Access had a $1.2-million budget for legal and political advocacy, as well as tens of thousands of members in states that sanctioned medical marijuana and in others looking to do so. ASA led seminars in strategic messaging and media outreach. It created a raid response program, using social media to rally instant crowds of patients to sites of police actions. When there were crackdowns on medical marijuana, ASA wanted the cops and the DEA, used to being hailed as heroes, to feel the loss of morale that came with getting jeered by the public.

In court, Elford took up the case of Felix Kha, a medical cannabis patient whose eight grams of marijuana had been seized by Garden Grove police during a traffic stop in Orange County. A prosecutor threw out the pot charges but refused to order the return of Kha's marijuana. In 2007, a California appeals court ruled that medical marijuana patients cleared of wrongdoing were entitled to the safe and speedy return of their herbal medicine. "Kha ... is a qualified patient whose marijuana possession was legally sanctioned under state law. That is why he was not subjected to a criminal trial, and that is why the state cannot destroy his marijuana. It is also why the police can't continue to retain his marijuana," declared the Fourth Appellate District Court in 2007. It became routine in California for people whose weed was seized by the cops to demand its return, often going to court to ensure they got it back.

California medical marijuana defendants became accustomed to public support, even celebrity treatment. Charles Lynch had opened a Morro Bay marijuana dispensary called Central Coast Compassionate Caregivers in 2006. The mayor, city council members, and the Chamber of Commerce came out for the ribbon cutting. But an irked local sheriff urged federal drug agents to raid the establishment. Lynch was convicted in 2008 of illegal marijuana distribution after prosecutors presented evidence of him serving a nineteen-year-old customer, a minor under federal law. Celebrities including talk show host Montel Williams, who turned to medical marijuana to treat symptoms of multiple sclerosis, and singer Melissa Etheridge, who used cannabis for breast cancer, rallied to Lynch's cause. Actor Drew Carey produced a sympathetic documentary for Reason TV, *Raiding California.* It focused on seventeen-year-old Owen Beck, a former high school football and soccer player and a bone cancer survivor. The teen told of his nausea from chemotherapy and his phantom pain from an amputation—"like someone had driven thousands of nails where my leg used to be." His mother and father described the family's decision to get him a medical marijuana recommendation and take him to Lynch's dispensary. They hailed Lynch for his respect and caring.

In 2010, United States district judge George H. Wu, departing from federal sentencing guidelines that could have sent Lynch to prison for seven and a half to nine years, gave him a year and a day. The judge said Lynch, who would appeal his conviction, was "caught in the middle of shifting positions by governmental authorities" and between state and federal attitudes on medical marijuana. In a stunning remark, Judge Wu said the problem "could be ameliorated" if the federal government reclassified marijuana from its status as a Schedule I drug with no accepted medical use.

Before a major ruling by the California Supreme Court, virtually no one knew about Patrick Kevin Kelly—other than a cadre of lawyers who saw his case as a test to limits imposed by the state legislature on California's voter approved medical marijuana law. Kelly had broken his jaw, suffered skull fractures, and busted his kneecap in three motorcycle accidents, landing "on my head every time." He also had fused neck vertebrae from his years as an oil-field roughneck, as well as hepatitis C, which he got as a result of a tattoo. Kelly took a prescription drug for nausea, but dropped it because it cost $1,250 a month—the same as his disability pay. So Kelly, after getting a marijuana recommendation, grew pot in the backyard of his modest, post–World War II bungalow in Lakewood, near Long Beach. He had six plants blooming with buds and surging a dozen feet high, and a seventh flowering plant, growing a few feet tall in their shadow, when narcotics officers busted down his door.

To Los Angeles County prosecutors, this was an easy case. The legislature, in a concession to law enforcement groups, had imposed a limit of six mature (bud producing) marijuana plants or twelve immature plants per medical marijuana patient. Kelly had seven mature plants. The 2003 Senate Bill 420, which went into effect on January 1, 2004, also said medical users could possess no more than eight ounces of dried marijuana. Deputies seized twelve ounces of pot from his home. The prosecutor read the state-mandated numbers to the jury. Kelly was found guilty of possessing more than an ounce of marijuana and illegal cultivation, under criminal statutes that don't consider medical use. He was sentenced to three years' probation and the two days he served in jail and was ordered to pay the court $750. His public defender apologized and said he would file an appeal. Kelly just wanted his name cleared and his 750 bucks back.

In January 2010, Oakland attorney Gloria Cohen, part of the legal team that took on the appeal, telephoned Kelly. She was ecstatic. "We're popping the champagne!" she told Kelly, informing him his conviction had just been thrown out by the highest court in California. "Thanks," he replied, still wondering about the $750. To medical marijuana advocates, the victory was huge. The Supreme Court said the legislature, in SB 420, had improperly amended Proposition 215 without the consent of voters, who approved the initiative. There was now no legal limit on the amount of cannabis a patient could possess under state law in California. Medical marijuana defendants could no longer be convicted in state court strictly on a number of plants or ounces. "I didn't understand the hubbub," Kelly said later as he reflected on the significance of the case. "I think with all the bumps in my head I didn't contemplate things very well. I'm glad it's helping people."

But many legal observers concluded that the state Supreme Court decision didn't prevent police from investigating medical marijuana cultivators with more than a half dozen plants for crimes such as possession for sale or illegal distribution. Most counties retained the six-mature-plant measure as a general policy, and prosecutors could still question whether harvests exceeding six plants reflected a patient's actual medical use. Marijuana was still federally illegal. Yet some physicians took to writing recommendations declaring patients' medical needs were consistent with growing ninety-nine plants. Some growers tilling massive gardens, and who had dispensary member cards for hundreds of medical users, figured they were safely in the clear. Not Patrick Kevin Kelly. He took to growing just five plants, one less than the former state standard. Despite the Supreme Court ruling, Kelly wasn't taking any chances on another raid by the cops.

California prosecutors and narcotics officers were not about to wilt in the face of unfavorable court decisions or the media spin of medical marijuana advocates. In San Diego, after the acquittals of Eugene Davidovich and Jovan Jackson, Steve Walter, the supervising narcotics prosecutor for Bonnie Dumanis, made clear that the district attorney would continue prosecuting retail pot purveyors, who were "using the medical marijuana law to justify a lot of people getting high." Despite courtroom defeats, Walter told *The Sacramento Bee,* "I don't take from that that we're not going to be able to prosecute a dispensary in the county of San Diego."

In fact, San Diego authorities had never given up on trying to convict Jovan Jackson. After his acquittal of marijuana charges stemming from 2008 purchases by undercover officers posing as cannabis patients at his Answerdam dispensary, Dumanis charged Jackson again based on officers' undercover buys at the still-open dispensary in July and December of 2009. This time, the prosecutor, Deputy District Attorney Chris Lindberg, got a judge to agree to a pretrial motion denying Jackson the right to defend himself as a medicinal marijuana provider under California law. Eugene Davidovich sent out an emergency update from the San Diego chapter of ASA. "A travesty occurred in San Diego today. Jovan Jackson a US Navy Veteran and medical marijuana patient was denied a medical marijuana defense in State Court," he wrote. "After the decision came this morning,

Steve Walter, Dumanis' #1, celebrated the Judge's decision with high fives and congratulatory hugs to Lindberg and the other DAs gathered in the courtroom to witness the Judge's decision."

In Jackson's second trial, the defendant and medical marijuana advocates were routed. "Ladies and gentlemen," Lindberg argued to the jury, "this case is about nothing more than selling drugs and making money," adding, "As the court told you during jury selection, medical marijuana does not apply" as a defense. Jackson was convicted on three charges of illegal marijuana possession and sales in September 2010. Three months later, San Diego Superior Court judge Howard H. Shore sentenced him to 180 days in jail, three years' probation, and a five-thousand-dollar fine. Facing a courtroom packed with Jackson's supporters, cannabis patients, and activists, Shore declared, "Medical marijuana is a scam."

The judge had accepted San Diego prosecutors' argument that Jackson's dispensary was illegal because his customers—the sixteen hundred members of his medical marijuana "collective"—didn't directly participate in cultivating the marijuana. Americans for Safe Access appealed Jackson's conviction. The medical marijuana movement was shaken. Meanwhile, another case, a fourteen-year-long saga involving a breast cancer survivor and her caregiver husband, would challenge—and haunt—the movement. It would test advocates' conviction, and their message, that compassion for medical marijuana patients could carry the day in court.

NINE

Martyrdom for the Missionaries

Years before he became a reluctant witness for the United States government, Michael Harvey was one of many seekers who had traversed the old Gold Rush passage to find the marijuana doctor with a healing touch born of her own suffering. People drawn to Dr. Marion P. "Mollie" Fry navigated Highway 49 after turning off of U.S. Highway 50 in Placerville in El Dorado County. They drove past wood frame houses dating back to the 1860s. They navigated hairpin highway turns, snaking through Coloma and past the replica Sutter's Mill, near where James Marshall discovered gold in 1848. They crossed the American River Bridge, ascending beyond the whitewater rafting outfitters and wine vineyards in oak-studded hills connecting two only-in-California towns, Lotus and Cool.

Just beyond the three-way stop in Cool, next to a rural post office, they reached the Whole Health Medical Marijuana Research Center of Mollie Fry. Long before the explosion of cannabis stores and medical pot clinics in California, the self-proclaimed "marijuana medic" was forging a decidedly new tradition in a family medicine legacy that extended back to the Civil War. Her grandfather, Dr. Frances Marion Pottenger, was a renowned tuberculosis researcher who founded a sanitarium outside of Los Angeles and helped spearhead the Easter Seals campaign. Mollie's own passion for medicine, her drive, and her spirit came from her mother, Dr. Caroline Fry, a specialist in psychiatric research and a free-living Malibu nudist.

Caroline Fry passed down another legacy—a history of breast cancer. At ten years of age, Mollie saw her mother wither away and die from the disease. The childhood trauma marked her life, making it only more terrifying when, in late 1997, she was diagnosed with fast-advancing cancer. She was given a 30 percent chance of survival. Surgeons removed both of her breasts, cutting deep into her chest wall, to save her.

Fry, who earned her medical degree from the University of California, Irvine, had put off her career while homeschooling her children in a faded blue ranch house on Waterfall Trail in Greenwood, a forested hamlet outside the mountaintop former mining camp of Georgetown. Fry's husband, Dale Schafer, a U.S. naval veteran, was a lawyer who represented injured employees, including cops, in workers' compensation cases. He would later become a candidate for El Dorado County district attorney as a medical marijuana advocate, a crusading convert rallying to the cause of his ailing wife.

After her radical mastectomy surgery, Fry, forlorn and frightened, endured five months of chemotherapy. She threw up constantly, losing up to half a pound a day. Her husband feared she was wasting away. A doctor told them marijuana might help. It did. She went from slipping into an emotional abyss to regaining weight and recovering her will to live. "Medical cannabis turned all of this around," she would one day proclaim in a federal courtroom in a legal epic that would span much of the life of the California medical marijuana movement.

A year after the passage of California's medical marijuana law, legally obtaining pot wasn't easy. Schafer would spend two and a half hours driving his wife to the San Francisco Cannabis Buyers Club of Dennis Peron. The cannabis club dispensed only an eighth of an ounce of marijuana at a time. On these trips, Fry arrived in various states of appearance—with her head bald from chemotherapy, or covered by a scarf, or later, in a wig—to make separate purchases on the same day. Perpetually sick from the drive and tormented by shooting pains, she found the journey intolerable. So Dale took to growing pot at home. As cannabis horticulturists went, he was—charitably—a work in progress. But the lawyer studied and found his touch, learning to produce a bountiful garden with multiple cannabis strains.

Mollie Fry, regaining her strength, found renewed energy and a cause. She opened a physician's clinic recommending medical cannabis—"God's medicine" she called it with spiritual conviction—to patients in 1999. Schafer set aside his workers' comp law practice to open a business called Cool Madness at her clinic. He dispensed legal advice on California medical marijuana law. And recalling the exhausting trips to San Francisco for medical marijuana, he began studying ways to provide for his wife's patients who were in need.

While medical cannabis dispensaries were still an anomaly in California, and state rules for delivering cannabis to medicinal users were ill-defined, federal law against marijuana was unambiguous. So was the U.S. Drug Enforcement Administration's searing distrust of medical marijuana doctors. It would be three years before the U.S. Ninth Circuit Court of Appeals recognized, in the case of Dr. Marcus Conant, physicians' constitutionally protected rights to discuss cannabis with patients—with the notable caveat that doctors had no constitutional shield for supplying marijuana or aiding patients in getting it. Schafer's desire to provide cannabis, as the spouse of a physician, was perilous. But the lawyer and doctor were all in.

In 1993, after a local raid on their pot garden, Valerie and Mike Corral had established the WAMM community to raise and share the plant that had alleviated Valerie's relentless seizures. Similarly, Fry and Schafer saw a larger cause in Molly's suffering and their decision in 1999 to open the Whole Health Medical Marijuana Research Center and advocate access to cannabis. But while the Corrals oversaw a small colony of severely ill patients tending to plants in Santa Cruz, the doctor and lawyer in California's Sierra Nevada inspired a vast pilgrimage—and a lucrative one, authorities would insist—of people seeking their services.

The couple appeared at pro-cannabis rallies at the state capitol in Sacramento, where Mollie lit glow sticks for patients "sick and dying because they couldn't have medical marijuana." She clutched a medical cannabis cross, jabbed animatedly at her hollowed chest, demanding acceptance for the plant she credited with saving her life. In time, Fry and Schafer traveled the state, testifying as expert witnesses on behalf of medical marijuana users charged in drug crimes. They came to believe a noble mission had been bestowed on them.

At the Whole Health center, they charged $150 to $200 per person for Molly's medical marijuana recommendations and Dale's legal consultations, taking in between $750,000 and $1 million from 1999 through 2001, federal authorities would assert. The couple ran radio ads offering a medical alternative to pills. "There is a choice," the spots said. "Medical marijuana." The first streams of patients came in mostly for conditions such as cancer or diabetes or rheumatoid arthritis. Soon Fry was more often seeing people who said they just needed a recommendation for pot to help them sleep or soothe their pain. The Medical Board of California would later take issue with her also recommending it to patients with histories of alcoholism, drug abuse, or mental illnesses, including schizophrenia.

"Does marijuana make you feel better?" Fry asked those who came to her. "How does it make you feel better?" Fry, who overcame cancer and chemo with cannabis, believed her torturous path had rewarded her with a gift of compassion. "I could touch people," she would say, "where they were hurting."

In January 2000, Michael Harvey, hurting from life in general, came to the clinic at the urging of a niece who was a paralegal for Schafer. Harvey had served two stints in the army and had worked at a foundry in Ohio and as a landscaper. The years had beaten him down. He had been fired from his last two jobs in Los Angeles. His niece suggested the doctor and lawyer might take a chance on him. So Harvey found himself in the waiting room of Dr. Fry. He filled out a medical form saying he was disabled by decades of alcohol abuse, memory loss, and headaches. Fry wrote in her records that he suffered from alcoholic dementia. Harvey told her staff he had been smoking marijuana recreationally since age eighteen, and Fry gave him a recommendation to use it medically. Fry and Schafer invited him into their home, providing a place to dry out from booze. He lived in their house and, later, a trailer on the property. He ate meals with the couple and their five children, including the three youngest, who were living at home. He went to church with them and exchanged Christmas presents. Schafer paid him a hundred dollars a week to help out as a handyman and shuttle his kids to gymnastics. Later, he would draft Harvey to tend to his marijuana plants and, ultimately, deliver cannabis to Mollie's patients. One day, with a letter of immunity from prosecution, the U.S. government would turn the beleaguered man into a key witness against the doctor and lawyer who took him in.

· · ·

From its opening in 1999, the Whole Health clinic drew the attention of the El Dorado County Sheriff's Department and a veteran narcotics detective named Robert Ashworth. Within weeks, the county probation department complained drug offenders under its supervision were failing tests for pot. They had marijuana recommendations from Dr. Fry. In his mind, Detective Ashworth didn't see people looking profoundly ill streaming into her clinic. He saw eighteen-year-old snowboarders and fifty-five-year-olds "who had been using marijuana forever." It seemed to Ashworth that Mollie Fry was handing out cannabis recommendations to everyone, out of a belief that pot could cure *everything*.

Mollie Fry preemptively reached out to the sheriff's department. On July 27, 1999, she called Ashworth in the narcotics division, asking him if she and her husband were under surveillance. Ashworth gave no indication that was the case as he accepted her invitation to inspect Schafer's marijuana garden. He showed up with his partner, Sergeant Timothy McNulty, at the house on Waterfall Trail on August 17. He sensed Fry's determination instantly. He found her "very, very emotional and very, very passionate." Fry, her hair now grown back thick with streaks of gray, spoke of surviving cancer and her healing mission as a marijuana doctor. The detective, a former military policeman and civilian cop from Montgomery, Alabama, found Schafer easygoing and personable. The two men took to chatting about the Little League team Schafer coached and to conversing warmly with each subsequent phone call or visit.

On the first encounter, the El Dorado narcotics officers asked the couple if they knew of nonmedical growers growing illegally in the county's backcountry. "I only know of the good guys," the tall, bearded lawyer assured Ashworth. Schafer promised he would keep an eye out for illegal grows and people acting in interests other than serving the ill under California's medical marijuana law. Meanwhile, he told Ashworth he wanted to give medicine he was cultivating to sick people who could neither grow nor afford their own cannabis. Schafer came away believing Ashworth thought that wasn't any problem. "I thought we were building a relationship," the lawyer would later say.

Before the men parted, Schafer had another question for the detective: Are we being investigated by the feds? Ashworth told him DEA agents weren't snooping in the couple's clinic or pot garden. At the time, it was true.

Before leaving, Ashworth noted the number of marijuana plants he counted on the property: twenty-one. He recorded the amount in a report to the El Dorado County district attorney. Over the next two years, the detective continued keeping tabs on the cannabis doctor and lawyer. "This was the best undercover operation I ever had," he said years later. "I never had to hide the fact that I was a policeman. Think about it."

El Dorado County in 1999 was trying to determine local policy for medical marijuana, for setting plant limits and measures to help officers discern who was growing medically and who might be trafficking criminally. Schafer joined with the district attorney, Gary Lacy, on a medical marijuana committee. He ran down California's attorney general, Bill Lockyer, at a political barbecue, getting him to mail him guidelines for patients using or growing marijuana under Proposition 215. Schafer called Ashworth frequently, occasionally passing along information on suspicious characters growing weed in the woods. The skeptical detective wondered if Schafer was worried about the competition.

In August 2000, Ashworth made another visit to Waterfall Trail. He inspected the couple's marijuana garden, including potted plants in a greenhouse on a slope behind the residence and others in the ground. He counted forty-three plants, bringing the cumulative total to sixty-four. His plant count, over separate visits and years, inched upward toward one hundred—a legal threshold that could trigger a five-year prison sentence under federal law, even if the total resulted from multiple visits, not just a single inspection or raid.

Their profile as a cancer-surviving doctor and her caregiver husband was bringing cannabis celebrity to the couple. *High Times* magazine sent a correspondent to their home. Photos from the visit were published online, showing the couple trimming marijuana buds in their living room with their youngest children, thirteen, ten, and eight. A caption for another picture described the kids in the garden "looking with tender care and love" at the plant "that saved their mom's life." Joining her mentor in marijuana medicine, Dr. Tod Mikuriya, the pioneering "doctor of last resort" for the movement, Fry signed on as one of the founders of the fledgling Society of Cannabis Clinicians. Locally, she established the Garden Valley chapter of the American Alliance of Medical Cannabis, offering seminars for marijuana patients in the mountain towns above Placerville.

Meanwhile, her husband took the fateful step of providing medicine to her patients. He began sending Michael Harvey in his four-wheel drive to locations ranging from the San Francisco Bay Area to South Lake Tahoe to deliver baggies of cannabis to patients who requested the extra service. In time, Harvey also went to the United Parcel Service drop box at Cool Corner Video and sent out shipments under Schafer's name. The handyman bypassed the U.S. post office next to the medical clinic because he figured that wasn't safe. Yet somehow delivering weed by UPS seemed okay.

Fry and Schafer rented an office in Oakland, booked hotel suites, and held events at private homes for the doctor to issue medical marijuana recommendations elsewhere. In the fall of 1999, at the Embassy Suites in South Lake Tahoe, they met a former office manager named Tracy Coggins and her boyfriend, a cannabis patient and marijuana aficionado named Paul Maggy. The twenty-eight-year-old Maggy was a dropout from Syracuse University, where he had studied mortuary science. He worked summers at a Tahoe bicycle store—and had a misdemeanor theft record for ripping off a customer.

Fry hired Coggins as her personal assistant to manage the office at the clinic in Cool. Schafer later took in Maggy to help him with Cool Madness. The family businesses paid Maggy eight dollars an hour, plus a five-dollar commission for each medical marijuana patient application he processed for Fry. Maggy also helped the lawyer create a new service called Home Health Horticulture. It provided four-hundred-dollar grow-at-home kits for marijuana patients that included lighting, nutrients, and six starter plants. Maggy later claimed he put Schafer in touch with two growers who supplied hundreds of marijuana clones. Maggy and Harvey took the cannabis seedlings in rock-wool growing cubes and set up irrigated, oxygenated cultivation trays for them in the family's garage. In the waiting room between Schafer's office and his wife's medical clinic, one of the seedlings was displayed growing under a fluorescent light, near a sign-up sheet for those who wanted to order the kits. Maggy would tell authorities Fry and Schafer established a full-spectrum service providing medical marijuana recommendations and furnishing cultivation supplies and starter plants while also delivering weed on demand to customers. The lawyer and doctor would dispute his account.

Fry wasn't naive about the risks of running a marijuana medical practice. She instructed her staff to keep an eye out for narcs posing as patients. Once suspecting a man in for an exam was an undercover officer, she led him through range of motion exercises. "Okay, lift up your shirt," Fry instructed him bluntly. "Let me see your wire." That time, there was none.

Maggy and his girlfriend were out by May 2000. Tensions had developed with Schafer over Maggy's demand for a pay raise and sales commissions on the grow-at-home kits. The lawyer was infuriated by Maggy's insistence that he deserved a fifty-dollar bonus for each growing kit sold for having researched and developed the idea. "You did not invent this," Schafer snapped at him, accusing Maggy of pursuing personal gain, not patient care. "You're just greedy." Schafer would later say he fired Maggy and Coggins. Maggy claimed they quit. In either version, they left abruptly. Maggy began growing marijuana and selling to medical users, working from lists of patients they took from Fry's office. In late November 2000, narcotics officers raided Maggy and Coggins's garden and seized eight hundred plants, arresting them for conspiracy to distribute marijuana.

A month later, officials of the United Parcel Service contacted DEA Special Agent Brian Keefe in Sacramento. Seven packages of marijuana, sent in Schafer's name by Michael Harvey, had been intercepted at a UPS sorting center in Rocklin, California. The DEA communicated the information to the El Dorado County Sheriff's Department. Suddenly, Ashworth's plant counts were indeed part of a federal probe. Undercover teams were targeting the clinic. As Schafer attended local working-group meetings to draft county medical marijuana policies with District Attorney Gary Lacy, Sheriff Jeff Neves, and Ashworth and McNulty, local authorities were reporting to agent Keefe and the DEA. Ashworth felt no compulsion to give the lawyer an update on his earlier question of whether the feds were after them.

Six weeks later, on Valentine's Day, real estate appraisers Todd and Doreen Zimmerman drove to Waterfall Trail to inspect the property for a home refinance loan. Doreen went inside to take measurements in the house. Todd started looking over the exterior of the house. He made his way to a concrete bunker, an old fallout shelter, built into the slope. He opened the door to an aromatic cannabis burst. Inside were three platforms teeming with marijuana plants, with lights, fans, and irrigation tubing. He freaked, slamming the door. He rushed into the house to retrieve his wife, trying to calm himself. They completed their measurements, working around bongs and germinating plants in Petri dishes in the master bedroom. They bid Schafer a hasty good-bye and drove away, glancing from the car to see two plant-filled greenhouses as they headed out. They stopped at the first pay phone in Cool, and Todd Zimmerman called the sheriff's department.

A day later, an undercover narcotics officer brought in from the Folsom Police Department in neighboring Sacramento County went to the clinic, wired up and posing as a patient. He asked an unsuspecting Dr. Fry for help in growing marijuana.

"I'm just trying to get started in that and, it's like, where do I start?"

"I can help you," Fry answered. "We have, um, my husband has a business. I wouldn't call it a business, actually, a service. Businesses are supposed to make money. This one loses money. We'll call it a service."

She went on to tell the undercover officer that Dale was growing marijuana as a caregiver for forty-five people and looking for ways to provide cannabis at lower-than-black-market prices. She told him they were the people to do business with—not another establishment up the road that was crawling with narcotics officers.

"We can provide you with clones. We can provide you with lights. We can provide you with nutrients. We can provide you with everything you need, and you don't have to go to Greenfire. Do not go to Greenfire!" Fry said.

"O.K.," the undercover said.

"Greenfire is staked out by the narcs," Fry went on. "They sit in a parking lot. You park. They write down your license plate number. Then they go in and compare your license plate number with the purchase order, and then they put you on a two-month rotation, and when you've had two months to get your plants going, they come in and bust you."

She invited him to sign up as a member of Home Health Horticulture and Research for the standard twenty-five-dollar fee. She told him about the four-hundred-dollar home growing kits offered and promised "our commitment to you in terms of trying to provide low-cost marijuana, organic quality." She added, "And then, whenever you need new clones, you just call us up."

In seven attempts, undercover drug agents failed to get the doctor or lawyer to sell them any pot. The best they could do was infiltrate a marijuana baking seminar Dale Schafer and Heather Schafer, his oldest daughter by a previous marriage, held in early September 2001 at the local Garden Valley Grange for people presenting medical cannabis recommendations. Dale and Heather showed the gathering how to make Rice Krispies Treats with hash oil. Officers, posing as patients, departed with some of the leftover treats.

On September 28, 2001, Fry and Schafer's fourteen-year-old son, Geoffrey Schafer, hollered to his parents that officers were swarming the house. Geoffrey was detained at gunpoint and handcuffed. Mollie Fry burst outside to see DEA agents and Ashworth's El Dorado County narcotics team. "I entirely submit. You are welcome to my house," the doctor announced before she was brought to the ground and handcuffed, trembling. She told a female DEA officer she was a cancer patient.

"You have cancer?" the agent asked.

"Of course I have," Fry responded. "Why the hell do you think I'm doing this?"

.   .   .

Detective Ashworth counted 34 marijuana plants on the property in the raid, bringing his cumulative count since 1999 up to 98. DEA agents seized another 12 plants from the bunker and the residence, bringing the total to 110—10 more than the threshold needed to get Fry and Schafer five years in federal prison if they were convicted at trial. The United States Attorney's Office in Sacramento also had Paul Maggy, who had been busted in a separate drug case, to bargain with on a plea deal, and who would testify that there had been hundreds of seedlings in Fry and Schafer's garage, along with a far-reaching marijuana conspiracy by the pot doc and cannabis lawyer. DEA agents also called on Michael Harvey, who had left his trailer and the family's employ months earlier. They interrogated him on the UPS deliveries and an alleged 250 plants grown in pots and on the hillside of Waterfall Trail after Ashworth's August 2000 visit. But U.S. authorities didn't rush to file charges. They knew they had sympathetic defendants in a breast cancer survivor and a media-savvy husband capable of stirring a public outcry. They were going to proceed with caution.

In 2002, Schafer ran for the office of El Dorado County district attorney. *The Sacramento Bee* and local *Mountain Democrat* newspaper in Placerville were closely following a rift in the district attorney's office in which the incumbent, Gary Lacy, was being challenged by one of his top prosecutors, Erik Schlueter, who was backed by the local sheriff's deputies union. To the press, Schafer was a colorful afterthought, worth a mention only because of the September 28 drug raid on his house and the profile of his stricken wife. As the three candidates debated at the town hall amid the old storefronts of Placerville, Schafer offered an upbeat antidote to the top contenders. Lacy and Schlueter sniped at each other bitterly, as both men touted their supporters in law enforcement and did all they could to ignore the pot lawyer in the room.

"I'm endorsed by the people who look in their rearview mirror and have a panic attack when they see a police officer," Schafer interjected. He said he was running for district attorney to offer compassion to people who eased their suffering with medical marijuana. He proposed protecting cannabis patients while directing prosecution resources to instead target methamphetamine labs and dangerous narcotics that were destroying families. Schafer drew a distinction. "I live with a marijuana patient," he told the audience. "These people are like you and me." He finished third in the June primary as expected, but with a surprising 15 percent of the vote.

Elsewhere in California, DEA agents were busting medical marijuana patients and providers. In August 2002, they raided and destroyed a six-plant garden of an Oroville woman, Diane Monson, who used cannabis to treat back pain. A month later, the feds generated their grandest public backlash by surging into the Santa Cruz garden of the Wo/Men's Alliance for Medical Marijuana. Federal prosecutors were wary of negative attention. In Sacramento, they waited as Monson and lead plaintiff Angel Raich brought their case to the U.S. Supreme Court. On June 6, 2005, writing the court's majority decision, Justice John Paul Stevens upheld the federal authority to prosecute medical marijuana, declaring that such prosecution didn't violate the commerce clause of the Constitution. Stevens noted the "strong arguments" of Raich and Monson "that they will suffer irreparable harm because, despite a congressional finding to the contrary, marijuana does have valid therapeutic purposes." But he wrote that the Controlled Substances Act "is a valid exercise of federal power, even as applied to the troubling facts of this case."

Two weeks later, Fry and Schafer were arrested on charges of conspiring to grow and distribute marijuana between August 1999 and September 2001. They refused a plea deal of no prison time for Dr. Fry and eighteen months for Schafer. "I married him for better or worse," Fry would later explain, sobbing. "I was not going to send him to prison. I could not live with myself." They also rejected the deal for another reason. The doctor and lawyer, and their legion of supporters, were convinced that their helping medical marijuana patients was not only right but righteous.

The trial began on August 2, 2007, with the proceedings offering only a backup chorus to the searing arguments outside the Sacramento federal courthouse, and on the airwaves, about federal intrusion into the matter of medical marijuana in California. By then, nine years had passed since Dr. Donald Abrams undertook breakthrough medical cannabis research during the AIDS crisis in San Francisco, and six years had gone by since the state-funded Center for Medicinal Cannabis Research began directing landmark California clinical trials on the medical efficacy of marijuana. A boom in cannabis dispensaries was well-established in Los Angeles and many other cities. A legion of medical marijuana physicians openly advertised their services across the state. But citing federal law, United States district judge Frank C. Damrell Jr. ruled that, in his courtroom, there was to be mention of neither California's Proposition 215 nor medical marijuana.

The judge's ruling, denying Fry and Schafer a medical marijuana defense, didn't apply on *The Christine Craft Show* on Sacramento's Progressive 1240 Talk City Radio. Craft broadcast daily trial updates from Fry, Schafer, or their lawyers, and she openly advocated that the jury reject the charges—and nullify federal law—on moral grounds. In court, lead federal prosecutor Anne Pings was furious. She demanded daily polling of jurors to ensure they hadn't heard Craft's call for them to "play dumb and vote not guilty."

The radio host persisted, and Pings railed to Damrell about snide on-air comments concerning U.S. prosecutors, and about Craft's appeal to jurors that "you don't have to do what the judge tells you. You can do what you want to." The assistant U.S. Attorney seethed when a woman claiming to have been disqualified during jury selection called Craft's show to complain that people selected for the panel didn't know about medical marijuana or Prop 215 or feigned ignorance.

"We are promised a jury of our peers," protested an ensuing press release by Bobby Eisenberg, spokeswoman for the Fry/Schafer Defense Committee. "Yet Fry and Schafer, medical marijuana advocates who upheld California law, are being judged by twelve people who swore they knew nothing about Prop 215 or marijuana being used as medicine." The notice announced a "jury nullification" rally outside the courthouse at "high noon."

Despite the judge's order, defense attorneys Tony Serra, representing Schafer, and Lawrence Lichter, representing Fry, sought to sneak the state medical marijuana law into federal court. In his opening statement, Serra began by describing Schafer "as law abiding all his life" and said, "Dr. Fry was the victim of severe, death-threatening breast cancer." Then he went on, "It was at or about the time that Proposition 215 was passed."

"Your Honor, objection!" said Pings's cocounsel, Assistant U.S. Attorney Sean Flynn, cutting him off. "May we approach?"

Out of earshot of jurors, Flynn protested to Damrell that it was clear where Serra was headed. "Your Honor, he's going to get into the medical value of marijuana. It violates the court's order [regarding] talking about Proposition 215. He's going to argue it helped her cancer."

Damrell told Serra he could tell jurors why Fry and Schafer grew marijuana, but said, "Whether it helped or not, stay away from that."

Then in his opening statements, Lichter spoke of Fry's chemotherapy and started to tell of her oncologist suggesting marijuana, saying, "As perhaps you've learned[,] . . . even before the Compassionate Use Act was passed in California, 67 percent of oncologists . . ."

"Objection!" Pings said.

Damrell had had enough. He sent the jury out, admonished the defense, and brought the jurors back in. He instructed the panel that the lawyers' discussion of the "distribution of marijuana for medical purposes under state law" was not to be considered. "Under federal law, it is not a defense to the charge of conspiracy to manufacture or distribute marijuana . . . in violation of the Controlled Substances Act," Damrell told the jury. "That a person engaged in such conduct for medical purposes, that is not a defense. . . . I will not permit testimony on these issues."

Flynn had outlined the government's case with a matter-of-fact narrative about crimes of two people who may have opened a medical office "to give people a piece of paper called a 'recommendation'" but then, motivated by greed, engaged in a far-reaching conspiracy to distribute marijuana. While the government had its 100-plus plant count from Ashworth and DEA agents, it also had the shocked home appraiser, Todd Zimmerman, to testify of seeing three shelves with 40 to 70 plants each, inside the hillside bunker. Prosecutors had Maggy to testify that Fry and Schafer had trays of 700 to 1,000 marijuana clones in their garage. They had Harvey to testify that he tended to 150 plants planted on the hillside behind that Waterfall Trail house after Ashworth's visit in 2000, and that the number of plants reached 250 by the fall harvest. "This is a case about two drug dealers who grew and distributed marijuana, Dale Schafer and Marion Fry, husband-wife, lawyer-doctor," Flynn began.

The government's witnesses included Jeffrey Teshara, a convicted robber testifying under a grant of immunity. Teshara said he got a medical marijuana recommendation from Fry and twice bought marijuana from the doctor after she told him to meet her at a nearby fire station and feed store. Another witness, Jody Bollinger, said she got a call from Heather Schafer at the clinic, asking her if she wanted a marijuana delivery. She said Schafer's oldest son, Jeremy, arrived carrying a backpack, pulled out two eighth-ounce baggies and sold them for ninety dollars. She testified he told her to make out the check to Dale Schafer "because, if there were any questions, I could say it was legal fees."

Calling Maggy to the stand, Pings led him in detailing his conviction for conspiracy to manufacture marijuana. Maggy had been looking at five years in federal prison, but served thirteen months on a plea deal—then got sent back for another ten months after testing positive for pot in a supervised release program. "Did I stand up for you at that time?" Pings asked him. "No," Maggy said. Then he stood up for the prosecution, testifying that Mollie Fry ran a high-volume business, pressuring her staff to bring in "a hundred patients a week." He testified of the hundreds of clones at the house and dispatching Harvey on deliveries of grow-at-home kits for Schafer. He told of seeing Schafer give out baggies of marijuana at his office. He said the lawyer also sold forty seedlings to a customer and gave a pound of pot—which he said Schafer bought for thirty-seven hundred dollars—to a South Lake Tahoe man to sell for forty-five dollars an eighth ounce, a markup of some two thousand dollars.

On cross-examination, Serra bore into him over circumstances of his break with Fry and Schafer. "Why did you leave?" Serra asked.

"I was afraid. Things were getting crazy," Maggy said.

"And you went out and started your own business."

"Yes I did."

"And that was to sell?"

"Sell marijuana."

"And what, in your mind, was the distinction between your selling marijuana and their selling marijuana?"

"I wasn't writing a recommendation for it," Maggy said.

Michael Harvey, the former houseguest and delivery man, was flustered on the witness stand. He said he didn't want to be there. But he testified he collected checks made out to Dale Schafer and that Fry weighed and gave him marijuana in ziplock baggies for the UPS packages he sent. He testified about gardens and potted plants on the family's hillside and his delivery runs, five to six days a week, for Schafer. He said he collected payments for the marijuana, plus a ten-dollar delivery fee for himself. Pings asked the overwrought man three times what the service resembled, before Harvey grasped the question and the answer she was looking for.

"Like delivering pizza," he said.

Serra went after the handyman with a fury, painting Harvey as a liar who denied to Fry he was cooperating with police against them.

"These good people took you in and fed you and gave you work, helped restore you to health and you looked them in the face and you deceived them, didn't you?"

Serra kept on. "You understand your status as you sit there, don't you?"

"My status?" Harvey asked.

"Yeah, you're a rat."

Mollie Fry was too emotionally fragile to take the witness stand. It was left to Schafer to characterize the couple as caring people getting railroaded by the testimony of rogue employees who sold pot to make money for themselves without his knowledge or consent. He asserted that he gave only marijuana he grew or acquired for free to Mollie's patients. He said Harvey, whom he took in because "it was the Christian thing to do," was permitted to charge only the delivery fee. Schafer said he neither authorized nor knew of any UPS shipments, and that his marijuana garden, from tiny seedlings to mature flowering cannabis, was never close to a hundred plants. He said his only intent was to help his wife and protect her. Mollie had no involvement in growing marijuana or providing it to sick people, Schafer testified, insisting: "I had an agreement she would stay completely away from it." And while Pings portrayed the couple as marijuana millionaires, adding up fees on patient recommendations issued between 1999 and 2001 (in Fry's medical practice that continued to 2007), Serra led Schafer through an accounting suggesting the couple was actually clearing only sixty thousand dollars each a year.

The defense also brought in character witnesses spanning years of Fry's and Schafer's lives. The last one was a courtroom shocker. Glaucoma patient Elvy Musikka was one of a handful of survivors furnished marijuana by the U.S. government's Compassionate Investigational New Drug program since 1976, after the lawsuit against the government by fellow glaucoma patient Robert Randall. She arrived at court carrying a metal tin of U.S. government-furnished joints produced at the University of Mississippi. Pings was aghast.

"Anything about her medical condition, the use of marijuana, the federal study, is totally inappropriate," the prosecutor argued. "I asked that she not be allowed to carry the prop."

"Tell her to leave that out in the hall," Judge Damrell told the defense.

Musikka testified that "all over the country, we love Molly and her husband." The jury never heard about her role in government-funded cannabis research and distribution—or her tin of joints.

On August 16, 2007, after eight days of trial and a mere three hours of deliberations, the jury convicted the lawyer and doctor on all counts.

On March 20, 2008, Fry rose before Damrell for sentencing. "Your honor, I stand before you as a woman who never intended to break the law. I am a doctor who at the time was dying of cancer." Her voice raw, she continued, "We set out to heal and to educate. We have caused no harm to anyone. There are no victims. . . . There are no ill-gotten gains."

Schafer told of driving his sick wife to San Francisco to get her medicine. He lectured on the history of federal marijuana prohibition in the face of hundreds of years of research showing its medicinal value. He said he and his wife were tried and convicted and were now about to be sentenced because they were people—seers—who early on recognized and shared the benefits of cannabis as medicine. He said, "I now feel like I know how Galileo felt as he looked through the telescope and saw that the sun was in the center of the solar system," drawing a parallel to Galileo's sentence to house arrest for his discovery.

Serra said the federal trial was a calculated assault on California's medical marijuana law. "Lady Justice weeps today," he said. "This is a horrible, historical martyrdom that is occurring and we're all part and parcel of it."

Pings countered that the government had offered leniency in a plea deal. "The United States gave them opportunities not to be here today," she said. "And if they are martyrs, it is because they have chosen to be martyrs."

As Damrell prepared to pronounce the sentence under federal guide-lines—five years in prison for each—the judge declared, "Both of you are martyrs. I think you should ask yourself the question: 'Martyrs of what?'"

He scolded them for even associating with "thieves, drug users," and "petty drug pushers," including some of the witnesses who testified against them. He declared it was the couple's own "self-aggrandizement" that led them to deny that they were acting outside of the law.

"You should have recognized that," Damrell said. "But you didn't because you felt . . . you were going to be missionaries for marijuana and that took over your lives. . . . I don't know what good comes out of it because I certainly don't want to see you go to prison for five years. That would not be my choice." And then he added, "But I'm sworn to uphold the law."

In November 2010, the U.S. Ninth Circuit Court of Appeals rejected Fry's and Schafer's argument that they were illegally entrapped by Ashworth and his partner, Sgt. McNulty, because the officers led them to believe what they were doing was legal and even encouraged them. "We decline to hold that appellants are entitled to lesser sentences because government officials failed to inform them their conduct was illegal," the court ruled.

Fry and Schafer arrived at the Sacramento federal courthouse to turn themselves in to the United States Marshals Service for prison on May 2, 2011. Their saga had gone on for fourteen years since Mollie was diagnosed with breast cancer, a dozen since they opened the Whole Health Medical Marijuana Research Center, nearly a decade since the September 2001 raid. Outside the U.S. courthouse, a throng of supporters waved signs—"Patients, Not Prisoners" and "Free Doc Fry!"—as the couple stood with their five adult children and the minutes counted down to their scheduled surrender. "We demand clemency for Dale and Mollie," shouted Don Duncan of Americans for Safe Access. "And we demand an end to the war on sick and dying patients!"

The couple's son Geoffrey Schafer, who unsuccessfully sued Ashworth and fellow officers for detaining him at gunpoint during the raid when he was fourteen, rose to salute his parents' sacrifice and to condemn the punishment they were to endure. "My only hope is that this travesty for my parents will light a fire under people," he said.

"Free God's medicine!" Fry shouted, as the doctor and lawyer headed off to prison.

By mid-2011, the vast California cannabis market was seemingly address-ing her wish. A medical marijuana industry in the Golden State was in full flower, with as many as two thousand dispensaries doling out marijuana to up to 1.1 million people who had recommendations from California physicians to use cannabis. By the time Fry and Schafer were sentenced, their case appeared to the movement as a tragedy from the past. But the feds would be heard from again.

TEN

Campaign for Cannabis

In late September 2010, an unlikely campaign appeared to be on the verge of making history. Just as voters in 1996 had rocked the politics of pot by making California the first state in America to permit marijuana for medical use, the Golden State was now seriously contemplating legalizing cannabis as an adult pleasurable pursuit. Voters were tuning in to the message of the Yes on 19 campaign: California was broke following an epic fiscal crisis. Cops were wasting millions of dollars busting and jailing pot smokers. Tax revenues from voter-sanctioned marijuana commerce could save jobs and critical public services.

Proposition 19 stood to authorize California adults to possess, share, or transport up to an ounce of weed (or more where local jurisdictions allowed it) and grow twenty-five-square-foot residential pot gardens. It would permit local governments to sanction retail sales of nonmedical marijuana and tax and regulate its cultivation, processing, and distribution. State voters seemed intrigued. They appeared to tune out the California Chamber of Commerce campaign that said legalizing marijuana for purely recreational use would create the reefer madness of a stoned California workforce. They seemed unfazed by claims of the police-funded No on 19 committee that the initiative would cost the state billions of dollars in federal funding for violating drug-free workplace rules and cause crime to surge. The campaign of initiative coproponents Richard Lee and Jeff Jones—partners in the cannabis cause since they united at the Oakland Cannabis Buyers Cooperative as the cultivator of the "house special" pot strain and the Supreme Court protagonist in the dispensary's historic legal saga—was drawing mainstream appeal and international attention.

Casual voters were unaware of the chaos the initiative was stirring inside the California marijuana movement itself. Medical marijuana dispensaries and pot doctors were threatened by broader legalization. Humboldt and Mendocino growers in the north coast Emerald Triangle were panicked over perils Proposition 19 posed for their medicinal and, more specifically, illicit cultivation. Longtime purists in marijuana activism saw the initiative as a politically crafted sellout that would add penalties for twenty-one-year-olds passing joints to twenty-year-olds and would fail to roll back a plethora of marijuana laws still on California's books. A countermovement, dubbed Stoners Against Proposition 19, emerged from the grassroots, championed by Dragonfly de la Luz, the pot-savoring ganja princess and cannabis chronnoisseur. And inside the cannabis community, a pitched battle roiled over the endorsement of a dead man.

Within the Proposition 19 camp, Jeff Jones, who worked on the campaign while shuttling between his Oakland and Los Angeles Patient I.D. Centers that issued identification cards for medical marijuana patients, regularly checked in with Richard Lee with urgency. Jones wanted to make sure the president of Oaksterdam University wasn't being raided by federal drug agents for having the nerve to bankroll an initiative to legalize pot. Both men thought it was a real possibility. In 2009, Lee pulled $1.3 million from his S. K. Seymour enterprises and rushed to put funds in the signature-gathering campaign for the initiative. He wanted to get the petition drive under way quickly. He feared that, once word got out, the Drug Enforcement Administration would come storming into his Coffee Shop Blue Sky dispensary, his marijuana nursery, and his famed cannabis trade school. Two decades after the former rock concert roadie started growing marijuana in Houston following his paralyzing fall, Lee saw his "suicide mission"—getting through another year without getting arrested for pot—as more magnified than ever, given his increasing public profile. So Jones called him frequently, making light of the risk.

"Are you still there?" he asked.

"Yeah," Lee answered. "They haven't busted me yet."

On the outside, the Proposition 19 campaign, with Lee, Jones, and a hired cadre of Democratic Party consultants, had the look of a serious political endeavor reflecting marijuana's arrival in California culture and politics. Its public relations face was that of Dale Sky Jones, who married Jeff Jones during the campaign. She was a former Seattle district manager for eighteen Famous Footwear stores and a former corporate trainer for Roadhouse Grill and T.G.I. Friday's restaurants. She had joined the cannabis movement as an office manager for a medical marijuana physician in Los Angeles and met her husband at an L.A. conference for the National Organization for the Reform of Marijuana Laws. The media came to know Dale Sky Jones—with her business suits, wavy reddish hair, public poise, and ready sound bites—for her message that Proposition 19 was something even "soccer moms" could embrace. She met with editorial boards of California newspapers, which had little inclination to endorse legalized pot, and urged them to consider the budget savings and tax benefits of a legal, regulated state marijuana industry. She testified at the capitol building in Sacramento, disarming the alarmist rhetoric of law enforcement officials with presentations on alternatives to existing drug policy.

On September 21, 2010, six weeks before Californians were to vote on the initiative, Dale Sky Jones squared off before a joint state senate and assembly legislative committee with testifying law-enforcement leaders, including Sacramento County district attorney Jan Scully. Delivering the message of the California District Attorneys Association, Scully said Proposition 19 was poorly written and vague, would subject the cities and counties that taxed and regulated pot to endless litigation, and would increase—not reduce—drug crime. "It will not impede the drug cartels that are coming across our border and actually growing on our state and public lands," Scully argued.

While the district attorney portrayed drug gangs in the woods, Dale Sky Jones wove a narrative about the end of alcohol prohibition and the emergence of California's world-renowned wine industry. "We don't have illegal grape-growing cartels in our national forests," she answered. "And they don't take out guns. They take out advertising."

Five days later, the California Field Poll showed Proposition 19 winning by a 49 to 42 percent margin among registered voters. On September 30, a poll by the Public Policy Institute of California put the initiative ahead by 52 percent to 41 percent. It appeared voters were buying in on potentially another transformative California marijuana initiative. This one stood to make the Golden State America's first state to move beyond medical cannabis, further challenging federal marijuana law and potentially inspiring new state-by-state efforts to accelerate increased legal tolerance of pot.

.   .   .

Dan Rush, the burly, f-bomb-dropping, chain-smoking, backslapping special operations director for United Food and Commercial Workers Union Local Number 5, allowed himself just one week a year—Thanksgiving—to relax.

Rush was a union man to the core. His father was a Teamster. His grandfather was a member of the International Association of Machinists. His grandmother was a member of Retail Clerks Local Number 1256. Dan Rush broke in as a "lumper," loading and unloading trucks at the Port of Oakland for the Teamsters. He was still a teenager when—after a worker had been run over and killed by a strikebreaker's truck during a 1970 grocery workers strike—he put a .44-caliber pellet in a wrist rocket. He let it fly toward another truck, one driven by off-duty Chicago police officers. The pellet shattered the windshield and put out a cop's eye, landing Rush in jail on a guilty plea for assault with a deadly weapon. He later grew up to make politics his weapon, rising in the California union movement as a coalition builder who delivered key endorsements and union clout for political candidates. He specialized in state ballot initiatives, backing an unsuccessful initiative for single-payer health care and twice helping defeat Republican-led "paycheck protection" measures targeting union dues and political contributions. Every Thanksgiving, Rush reenergized himself by reading the California Secretary of State's list of ballot measures approved for signature gathering for the next election cycle, looking for his next cause to defeat or champion.

As he scanned the list in November 2009, Rush noticed multiple petition drives to qualify initiatives to legalize marijuana in California. His eyes stopped on one measure and, notably, its campaign address, 1600 Broadway in Oakland, the site of Richard Lee's Oaksterdam University. It occurred to Rush that the downtown area around the school of pot—just blocks from where his grandmother had worked for Retail Clerks Local Number 1256—was experiencing a renaissance, with new business activity and street life. Rush was struck by something else. His thirty-three-thousand-member United Food and Commercial Workers Union Local Number 5—part of the 1.3-million-member UFCW International—represented an array of grocery workers, meat cutters, drugstore clerks, and other professionals and laborers in a retail, agricultural, pharmaceutical, and food-processing union. Medical marijuana in California was creating employment in a cannabis retail, agriculture, medicinal, and food-processing industry. Rush was a recovering alcoholic, sober more than a decade, with little interest in pot. Yet he saw a potential reservoir of jobs—union jobs—with medical marijuana and, especially so, with further legalization.

Three days after Thanksgiving, Rush put on his leather jacket, strapped on his chaps, and rode his motorcycle to Oaksterdam University. He figured he might encounter "a bunch of wing-nut fucking hippies" or—worse—not a single person working on a Sunday.

He swaggered into the Oaksterdam campaign office to see a throng of volunteers and field coordinators hunched over laptops and working phones beneath a logo heralding the pot college's place in building a new California economy: "Quality Training for the Cannabis Industry." He found the campaign consultant Douglas Linney, a political strategist for environmental coalitions and progressive candidates and causes, and Dale Sky Jones, Oaksterdam's chancellor. This is real, Rush thought. Nevertheless, he announced to them that their campaign had no chance of winning without union support. Rush offered a bold proposal: employees of Oaksterdam University, its nursery and gift shop, the Coffee Shop Blue Sky dispensary— and the rest of Richard Lee's S. K. Seymour enterprises—should sign up as card-carrying members of the United Food and Commercial Workers Union.

"Get your workers to join my union, and I'll get my union to endorse your initiative," Rush promised.

Richard Lee embraced the idea and then found himself having to talk some of his own employees—who already got good wages, health care, and a 401k plan—into unionizing. Lee argued that the political cause of cannabis would advance with unions on board, and that that organizing could add protection "to keep us all from getting busted." In May 2010, with commitments from the Oaksterdam industries and the employees of Jeff Jones's Patient I.D. Center, Dan Rush rushed out a press release: the UFCW had just brought America's first marijuana workers into the union movement. The media jumped on the story. Rush set off to organize more workers in California dispensaries, pot greenhouses and farms, testing labs, cannabis kitchens, and budding marijuana business services, seizing the present and prepping for the future under Proposition 19 and legalization beyond medical use.

Oaksterdam University became both a nerve center for the campaign and a nexus for cannabis dreamers wanting to steer the California green rush. Matthew Witemyre, a young University of Florida political science graduate who worked on the Howard Dean presidential campaign and for the Marijuana Policy Project, moved to California and enrolled in a thirteen-week-semester program at Oaksterdam University. He stayed on to teach courses there in cannabis advocacy and civics. And as the Proposition 19 drive was kicking off, he met George Vianchini, a former video store owner from Marin County who came to the school to study legal structures for cannabis businesses. In the summer of 2010, in a suburban dwelling tucked amid golden hills north of San Francisco, the two men launched a marijuana-processing factory called Medi-Cone. The start-up business packaged cannabis—much of it bred from signature strains from the Oaksterdam nursery—for medical marijuana dispensaries and prepared for a potential future of supplying retail stores selling pot for adult recreational use.

After consulting with attorneys on California medical marijuana law, Vianchini and Witemyre organized Medi-Cone as a nonprofit cooperative. They also called in Dan Rush to unionize their workforce. Soon, members of the UFCW were rolling joints with rice-paper cylinders imported from Amsterdam, inserting them into Doob Tubes, and sealing them in cardboard-and-plastic medical marijuana "multipacks" ready to slide onto the hangers of cannabis stores. Witemyre, earning a union rate of twenty-five dollars an hour as Medi-Cone's chief of staff, had his doubts that Proposition 19 could pass. But if it did, he envisioned Medi-Cone flourishing in an expanded marijuana economy as a retail production factory they could some-day offer to big investors coming in.

While Proposition 19 provided fertile ground for Rush and UFCW organizing, Jeff Wilcox, the largest nonunion general contractor in the San Francisco Bay Area, prepared to wager a substantial bet on cannabis. Wilcox had battled for fifteen years with the Carpenters Union, steadfastly refusing to let the union organize his hourly employees constructing office-building interiors. The Carpenters hated him, and Wilcox fairly delighted in "fighting them tooth and nail and never losing a fight." Wilcox was also a medical marijuana patient, having gotten a physician's recommendation for construc-tion-related back pain. He owned a four-building, 172,000-square-foot ware-house complex near the Oakland waterfront and the Harborside Health Center, the dispensary that executive director Steve DeAngelo billed as the world's largest marijuana provider.

Wilcox contacted city council members and other Oakland officials. He told them he was prepared to invest $20 million to convert his warehouses into a medical marijuana cultivation center and business park with indoor farms that could supply the California cannabis market and generate a bounty in tax revenues for the city from medical cultivation alone. Recognizing Oakland's union-friendly politics, Wilcox pledged a unionized workforce. He placed a call to Dan Rush.

"My name is Jeff Wilcox," he said. "I want to join your union."

Rush and Wilcox met at Quinn's Lighthouse Restaurant and Pub over-looking the Oakland estuary. Wilcox presented his business plan. He told about the 414 cannabis union jobs he could create—with average wages of seventy-three thousand dollars, plus benefits. Rush looked into the eyes of the man who was supposed to be the archenemy of labor.

"I think I love you, brother," Rush said.

Rush brought Wilcox to Oaksterdam University and introduced him to Richard Lee. Wilcox wrote out a ten-thousand-dollar check to the Proposition 19 campaign, the first installment of the fifty thousand dollars he would donate. Lee looked at him warily. Jeff Wilcox didn't personify what Lee envisioned for his campaign to tax and regulate adult marijuana use in California. Lee saw Oakland, and California, flowering with small mari-juana businesses and cozy, Amsterdam-style pot pubs, not a massive corpora-tization of cannabis. He casually told the wealthy general contractor he was welcome to volunteer with the Proposition 19 phone bank.

"You're not going to brush me off," Wilcox said. "I'm going to help you."

Wilcox felt a "primal instinct" that he and Lee were natural partners. He believed that what Lee was doing with Proposition 19 was huge, and that so was Wilcox's effort to bring the California cannabis economy to its com-mercial and industrial future. Members of the Oakland City Council were drawn to Wilcox's vision with a similar passion. A year after city voters had enacted America's first marijuana tax—a 1.8 percent levy on dispensary receipts—the city council had put on the ballot a measure to increase its local medical marijuana tax to 5 percent and boost taxes to 10 percent for sales of nonmedical cannabis if Proposition 19 passed. Awed by revenue figures in Wilcox's business plan, the city council approved a plan to issue four licenses for industrial marijuana farms, with Wilcox just one of the potential suitors.

If there were to be tax proceeds from pot, other cash-strapped California local governments decided, they wanted in as well. Nearly a dozen cities rushed companion measures for Proposition 19 onto the November ballot, in many cases asking voters to impose local taxes on existing medical marijuana sales and higher levies for a recreational market. Council members in Sacramento, working on a plan to cut the number of dispensaries in the city from thirty-eight to twelve, suddenly decided that thirty-eight was just fine—particularly if voters were to approve a 4 percent local medical mari-juana tax and a 10 percent tax for nonmedical sales under Proposition 19. The city of Long Beach readied a local measure to reap a 15 percent tax from retail sales for adult marijuana use. Even without the passage of Proposition 19—and especially with it—Oakland, long suffering from economic neglect, envisioned that its warehouse marijuana farms could yield a massive windfall from weed in marijuana taxes, state sales taxes, and other badly needed revenues. But Proposition 19 and Oakland's commercial cannabis ambitions further splintered marijuana advocates over the initiative. The ballot measure, and the wagering over an expanding marijuana market, sent tremors felt by the United States Justice Department—and the White House—in Washington, D.C.

· · ·

Richard Lee and Jeff Jones had drafted Proposition 19 with their political consultant Douglas Linney; Robert Raich, one of the attorneys in the Oakland Cannabis Buyers Cooperative case; and cannabis advocates Chris Conrad and Mikki Norris, publishers of the movement newspaper *West Coast Leaf*. But as they were writing the measure, they were shunned by much of the California marijuana advocacy establishment, which considered their effort ill-advised and, worse, a surefire loser. So it was left to Lee, the former rock concert roadie from Houston, and Jones, the son of a bus company owner from Rapid City, to bring forth the "Regulate, Control and Tax Cannabis Act of 2010" and declare the initiative's findings. Proposition 19 asserted that "California's laws criminalizing cannabis have failed and need to be reformed." It argued the state should free up police resources and "stop arresting thousands of nonviolent cannabis consumers." It claimed that "there is an estimated $15 billion in illegal cannabis transactions in California each year," and that "taxing and regulating cannabis, like we do with alcohol and cigarettes, will generate billions of dollars in annual revenues for California to fund what matters most to Californians: jobs, health care, schools and libraries, roads and more." The appeal struck a chord as California's fiscal deficit topped $25 billion and Governor Arnold Schwarzenegger, the legislature, and the 2010 gubernatorial candidates, Democrat Jerry Brown and Republican Meg Whitman, fought over what programs and state employees to slash, and how.

Dan Rush kept his promise. He delivered the endorsement of UFCW Local Number 5, and then bore down on the state's largest union representing public employees. Board members of the Service Employees International Union told Rush they might be desperate over California's fiscal crisis but not desperate enough to publicly endorse legalizing pot. Undaunted, Rush stalked SEIU labor halls. He made direct pitches to the mostly public-sector workers. He buttonholed Bill Lloyd, president of the SEIU's California State Council. "Bill, what if I can get you $1.5 billion in tax revenue to go into the state's general fund?" Rush asked him, promising a fiscal elixir from recreational marijuana.

Rush wasn't entirely blowing smoke. The state's taxation agency, the Board of Equalization, famously declared that legalizing marijuana could generate $1.4 billion for California coffers. The board's estimate was based heavily on an added fifty-dollar-per-ounce state tax on potential marijuana sales—a proposal by a San Francisco assemblyman, Tom Ammiano, that wasn't included in Proposition 19. But the state tax agency also took note of money already flowing in from medical marijuana, up to $105 million in 2010 California sales taxes from as much as $1.3 billion in marijuana dispensary transactions. Ultimately, Rush lured in the Service Employees International Union. Though it declared no interest in organizing cannabis industry workers, the powerful union, with seven hundred thousand California members, agreed to support Proposition 19—and endorsed taxed and regulated marijuana in the Golden State.

Richard Lee sensed another major breakthrough when his phone rang at Oaksterdam University in the summer of 2010. A representative for Alice Huffman, president of the California State Conference of the NAACP, said Huffman wanted to meet with him. When Huffman arrived at his cannabis college office, Lee was prepared to make a hard sell for his initiative. He didn't have to.

"I have had an epiphany," Huffman told him.

The state NAACP director then spoke, with little interruption from Lee, on the historic persecution of African Americans under state and national drug laws. Huffman later convened a press conference in Sacramento. She presented a research report funded by the pro-legalization Drug Policy Alliance. In California's twenty-five largest counties, the report said, blacks accounted for 7 percent of the population but 20 percent of marijuana possession arrests—even though a higher percentage of whites used pot. Huffman argued marijuana legalization was necessary to end the inequities of prohibition that disproportionately jailed and stigmatized people of color. "We at the NAACP see this as a civil rights issue," Huffman declared as she delivered the organization's endorsement of Proposition 19. "This is not a drug rights issue."

The response from Bishop Ron Allen in Sacramento was furious. Allen was president of the International Faith-Based Coalition, with thirty-six hundred member-congregations, including hundreds of fellow African American pastors. Allen was a recovered crack addict. He preached against an affliction of drugs in minority neighborhoods. He railed to *The Sacramento Bee:* "If anyone should know of the effects of illicit drugs in the black community, it should be one of our most respected civil rights organizations." Allen went on CNN and Fox News, demanding Huffman's immediate resignation. The pastor's ire over the NAACP endorsement became the perfect national media metaphor for framing Proposition 19 in the larger context—and crosshairs—of America's drug debate.

But it was inside the California cannabis community where the turbulence over Proposition 19 reached its zenith. Dennis Peron, the father of Proposition 215 and a living symbol of the medical marijuana movement, railed that Proposition 19 diminished rights and actually enabled drug prohibition. Peron blasted the initiative for adding a criminal penalty—a fine of up to one thousand dollars and up to six months in county jail—for people over twenty-one who provided marijuana to anyone eighteen to twenty years of age. (The measure had left intact existing laws against giving marijuana to minors under eighteen.) And Peron said politically crafted language prohibiting "smoking cannabis in any space while minors are present" would be construed to mean no California parent could smoke a joint in his or her own house. Peron also held a fierce belief that all marijuana use was medicinal—that anyone consuming cannabis was doing so "to alleviate something." He raged over a ballot initiative based on a notion of recreational use. "Marijuana has been a medicine for thousands of years," he said. "All of a sudden it's not a medicine?"

Peron's opposition was particularly awkward for Richard Lee, since the Oaksterdam president hired Peron as a featured university lecturer, one who enraptured students with his personal story and firsthand history of California's cannabis movement. Things got more uncomfortable when Peron led anti-Proposition-19 picketing outside Lee's Coffee Shop Blue Sky dispensary and trashed the initiative while speaking to students. Lee called Peron in and said he had to let him go. The Oaksterdam president said he respected Peron and his right to speak out against the initiative—he just wasn't going to pay him to do it at his university. "I would have fired me too," Peron concluded.

Proposition 19 split the marijuana movement into multiple constituencies. There were purist supporters of medical marijuana only. There were advocates demanding legal recognition for marijuana's place in society as a recreational pleasure. There were many others who supported broader marijuana liberalization yet wondered whether this initiative was the correct vehicle to achieve it.

Valerie Corral, who had braved the federal raid on the garden she and her husband established so that severely ill people could grow and consume cannabis at little or no cost, was particularly torn by Proposition 19. The cofounder of the Wo/Men's Alliance for Medical Marijuana reviled the commercial dispensaries that had triumphed over the organization's collective cultivation model. She saw many as greedy enterprises that overcharged the sick for marijuana as the dispensary operators lived the financial high life. While the city of Oakland and would-be cannabis entrepreneur Jeff Wilcox envisioned a booming economy for legal pot, Corral wondered whether broader legalization could bring some populist economic justice for patients.

Corral hoped Proposition 19 and recreational marijuana would cause retail prices of marijuana to plummet and—by extension—make it more affordable for those who needed it as medicine. "Something has happened to our movement, something that is dark and denigrates the issue," she reflected as the vote approached. As Proposition 19 drew attention by illuminating a thriving marijuana marketplace, she grieved, stating that the California cannabis movement "did not happen so that people could get rich." But Corral feared that Proposition 19, by allowing local governments to regulate pot commerce, could also backlash badly on medical marijuana and trigger more crackdowns on cannabis patients. She didn't endorse the measure. Ultimately, she would warily vote yes, deciding against handing any perceived victory to the prohibitionists who had long made life difficult for people needing marijuana.

It was the late Jack Herer, the celebrated "Hemperor," former Grass Party presidential candidate, and author of the famed anti-marijuana-war manifesto, who particularly haunted Proposition 19 in the cannabis community. Within the movement, questions over how the Hemperor might view the initiative from the afterlife seemed critical. The author of *The Emperor Wears No Clothes,* who had decried government and corporate conspiracies behind a war on marijuana and hemp and against the cannabis seeds that "will save the planet," had mounted a relentless effort to legalize marijuana in California since 1972. Herer failed to qualify his own initiative for the 2010 ballot. It called for a repeal of all California marijuana laws and immediate release from prisons for "all persons . . . charged with or convicted of any nonviolent cannabis hemp marijuana offenses." Herer had blasted Richard Lee's rival "tax and regulate" measure as a compromise with prohibition. As he took to the stage at the Hempstalk Festival in Portland, Oregon, in September 2009, the movement knew where Herer stood on taxing cannabis: there were to be no levies ever placed on nature's most prized herb. "There is nothing fucking better for the human race than having marijuana morning, noon and night," Herer roared to the crowd, advocating cannabis without restrictions. He stepped off the stage and suffered a massive heart attack. He died the following April.

Dragonfly de la Luz was in South America to watch a solar eclipse on Easter Island when the spirit of Jack Herer inspired her. The ganja princess began writing her own manifesto, a tirade against Proposition 19. Evoking Herer and Dennis Peron, she delivered a nineteen-point argument on why "pro-pot activists oppose Prop. 19." She declared that the initiative simply "does not reflect most people's ideas of what legalization would be," urging cannabis chronnoisseurs to study it and "VOTE KNOW." Dragonfly uploaded her treatise to a new website, for a group called Stoners Against Proposition 19. It was a sensation.

The No on 19 movement also drew in Lanette Davies, director of Crusaders for Patients' Rights in Sacramento and co-operator of the Christian-run, bud- and Bible-distributing Canna Care dispensary. Davies hired a truck with a giant No on 19 sign and had it circle freeways around California's capital city. "I am against this because I feel patients have been sold a bill of goods that is going to take their freedom away," Davies announced. A new Sacramento advocacy group for medical marijuana dispensaries, the California Cannabis Association, led the chorus composed of a frightened medicinal industry. The Cannabis Association declared provisions in Proposition 19—which allowed local governments to ban stores selling nonmedical marijuana—would also allow them to drive out existing medical marijuana dispensaries. Other advocates claimed that letting Californians over twenty-one grow twenty-five square feet of marijuana at home would restrict medical users who needed much more than a five-foot-by-five-foot growing space. Dr. Jean Talleyrand, director of California's largest medical marijuana physicians' network, MediCann, which surely stood to lose out if people no longer needed a doctor's recommendation to legally consume cannabis, seized on claims that scores of dispensaries could close. "Patients who use medical cannabis to treat medical conditions could be denied safe access to their medication," Talleyrand declared, calling for a no vote.

Jeff Jones was livid over how people in the industry were turning against the initiative. He saw many as spreading inflammatory claims to protect their own economic self-interests over the broader cannabis cause. Proposition 19 proponents pointed to initiative text supporting "easier, safer access for patients who need cannabis for medical purposes" and facilitating making marijuana available for increased medical research. The campaign asserted that legalizing marijuana beyond medical use would affect neither existing dispensaries nor any rights of medical marijuana patients granted under the 1996 Proposition 215, the Compassionate Use Act. But the initiative language was too vague for some in the medical movement. Jones even found himself challenged in editorial board meetings with pot-friendly alternative weeklies and magazines over Proposition 19's impact on medical marijuana. "Dude, I'm from the medical community," the man who undertook a U.S. Supreme Court challenge over patient rights to medical marijuana found himself having to argue. "Do you think I'm here to undercut Proposition 215?" Don Duncan, California director for Americans for Safe Access, eventually said Proposition 19 wouldn't impact Proposition 215. But the fact that the California-born ASA notably took no position on the measure—saying nonmedical legalization wasn't its cause—further undercut Proposition 19's cannabis-community support.

In California's Emerald Triangle, fears over Proposition 19 were fanned by a wild rumor that Big Tobacco was buying up north coast acreage for massive cultivation that would put Humboldt and Mendocino pot growers out of business. Frank Lester, a spokesman for R. J. Reynolds Tobacco, told *The Sacramento Bee* that it had no interest in cashing in on the initiative. "We're not in the trade of selling marijuana, nor will we ever be," Lester said. But the rumor wasn't going to die. And when Emerald Triangle growers weren't panicked over tobacco companies, they were alarmed by Proposition 19's seeming collusion with Oakland's plans for industrial cannabis farms.

At his Arcata iCenter dispensary, Stephen Gasparas fretted that, one way or another, "factory bud" was on the way and would threaten the character of the region. The marijuana émigré to the enchanted cannabis culture of the north coast also feared new state and local taxes on marijuana that could come from Proposition 19. And legal recreational use suddenly made the pot-aficionado-turned-medical-marijuana-businessman uncomfortable. There was more respect for cannabis customers coming in with physicians' recommendations for medical use, Gasparas suggested, than partiers "coming in for a six-pack of joints and a six-pack of Miller."

Elsewhere in the Emerald Triangle, mounting fears of bottomed-out pot prices, ultimately underscored by a Rand Corporation study that suggested the price of a joint in California could tumble to $1.50 with legalization, terrified people in the illegal market. "Legalization of marijuana will be the single most devastating event," declared Anna Hamilton, a musician and local radio host, speaking to the fears of the region raised on illicit pot production.

Richard Lee traveled to the north coast, trying to give the Emerald Triangle confidence in his initiative. In Mendocino, he picked up at least general rhetorical support for the notion of legalization from veteran marijuana farmer Tim Blake of Laytonville's Area 101, the host of the Emerald Cup outdoor cannabis festival, and Matt Cohen, the model grower for Mendocino's effectively taxed and regulated cultivation program, in which the sheriff affixed fifty-dollar plant-registration tags on ninety-nine-plant-limit gardens of certified medicinal growers. Blake and Cohen suggested the initiative merely signaled an inevitable future. They argued at a local forum that Mendocino and Humboldt Counties must seize their destinies as pot tourism hubs with cannabis tastings, visitor-friendly ganja boot camps, and gourmet bud and breakfast inns, modeling their wine-producing cousins to the south by becoming the Sonoma and Napa Counties of cannabis. Lee joined in touting the tourism benefits of marijuana legalization. He was doing better in the region until he answered a question during an interview with the *Journal* of Humboldt County on the Emerald Triangle's place in the coming legal California pot market. Lee said local growers harvesting legendary sun-grown marijuana "may have to start making a lot of hash out of that," suggesting an unglamorous future in manufacturing cannabis concentrates. His let-them-make-hash remark ignited the fury anew.

Humboldt County outdoor cultivator Joey Burger saw the threat of an Oaksterdam cartel, with or without legalization beyond medical use. "They're taking market share from people who spent a generation risking their lives and land," he fumed. As the Proposition 19 vote approached, Burger formed the Humboldt Growers Association. He started lobbying county officials to approve a taxed and licensed outdoor cultivation program to protect the region's growers—and Humboldt's proud marijuana traditions—against cavernous indoor farms in Oakland.

The rift in the California cannabis community brought Dragonfly de la Luz to the public radio airwaves in Mendocino County for a debate with Chris Conrad, a cannabis author and Oaksterdam University professor who had been a protégé of Jack Herer. Dragonfly invoked Herer's name in warning that Proposition 19 would sacrifice the pot-growing arts of California and the Emerald Triangle on an altar of corporate cultivation. She said it would "tax cannabis so much you can't afford to get high." Conrad explained he had helped draft Herer's initiative for more sweeping legalization. But, he said, the fact that Herer's initiative didn't qualify for the ballot was no reason to betray a landmark opportunity presented by Proposition 19. "It would be foolish to say let's throw this away.... Let's keep it illegal," Conrad argued. "The fact is, this is an opportunity to do something the whole world is watching.... This is the moment history has been pointing us towards."

Ultimately, the adult children of Jack Herer sought to mend the rift over Proposition 19. They put out a letter insisting that, while their father wanted more, he would have come around and backed the tax-and-regulate initiative because "the last thing Jack Herer would want is for Californians to vote to keep cannabis illegal." Written by his second-oldest son, Dan Herer, the letter said, "Unfortunately, Jack passed away before Prop. 19 made the ballot; so many people think he would still oppose it. We don't believe that." Through his family, and from the grave, the Hemperor of the marijuana movement was on board.

. . .

Despite the tumult in the cannabis community, the absence of newspaper endorsements, and a lack of support from any major California elected official, Proposition 19 was still resonating with voters. A month before the election, Stephen Colbert of Comedy Central took note of the initiative's popularity in the polls. "There is one candidate out there in this election who does not need my help, 'the Honorable Mary Jane Von Spliffenberg,' also known as California's Proposition 19 to legalize mari-ju-wana,'" the spoofing political host announced on his *Colbert Report* program. "If Proposition 19 were a human, it would be the most popular candidate in California."

Among those also sensing the initiative's support was Governor Arnold Schwarzenegger, the former bodybuilder who once famously smoked a joint in the documentary *Pumping Iron*. Pressured by the initiative's possibility of passage, Schwarzenegger handed a major victory to marijuana advocates. The Republican governor signed legislation, Senate Bill 1449, by Senator Mark Leno, a Democrat from San Francisco. It reduced possession of an ounce of marijuana from a misdemeanor to a noncriminal infraction. In 1975,

California had downgraded simple marijuana possession from a felony to a misdemeanor with an infraction-level fine of one hundred dollars. The new bill meant thousands of Californians facing marijuana misdemeanors would no longer be processed through the courts and criminalized. In his bill-signing statement, Schwarzenegger declared, "Unfortunately, Proposition 19 is a deeply flawed measure . . . that will adversely affect California's businesses without bringing the tax revenues to the state promised by proponents."

Proposition 19 opponents seized on the bill to argue the initiative was no longer needed. Inside the campaign, Jeff Jones felt conflicted. He feared the governor took the air out of a key initiative argument against wasting police resources on minor pot offenses. But Jones also believed that Proposition 19 had just coerced Schwarzenegger into signing the most significant California marijuana-decriminalization bill in thirty-five years.

A second Rand Corporation study deflated another argument of the Proposition 19 campaign—that legalizing marijuana in California would strike a blow against Mexican drug traffickers and drug violence south of the border. The Santa Monica think tank concluded that legal pot in California would likely make only a 2-to-4 percent dent in what Mexican cartels reap from marijuana, cocaine, meth, and heroin. The White House's Office of National Drug Control Policy issued a statement by director R. Gil Kerlikowske praising these findings and underscoring the Obama adminis-tration's close watch on Proposition 19. Weeks earlier, nine former Drug Enforcement Administrators, including Robert Bonner, a former U.S. Attorney for Los Angeles and federal judge, had written Attorney General Eric Holder. They called on America's top law enforcement officer to come down hard on Proposition 19 by attacking the core argument for the initia-tive: tax revenues for California. "Proposition 19 suggests that marijuana sales will be taxed and revenue collected by the state," the DEA administra-tors wrote Holder. "It is unlikely that any taxes will be paid, for doing so would admit criminal violation of federal law and expose the seller to federal prosecution." The missive ignored the fact that California was already col-lecting millions of dollars in sales taxes on medical marijuana. But it hit at Proposition 19's central pitch by equating paying taxes with admission of a crime.

When Holder replied to the former DEA administrators' letter on October 13, he delivered a body blow to Proposition 19. The attorney general declared the U.S. Justice Department wouldn't stand idly if the initiative were passed by California voters. "Let me state clearly that the Department of Justice strongly opposes Proposition 19," Holder began. He said he would enforce the Controlled Substances Act "against those individuals and organizations that possess, manufacture or distribute marijuana for recreational use, even if such activities are permitted under state law."

The Holder announcement, while hardly unexpected, shook the campaign. Dale Sky Jones took note that "when we weren't a threat, they didn't pay attention"; and now that the initiative was leading, "they're going to do everything to stop us." Dan Rush looked over the meticulous crafting of Holder's letter, at how it struck squarely at Prop. 19's appeal regarding taxation and regulation. "We're screwed," he thought. Holder's announcement reaped front-page play in newspapers across California. Meanwhile, a mounting conflict with the feds only elevated Proposition 19's appeal as an international story. Journalists and film crews from Japan to Brazil to Finland had descended on California for the marijuana legalization vote. A Los Angeles–based Israeli documentary filmmaker, Dan Katzir, was trailing Richard Lee. He caught him reflecting by Oakland's Lake Merritt. "I'm more of a target than ever," Lee offered. "If we win, they bust me for retaliation. And, if we lose, they bust me because it's open season on me. I'm dead either way."

By Halloween, Proposition 19 appeared to have lost its appeal with voters. The California Field Poll showed it losing by a 49 to 42 percent margin. Emboldened, the No on 19 campaign stepped up attacks on provisions in the initiative that said people couldn't be "punished, fined," or "discriminated against" for using marijuana. The opponents characterized the language as a gateway permitting high workers and on-the-job pot smoking. Their attacks ignored a 2008 California Supreme Court decision in the case of a Sacramento telecommunications employee and medical marijuana user, Gary Ross, who was fired over results of a drug test taken as a condition of employment. The Supreme Court had upheld the firing—and employers' rights to set workplace rules for drugs. But a California Chamber of Commerce radio ad, stoking the fears of employers, sizzled: "Imagine coming out of surgery and the nurse caring for you was high, or having to work harder on your job to make up for a coworker who shows up high on pot. It could happen in California if Proposition 19 passes." The depiction of the stoned nurse would linger in the final stretch of the campaign.

Short on cash for a closing advertising blitz, Dan Rush approached representatives of Snoop Dogg. He asked if the pro-pot rapper, later to be known as Snoop Lion, could put up a video endorsement saying something "hip and sensible" about the promise of legalization, hoping a viral web spot could rally college students and other younger voters to the ballot box. A few days before the election, Snoop was on YouTube wearing a knit cap with floppy dog ears. His eyelids appeared heavy from pot. "I'm urging everybody to go out there and vote on November 2. Speak your mind. Speak your voice," he said. Snoop then raised a joint. He took a couple of hits and paused to exhale. "And Proposition 19—you know where I stand on that. *Very high.*"

Dan Rush watched the web video and cursed with horror. "That just scared the hell out of every mom of a teenager in the fucking country," he steamed.

Neither a late $1-million contribution from billionaire philanthropist George Soros nor television spots—featuring retired San Jose Police Chief Joseph McNamara declaring the war on marijuana a failure—could rescue Proposition 19. The initiative lost by a 53.5 percent to 46.5 vote margin. Richard Lee put out an election night statement, noting the unprecedented, historic support. "The fact that millions of Californians voted to legalize marijuana is a tremendous victory. . . . Proposition 19 has changed the terms of the debate," he said. "Millions now understand it's time to develop an exit strategy for the failed war on marijuana." Lee quipped to reporters that the sparsely funded initiative, for which he was the largest contributor, with $1.6 million, drew more votes than the $140-million campaign of the Republican gubernatorial candidate, Meg Whitman. Lee's checking account was now empty. But he believed others would step in for a future legalization drive—this one with a bigger, broader donor base and a unified cannabis community.

As Proposition 19 went down in defeat, Richard Lee achieved unantici-pated returns for his tax-cannabis cause. As voters statewide rejected the measure to tax cannabis, nine cities overwhelmingly approved local measures to tax cannabis. Cities, including San Jose and Sacramento, Stockton and Berkeley, approved levies on medical marijuana dispensaries. Oakland increased its medical cannabis tax. The cities were now invested in the pot economy. The attention drawn by Proposition 19 revealed to the world what already existed: a billion-dollar medical marijuana industry making mari-juana widely accessible in the Golden State. Proposition 19 also alerted the federal government to California's ambitious, unfolding commercialization of cannabis. There would be a price to pay.

ELEVEN

A Mile High and Beyond

Dan Rogers didn't anticipate that his years as a corporate nomad would culminate in a pilgrimage to Oaksterdam. The graduate of Fort Lewis College in Colorado had built a fifteen-year career in the financial world as a credit analyst and risk underwriter for Bank of America, as a bank auditor for the Federal Deposit Insurance Corporation, and ultimately, as an investment banker and equities trader in Toronto. Then a crashing economy put him out of work. Rogers packed up his belongings, and his savings, and returned to Colorado, figuring he would toast the end of his finance career by opening a liquor store. And then a friend and business associate came to him with a more surefire idea: marijuana.

Colorado by 2009 was following California's lead—and exploding with America's second great green rush. Nearly a decade after Coloradans passed Amendment 20, the state's 2000 Medical Use of Marijuana Act, dancing humans dressed as marijuana joints were enticing customers into new pot stores opening with such density on Denver's South Broadway Street that the district was dubbed the "Green Mile" and "Broadsterdam." Between January 2009 and May 2010, a sizzling pot market rose to meet the demand. Some 250 marijuana stores opened in Denver, another 100 in Boulder, and more than 700 statewide, and the number of registered medical marijuana users in Colorado jumped from fewer than ten thousand people to more than one hundred thousand.

And so Rogers, the former finance major, traveled out to California and Oakland's fabled Oaksterdam district for accelerated studies in cannabis. He got an after-hours tour of Steve DeAngelo's Harborside Health Center and its vast medicinal selections and holistic services promoting wellness for medical marijuana patients. He soaked in the Amsterdam-style coffee-and-cannabis ambiance of Richard Lee's Coffee Shop Blue Sky. And he enrolled in a three-day slate of classes at Oaksterdam University. He took meticulous notes as Lee lectured on coconut fiber nutrients, on hydroponic cannabis cultivation, and on anticipated plant yields from indoor growing. And he felt the searing gaze of California medical-marijuana-movement icon Dennis Peron. "Don't get into this business to profit from it," Peron told Rogers's Oaksterdam session. "Don't be a profiteer." The investment banker and equities trader from Colorado took in Peron's words and, in particular, how he delivered them—"looking directly at me."

But Colorado would build on California's model and deliver the message back to America's marijuana epicenter that medical marijuana was, indeed, about profit. Colorado, with no more than one-sixth of California's cannabis market, would go far beyond the Golden State in creating an intensely regulated, unabashedly for-profit industry in which medical marijuana entrepreneurs could pocket their earnings. Unlike California, Colorado was also about oversight and rules. Reacting to its unbridled marijuana market, Colorado chose to create an industry with state-licensed medical marijuana workers, video surveillance, supervised factory cultivation, and a state medical marijuana policing agency. Colorado didn't settle for hazy California language about purportedly nonprofit "collectives" accepting patient donations or reimbursement for costs of cultivating and distributing marijuana. It boldly adopted America's first state-sanctioned program for the commercial production and sale of cannabis.

The developments sent shudders felt on the West Coast. As the birthplace of the medical marijuana movement and home of the nation's most potent marijuana economy, California was thought to be teaching the rest of America. However, the California marijuana movement was splintered after the defeat of the Proposition 19 legalization measure. It was also unnerved by the U.S. Justice Department's renewed saber rattling over the initiative and California's mushrooming, overwhelmingly unregulated cannabis commerce. Colorado would come to present an alternative of state regulation that could provide seemingly unambiguous guidelines for local police and, potentially, a state's rights defense against incursions by the federal government. So in early 2011, California marijuana advocates, attorneys, dispensary operators, and growers convened in a summit, plotting the state's cannabis future after Proposition 19 and arguing over how to establish better legal protections for those distributing medical marijuana. Colorado stoked the California discussion, and many California advocates utterly hated the details coming out of the Rockies.

When Dan Rogers returned to Denver with his newly minted Oaksterdam University diploma in 2009, fear was mounting in Colorado that the state was about to be overrun as a California cannabis colony. Illicit marijuana from California was flowing to Colorado communities that were opening new pot stores. An eleven-pound shipment of marijuana, sent by California growers to two wannabe Colorado medical marijuana operators, was intercepted at the post office in Snowmass Village near Aspen. In Denver, as Rogers was setting up the first of this three Greenwerkz marijuana stores in the state, he found himself fielding, and fending off, unsolicited calls from people in town claiming they could stock his dispensary with exotic California cannabis selections.

California entrepreneurs were also traveling to Colorado, looking to invest or secure paid consulting services in the state's accelerating new trade. Denver's alternative weekly, *Westword,* brimming with ads for Colorado marijuana stores, reported on out-of-state "Ganjapreneurs . . . cashing in on Colorado's booming medical pot business." *Westword* detailed the efforts of a Los Angeles dispensary chain seeking to partner with Colorado marijuana outlets. It also declared that Oakland's Harborside Health Center, "the Neiman Marcus of Dispensaries," was coming to Colorado. Harborside's flirtation in the Rockies was limited to a consulting service, called Harborside Management Consultants, which engaged in talks with an upstart Colorado dispensary, Local Product. But the specter of the Californication of Colorado's cannabis industry was stoked as Don Duncan, in Colorado for the Harborside consulting group, announced, "We've been looking at Colorado for several years now, watching the scene. I would say right now, in the state of Colorado there is a vacuum that needs to be filled. It's an exciting place to be." A handful of California cannabis speculators, arriving in 2009 or earlier, found niches in Colorado medical marijuana businesses. However, Harborside Management Consultants, later named CannBe before the consulting and lobbying group folded in 2011, left without any pot-management agreements in the Centennial State—and with Duncan questioning whether the untamed, unpredictable market in the Rockies was worth the risk.

Coloradans saw the south Denver district, including the new Broadsterdam, transform like a marijuana mining town with unpermitted and unregulated pot stores that sprung up in shabby lean-tos and abandoned storefronts hastily adorned with neon pot leaves and, in one case, a dispensary sales window consisting of a flapping plastic trash bag. It wasn't just newcomers from California but also people from multiple states and all corners of Colorado who were streaming in to sell pot. "This reminds me of 1899 in Cripple Creek, Colorado, when somebody struck gold," Colorado state senator Chris Romer complained in a CNN interview. "Every 49er in the country is making it for Denver to open a medical marijuana dispensary." So Romer reached out to a Republican state representative, Tom Massey, from rural Poncha Springs in central Colorado. He partnered with him on 2010 legislation—House Bill 1284, or the Colorado Medical Marijuana Code. The legislation would position Colorado as a scalable rival to California in the brashness of its marijuana commerce while imposing unprecedented rules on a state-sanctioned cannabis trade.

The Colorado lawmakers called on Matt Cook, an ex-cop from Colorado Springs and head of the Liquor and Tobacco Enforcement Division for the Colorado Department of Revenue, to draft the rules. As Cook took to the task, he was berated by fellow cops at a conference of the Colorado Drug Investigators Association. The event featured special guests, narcotics officers from California's Mendocino and Humboldt Counties. Even though Mendocino by 2010 was looking to license willing medical marijuana cultivators, the Emerald Triangle narcs openly laughed at Cook for thinking Colorado could impose statewide regulation on something as wild and undisciplined as marijuana.

Cook pored over California's 2003 Senate Bill 420, with its vagaries on medical marijuana collectives and total lack of language addressing storefront dispensaries. He saw California marijuana businesses handling hundreds of millions of dollars in transactions, with little tracking of where the cash went. He saw thousands of pounds of marijuana winding up in the display cases of California dispensaries with no sense of how it got there. Working with Cook, Massey endorsed the ex-cop's map for stringent rules, including audits and surveillance, to ensure "no product is going out the back door," from marijuana stores to the black market. Massey also hoped effective state regulation would ease the feds' fears over illicit trafficking to nonmedical users and convince the U.S. Justice Department "to turn a blind eye" to Colorado. Pat Steadman, a Denver state senator who partnered with Massey on a follow-up medical marijuana regulation bill, also came to believe there was no point in lying about marijuana stores making money. Steadman looked at California's nonprofit collectives "as just kind of a sham." He concluded, "You might as well call it what it is: People are in business and making money. And the market is going to control prices at the end of the day."

In 2010, the Colorado Legislature sanctioned a lucrative integrated production system for medical marijuana, in which only Colorado residents could work or invest. Colorado dispensaries—state-licensed as "medical marijuana centers"—were required to grow 70 percent of the marijuana they sold. Any remainder had to be purchased from other state-certified dispensary cultivation centers. Factory bud—so feared in California's Humboldt and Mendocino Counties during the Proposition 19 campaign—was soon being cultivated in vast quantities in the Mile High City as dispensaries in and around Denver leased out warehouse space for commercial marijuana production. Grow rooms were videotaped. Plants were tagged for state inspectors—in some cases with radio frequency trackers. Shipping manifests from cultivation rooms had to be filed with the state, and the routes preapproved, before the product was packed, weighed, and delivered to marijuana stores—where the inventory manifests were rechecked and the pot reweighed as it was off-loaded under more video surveillance. The electronic eyes of Colorado's new Medical Marijuana Enforcement Division, with Matt Cook as its first senior director of enforcement, followed Dan Rogers via a slew of cameras in a cultivation center he built in an old printing factory near downtown Denver. Cameras recorded every move of Rogers's employees perfecting citrus-scented Lemon Diesel marijuana or two of their signature breeds, Reclining Buddha and Heartland Cream. Still more surveillance cameras tracked each counter transaction at his three Greenwerkz marijuana stores, in Denver, Edgewater, and Glenwood Springs. Under Colorado's law, Rogers had to be able to account for every plant, every gram, and every sale.

Colorado's regulated cannabis industry provided an enticing business lure for former California restaurateurs Scott Durrah and Wanda James. For years, Durrah, a master chef from the New School of Cooking in Los Angeles, and James, a marketing executive and onetime California congressional candidate, ran the acclaimed Jamaican Café on the Santa Monica Promenade. After moving to Colorado, they opened the Caribbean-cuisine 8 Rivers restaurant in Denver and, later, a traditional Southern eatery, Jezebel's. With state lawmakers contemplating sanctioned marijuana commerce, Durrah and James partnered in a new Denver dispensary, Apothecary of Colorado. The dispensary featured a gourmet shop for cannabis food products. And after a customer dying of cancer asked if Durrah could prepare him a medicinal meal so the man could dine with his wife without the oblivion of morphine, Durrah and James were inspired to move on to another cannabis venture.

They became licensed manufacturers of infused products under Colorado's medical marijuana law, packaging flavorful marijuana mango salsas; marinara and green chili sauces; apple butter; pot-potent gluten-free jams; and their special cannabis indica, peanut butter, and jelly cups and sativa-granola bars. Durrah drew national media attention in a CNBC documentary, *Marijuana USA,* featuring him in the kitchen teaching classic-cuisine preparations with marijuana—a Julia Child of cannabis cooking. Durrah and James marketed their Simply Pure state-licensed cannabis kitchen as a source of "well-crafted natural cooking and cannabis[,] . . . the perfect combination for a healthy lifestyle." James, a political fund-raiser for 2008 Democratic presidential candidate Barack Obama and officeholders including Colorado congressman Jared Polis and Governor John Hickenlooper, saw a political message in the couple's involvement in delivering state-monitored shipments of cannabis confections to 350 Colorado marijuana stores. The two former California restaurateurs, who, James said, made sure they came to "know every elected official" in Colorado, "figured we could bring a face to cannabis that people couldn't demonize." James asserted that Colorado's state-regulated marijuana industry wasn't California: "It's not Hollywood. It's what Middle America is all about."

But nowhere else in Middle America, or worlds beyond, was there an estimated 1 million square feet of warehouse space—in and around Denver—getting leased out for the commercial cultivation of pot. A cavernous, shuttered Drive Train Industries truck-and-tractor-parts plant was converted to house separate indoor marijuana farms for at least eight marijuana stores, just some of hundreds of retail outlets beginning cannabis production. In the midst of a searing real estate downturn, in which his sales of high-end residential properties all but died, Denver broker John Wicken found a surging new market. Vacant old brick warehouses and industrial shops, which five years earlier were being converted into artist lofts and live/work spaces for urban professionals, now sprouted newly leased cannabis grow rooms. Wicken saw pot steadying the real estate economy. "There are buildings with 40,000 square feet sitting empty," he observed. "Who else is going to take it?"

The new Colorado rules came with ominous trade-offs and economic challenges for cannabis entrepreneurs. Many Colorado pot businesses went under, unable—or unwilling—to afford state requirements for exhaustive video surveillance of marijuana transactions and shipments, including storing a minimum of twenty days' worth of surveillance records for police inspection. Scores of people were also driven out of the business under rules that barred paroled felons from working in the Colorado marijuana industry in any capacity for five years, and which banned for life anyone convicted of a drug felony. Colorado also imposed strict limits on private pot gardens, allowing six marijuana plants per registered medical user. Nonprofit caregivers were allowed to raise plants for a maximum of five people, six plants for each; for-profit marijuana stores could cultivate only six plants per user-member. Colorado marijuana consumers could shop at any cannabis store but had to designate a single store as their provider and cultivator. In California, dispensaries compiled lists of tens of thousands of patient members, who faced no restrictions on the number of storefront collectives they could join. California growers with duplicate patient names claimed to legally provide medical marijuana as patient cultivators for multiple dispensaries. That couldn't happen in Colorado.

As Colorado's marijuana trade ballooned to as many as a thousand dispensaries, small growers were all but shut out of the market. Cannabis in Colorado became an increasingly corporate venture. The new faces of the industry were people such as Norton Arbelaez, a state resident and Tulane University law school graduate who brought in partners to invest nearly $1 million in his upscale River Rock marijuana store and cultivation center in a converted Denver bus terminal. There, Arbelaez greeted not only cannabis consumers but also Colorado's new, truly unique, medical marijuana narcs. Colorado cops and retired Drug Enforcement Administration officers, licensed as medical cannabis police for the Colorado Medical Marijuana Enforcement Division, came in on inspections dressed in bankers' suits and tasseled shoes. They expressed little interest in or alarm at the piney smells of Arbelaez's featured Jack Frost Sativa. But they carefully looked over his thirty-two video surveillance cameras, including a scanner with face recognition technology, reviewed his sales transactions, and cataloged plants marked with state bar codes. It would cause Arbelaez to reflect on Colorado's compromise for state-sanctioned cannabis commerce. "We've waived our Fourth Amendment protections," he concluded. "We've given every piece of personal information to the state. It's Big Brother. Let's not kid ourselves."

By 2011, state licensing fees on 730 retail marijuana stores and more than a thousand cultivation centers and other cannabis businesses funded the $10 million budget of the Medical Marijuana Enforcement Division, a new department in the state's Department of Revenue, which also oversaw liquor and gambling. By 2011, Colorado had forty-two hundred fingerprinted, background-checked, state-licensed, and identification-card-wearing medical marijuana employees. In Denver, local medical marijuana taxes and fees nearly covered the city's budget for the nation's largest municipal park system. In 2010, then-Colorado governor Bill Ritter, a former district attorney who opposed medical marijuana, turned to the state's Medical Marijuana Program Cash Fund during a fiscal crisis. He found $9 million in revenues—fees charged on medical marijuana users as part of a mandatory state patient-registration program—to cover nearly one-sixth of Colorado's budget deficit. And it was a brave new world in the Rockies for former DEA agent Paul Schmidt, too. The man who once directed federal raids on pot fields in Oregon found himself schmoozing with Colorado medical marijuana operators as a supervisor in the Medical Marijuana Enforcement Division. So strange, he thought; "I used to call these people defendants. Now I call them an industry."

Colorado's integrated commercial cultivation rooms and marijuana stores and competitive, for-profit market also drove down the price of pot. Compared to California, Colorado medical marijuana consumers often paid one-third to one-half less per eighth of an ounce of herbal medicine.

. . .

Colorado provided an inviting, fertile ground for Dan Rush, the California union man who had seized an opportunity during the Proposition 19 campaign to organize the first marijuana workers in America and sign up several hundred pot employees in California for United Food and Commercial Workers Union Local Number 5. After the initiative's defeat, Rush was summoned to the North American union's Washington, D.C., headquarters. He was knighted with a new title: director of the Medical Cannabis and Hemp Division for the United Food and Commercial Workers International Union. His commission was to bring marijuana cultivators and pot retail workers across the budding plain of medical cannabis states into the union movement.

When dispensary operators in Fort Collins faced closure under state regulations that allowed cities to decide whether or not to permit marijuana stores, they summoned the union man from California. Working with Colorado's UFCW Local Number 7, Rush organized some four hundred pot workers in eighteen of Fort Collins's twenty-two marijuana outlets. The union energized a local ballot challenge to the city's dispensary ban. When the bid was narrowly defeated, Rush and the Fort Collins operators turned the result into a media event about the loss of well-paying middle-class jobs and promised to build Colorado's cannabis economy. "If you're a dignified employer and a compliant employer in this industry, we'll organize your workers and help stabilize the industry," Rush declared. Despite the loss of four hundred union jobs in Fort Collins, he would organize nearly a thousand more Colorado pot workers.

Rush headed on to Michigan, where voters had approved medical marijuana use in 2008. Even though a 2011 Michigan Court of Appeals ruling declared medical marijuana stores weren't allowed under Michigan's law, Rush got four hundred aspiring cannabis industry workers in Michigan to sign up as associate members of the United Food and Commercial Workers Union—waiting for a day when Michigan's pot economy reached maturity and acceptance. Elsewhere, California players had mixed results in America's emerging medical marijuana landscape. In Washington, D.C., a Sacramento medical marijuana provider, the Abatin Wellness Center, and its celebrity partner, talk show host and cannabis patient Montel Williams, were awarded one of five dispensary licenses in the nation's capital. In Maine, California's renowned Berkeley Patients Group dispensary wound up in bitter litigation, with dueling lawsuits and an out-of-court settlement, after it helped finance one of the state's eight approved dispensaries, only to have operators cut a deal with another investor.

As other states emulated California by approving medical marijuana use, cannabis advocates exploited California as a political foil to advance their cause. In Oregon, which had legalized medical marijuana use two years after California's Proposition 215 passed, voters in 2010 considered a ballot initiative—Measure 74—to allow state-regulated marijuana dispensaries. Police strongly opposed it, pointing to Los Angeles' explosion of pot stores and failed efforts to rein them in. Medical marijuana supporters, too, pointed to California, as their argument for passing Measure 74. "We need to stop this underground growth of unregulated dispensaries before we do become another California," Cheryl Smith, executive director of a Eugene medical marijuana advocacy group, the Compassion Center, told the *Eugene Weekly.* Oregon voters rejected Measure 74; afterward, unlicensed dispensaries flowered in the state. (Three years later, in 2013, Governor John Kitzhaber would sign legislation to legalize medical marijuana stores.) In Washington State, which approved medical marijuana in 1998, more than a hundred dispensaries with no specific approval under state law opened in Seattle in 2011 claiming protection—with support of the city—under a 2011 state amendment allowing small scale "collective gardens." In Montana, which allowed medicinal use in 2004, federal authorities began targeting unregulated state dispensaries. Raids on Montana pot stores in early 2011 triggered worries in other medical marijuana states, including California.

New states approving medicinal use came to boast of restrictions on access to marijuana. In New Jersey, where the legislature approved a 2010 medical marijuana law allowing cannabis use by people with terminal illnesses or a specified "debilitating medical condition," the state's plan to license six nonprofit marijuana distribution centers was billed as an antithesis to California's wild cannabis capitalism and Colorado's lucrative state-regulated commerce. "Certainly, we're going to be the most restrictive state in the land," Democratic state senator Nicholas Scutari, primary sponsor of the state's Compassionate Use Medical Marijuana Act, asserted on New Jersey public television's *NJ Today*.

By the start of 2012, Washington, D.C., and sixteen states, including, among others, Alaska, Arizona, Connecticut, Delaware, Hawaii, Nevada, New Mexico, Rhode Island, and Vermont, had followed California's lead in legalizing marijuana for medical use. In November 2012, voters would make Massachusetts the eighteenth medical marijuana state, and governors in New Hampshire and Illinois would sign legislation in 2013 to legalize medicinal cannabis use, bringing the number of states to twenty. More than 110 million Americans—exceeding one-third of the national population—would live in places endorsing marijuana as medicine. In 2011, results from a 2007 to 2010 national survey by the Substance Abuse and Mental Health Services Administration revealed that the number of current marijuana users in America had spiked, from 14.4 million people in 2007 to 17.4 million in 2010. The White House Office of National Drug Control Policy expressed alarm. "Emerging research reveals potential links between state laws permitting access to smoked medical marijuana and higher rates of marijuana use," proclaimed its director, R. Gil Kerlikowske. Yet marijuana advocates pushed for more liberalization. Seizing on the near-success of California's Proposition 19, they qualified ballot measures in Colorado, Washington State, and Oregon seeking to legalize marijuana regardless of medical need.

. . .

In late January 2011, concerned California marijuana advocates and industry professionals gathered at a conference in Berkeley called "Marijuana Reform:

Next Steps for California." It was billed as a debriefing, and reunifying, event after the divisive Proposition 19 campaign. Dale Sky Jones, Oaksterdam University's chancellor and the initiative's spokeswoman, called for the movement to advance the legalization cause once again, this time working together after "the vote heard around the world." But the conference coordinator, Dale Gieringer, California director of the National Organization for the Reform of Marijuana Laws and an early, private critic of Proposition 19, pointed to a more pressing challenge. More than fourteen years after the passage of Proposition 215, cops were still raiding medical marijuana providers. In late 2010, local drug task forces staged sweeping raids on medical marijuana dispensaries in San Jose and around the upper Central Valley college town of Chico. California marijuana advocates had fought recurring battles with the federal government since before voters approved the nation's first medical marijuana law in 1996. Even though the feds had signaled in late 2009 that they wouldn't target medical marijuana patients operating in compliance with state law, many California cops and prosecutors insisted there was nothing in state law to cover California's marijuana stores or the thousands of marijuana growers who believed they could sell pot to dispensaries simply by registering as medical cannabis patients.

In 2011, with Colorado's state-regulated medical cannabis industry valued at $250 million, the California branch of NORML estimated the Golden State's retail medicinal market at $1.5 billion—and possibly as high as $4.5 billion. It all appeared to hang on a nebulous legal thread of California's 2003 Senate Bill 420, which sought to guarantee safe and affordable access to marijuana under Proposition 215 by declaring medical marijuana patients could "associate" to "collectively or cooperatively cultivate marijuana for medical purposes." Tamar Todd, a staff attorney for the Drug Policy Alliance, warned attendees at the Berkeley conference that California was the state most at risk for a renewed federal crackdown. "As for now, California is the most vulnerable because it is the most gray about what is legal and illegal," Todd declared.

Gieringer, one of the architects of Proposition 215, had looked at Colorado's regulated cannabis commerce. There was little he liked. He thought marijuana stores running state-supervised cultivation rooms would never fly in California, with its vast cannabis culture and diverse home- and country-grown medicinal offerings. But Gieringer took note that the feds, so far, were mostly leaving Colorado's thriving cannabis industry alone. He called for rules to fit California. "We need a well-regulated, safe and responsible medical distribution system," Gieringer argued. "We really need to bite the bullet on this." San Francisco assemblyman Tom Ammiano took the podium to call for input, and California solutions, for an "omnibus cannabis bill" to license, regulate, and protect medical marijuana distribution. But the enthusiasm in the room was muted.

Steph Sherer, who had become the Washington, D.C., executive director of Americans for Safe Access and a leading national voice for medical marijuana patients, decried the potentially onerous costs of regulation, including taxes and licensing fees, on sick people benefiting from cannabis. Sherer was infuriated that many California cities had exploited the political cover of Proposition 19 to impose new local taxes on medical marijuana sales, on top of existing state sales taxes paid by dispensaries. "For those of you who are asking for taxes, it's crazy, it's outrageous," she told the Berkeley gathering. "That tax is falling on patients. Don't piggyback a program on our backs."

Few were more wary of Colorado-style regulation than marijuana cultivators from Ukiah to Arcata in California's Mendocino and Humboldt pot country. There, the idea of state oversight reignited worries of lost cannabis traditions and livelihoods as harshly as the Proposition 19 campaign and Richard Lee's let-them-make-hash insult. North coast growers needed only to look at the fallout in Colorado's free-spirited marijuana mountains above Boulder and Denver to see what they feared on full display.

More than eighty-two hundred feet above sea level, the town of Nederland, the Arcata of the Rockies, passed a symbolic vote in 2010 declaring all marijuana legal in the old hippie haven and silver town that *Rolling Stone* magazine dubbed "Stonerville, USA." Before state regulation, the pot economy boomed in Nederland, with as many as fourteen local marijuana stores opening—one for every hundred residents. People from as far away as Durango, seven hours to the west, drove into town to sample Nederland's boutique mountain bud. In 2010, local sales tax earnings from marijuana soared, accounting for 10 percent of Nederland's total. Restaurants, shops, and the town's only hotel also filled with pot tourists. Hoping to cash in further, Nederland's board of trustees imposed an additional five-thousand-dollar fee on new cannabis stores—just as the State of Colorado was enacting licensing fees and the strictest oversight in America.

Kathleen Chippi, a fiery advocate for cannabis without restrictions, had two thousand member-customers signed up with her One Brown Mouse pot store in Nederland. She shut her doors rather than pay the costs of Colorado-mandated video surveillance or submit to state-supervised cultivation or the monitored transit loathsome to local mountain growers. To Chippi, it was now harder in Colorado to deliver pot than plutonium. "I refuse to give up my fucking constitutional rights to the Colorado Department of Revenue," she declared, cursing the government, intrusive oversight, and abusive taxation of marijuana. Things became worse for Mark Rose, a former hospital technician who was making a living in Nederland from his mountain-grown strains of Chem Dawg and Sweet Island Skunk and partnering in a local dispensary, Grateful Meds. It had been a dream for Rose, who celebrated as seemingly every pot grower in town—from "twenty-one-year-old skateboarders to seventy-two-year-olds supplementing their Social Security income"—enhanced his or her livelihood with cannabis. But the state ordered marijuana stores to grow their own product, Rose protested, because "they just couldn't stand the idea of some hippies sharing the wealth." Grateful Meds had to shut out local growers for a video-monitored cultivation room in Denver. For Rose, there was another, searing indignity. A decade earlier, while briefly moving to Ohio, Rose was pulled over for a traffic stop and found to be carrying a pound of Nederland's finest herb, a felony. Under Colorado's new marijuana rules, he was considered a drug criminal and was banned for life from working in the state's medicinal industry.

In Sacramento, a marijuana industry lobbyist, Max Del Real, forming a trade association called the California Cannabis Business League, invited Matt Cook to California to meet with dispensary operators and advocates. Del Real pushed for a clear break from Senate Bill 420 and its language that "nothing . . . shall authorize any individual or group to cultivate or distribute marijuana for profit." "We have to take medical cannabis towards business success and that means a for-profit industry," Del Real declared. But tales of growers in Colorado's marijuana mountains getting wiped out by state regulation frightened the north coast Emerald Growers Association, a new group advocating local rules to protect outdoor medical marijuana growers. "There's going to be a statewide initiative with the Colorado model," association director Alison Sterling-Nichols, a former campaign consultant for Humboldt district attorney Paul Gallegos, warned local cultivators in an urgent meeting. She knew that few in California's Emerald Triangle would stand for obtrusive video surveillance and corporate weed. Through the association, Humboldt and Mendocino pot farmers began to fight to ensure that any state regulation protected their access to the medical marijuana market.

Despite promises of protection under Colorado regulation, former California restaurateurs Scott Durrah and Wanda James wound up folding their Simply Pure cannabis kitchen after their bank suddenly refused to service their accounts because federal regulators still viewed deposits from state-sanctioned medical marijuana as akin to money laundering from drug trafficking. The couple stepped up their political activism by signing on to another cannabis cause: legalizing marijuana beyond medical use in Colorado.

Despite state medical cannabis regulators' promise to curb illegal marijuana diversion, a report from a Rocky Mountain High Intensity Drug Trafficking team charged that Colorado was chasing California as an illicit leader in shipping pot across America. Colorado's new medical cannabis cops also ran into fiscal challenges in their efforts to govern the state's marijuana industry. After overestimating licensing revenues on marijuana stores and cultivation centers, the Medical Marijuana Enforcement Division had to slash nearly half of its staff.

And Dan Rogers, the former equities trader who graduated from Oaksterdam University to become a Colorado marijuana entrepreneur, got a letter from Colorado's United States Attorney, one of twenty-three initial missives advising operators of federal laws against drug trafficking within one thousand feet of schools. Rogers wrote back, explaining that a surveyor showed his Denver store well outside that distance from a local middle school. He got an unfailingly polite response from U.S. Attorney John F. Walsh. "I appreciate the spirit in which you have sent your letter. . . . I shall make certain your intentions are noted by the appropriate persons performing the due diligence in our enforcement efforts," Walsh wrote. Roger went ahead and closed his Denver dispensary, reopened it at another location, and continued operating his three cannabis stores and their cultivation facilities.

In California, the fractured marijuana movement belatedly united on a plan for state regulation. But by then it would face leery lawmakers, disinterested cops, and an unfolding crackdown on America's largest marijuana economy.

TWELVE

Cultivating Trouble

Days after the defeat of the Proposition 19 marijuana legalization initiative, Oakland city attorney John Russo got a visit from an old friend who was a high-ranking official in the United States Justice Department in Washington, D.C., and who just happened to be in town. Their friendship was untarnished by the fact that the justice official worked by the rules of federal marijuana prohibition and Russo had built a legacy as a politician and lawyer declaring the government's cannabis policy to be "utter nonsense." In 1998, Russo had been a member of the Oakland City Council, which voted to declare a public health emergency and designate the Oakland Cannabis Buyers Cooperative to be the city's agent for medical marijuana distribution after it was targeted by federal authorities. Later, as the elected city attorney, he wrote amicus briefs in Oakland's support of the cannabis club's challenge to federal intolerance of marijuana as a state-permitted medicine. He was among the protagonists as pot-progressive Oakland set a limit of four taxed, licensed, and locally regulated dispensaries, avoiding getting overrun by cannabis stores while preserving its place as a beacon for marijuana activism and as home to the world's largest medical marijuana provider—Harborside Health Center—and America's most famous school of pot, Oaksterdam University. Russo had also been an ebullient public backer of the Oaksterdam-generated Proposition 19—just as, behind the scenes, he was cautioning Oakland officials about unbridled commercial cannabis ambitions.

As his friend from the Justice Department took a seat on a sofa in the city attorney's office and they chatted warmly about their children, Russo sensed what was coming. One week to the day after Californians voted down Proposition 19, Oakland city staff had drafted a request for applications for four city permits for "large scale Medical Cannabis Industrial Cultivation and Processing Facilities." Oakland was spiritedly moving forward. This city, long hard-bitten by crime and economic malaise and mostly left behind as other San Francisco Bay Area communities reaped the benefits of California's technology boom, was determined to become the Silicon Valley of cannabis. It set out to license massive industrial pot farms operating under eco-friendly city mandates of "zero waste," "efficient energy," and "carbon neutrality." In the weeks before the November 2 election, Russo had fielded telephone calls from the United States Attorney's Office in San Francisco about Oakland's marijuana production plans, approved by the city council in July. The messages were terse and direct: the federal government wasn't going to tolerate this. Now Russo's friend from Justice was there to tell him so in person—and to let him know what Oakland was risking.

A year earlier the administration of President Barack Obama had appeared to declare a truce on medical marijuana when Attorney General Eric Holder announced the government wouldn't prosecute "patients with serious illnesses," and his deputy, David Ogden, sent out a memo formally directing local U.S. Attorneys "not to focus federal resources on individuals whose actions are in clear and unambiguous compliance with existing state laws providing for the medical use of marijuana." Across California, a purportedly nonprofit medical marijuana industry boomed, with stores handling millions of dollars in cannabis transactions. Dispensaries and cannabis speculators exuberantly interpreted the feds' promise not to prosecute state-permitted "patients and caregivers" as safe passage for opening medical marijuana businesses. They seemed to look past a critical caveat of the Ogden directive: "Prosecution of commercial enterprises that unlawfully market and sell marijuana for profit continues to be an enforcement priority."

The federal truce on medical marijuana was fragile. And the surging California pot market, spotlighted in international medical coverage during the Proposition 19 campaign, had riveted the attention of the Justice Department. Yet Oakland's eyes still sparkled over the business plan of a wealthy construction contractor, Jeff Wilcox, who promised to convert his warehouse complex to include a hundred-thousand-square-foot marijuana factory farm producing twenty-one thousand pounds of "medical grade cannabis" per year to supply the California market. The venture was expecting to reap $47 million to $71 million a year while still claiming not-for-profit status. Oakland wanted to quadruple down on its bet by issuing permits for four factory farms, with Wilcox just one of the contenders. The city put out its request for applications. And John Russo's friend from Washington, D.C., told him that if Oakland went forward, the federal government's medical marijuana enforcement stand-down in California was over.

The city attorney had earlier tried to warn the Oakland City Council to proceed cautiously. In July, when the city considered the cannabis industrialization plan, Russo urged the council to delay approval to see if the Proposition 19 initiative to tax and regulate marijuana was passed by voters. Russo thought the initiative might provide some cover under California law for marijuana industrialization. Otherwise, he didn't see anything in the Proposition 215 medical marijuana law or the state's Senate Bill 420, the so-called Medical Marijuana Program Act, to permit such an endeavor. But Jeff Wilcox stoked Oakland's civic sense of cannabis destiny. His AgraMed venture promised not just industrial cultivation but also a vast marijuana business park with growing rooms, a marijuana edibles bakery, a cannabis jobs training center, a research laboratory, and retail space. It was to generate $3.5 million in yearly medical marijuana tax revenues for Oakland, on top of a surge in state sales taxes and other revenues from a resulting economic boom. In 2010, Oakland laid off eighty cops in budget cuts to help trim a $42-million city deficit and anticipated an even bigger deficit for the next budget year. Despite Russo's cautions, the city council wasn't going to forestall a fiscal cure through cannabis.

After the council voted unanimously to set in motion plans for commercial marijuana production, other suitors for the four lucrative cultivation permits began to make their presence known. One was a dashing young ganjapreneur named Dhar Mann, son of a politically influential family that ran Oakland's largest taxi cab franchise. With considerable fanfare and a welcoming party of public officials, he opened a big-box Oakland store called iGrow. It was billed in media accounts as the world's largest hydroponics store and—though it sold no pot—as the "Walmart of Weed." Mann set off to establish franchises in medical marijuana states for a chain, later named weGrow, that hyped itself as the "First Honest Hydro Store," displayed real marijuana plants, and openly discussed medicinal cultivation with customers. Mann also got the word out in Oakland that he had warehouse space ready for growing cannabis. Meanwhile, another contender, a mysterious player whose first name stood for *yes and no* and last name was *maybe* spelled backward, was already operating a vast indoor marijuana farm in the city.

Yan Ebyam, given his name by hippie parents in Mendocino County, was the CEO of a company called Marjyn Investments. It shared a Los Angeles business address with an L.A. immigration lawyer, Nathan Hoffman, who had taken up working with Southern California medical marijuana dispensaries. Initially unnoticed, Ebyam and Hoffman contracted with an East Oakland industrial plumbing and metal fabrication company to lease warehouse space for a marijuana-growing operation that soon blazed with 450 indoor lights. They dubbed the venture Bronze Horizon. They would eventually register with the California secretary of state the names of other potential ventures, in hues of a dozen "horizons"—from Emerald to Gold to Pink—to supply the California medical marijuana market.

Whether it was to come from Oakland's commercial farms or the big-market dreams of people such as Ebyam and Hoffman, California's pot economy was ripe for the industrialization of cannabis. In Southern California, the overflow of dispensaries in Los Angeles spilled into neighboring Orange County, where Hoffman represented dispensary clients in Garden Grove and beyond. A vast demand for product needed to be satisfied. Pot speculators, and some cash-strapped cities, saw opportunity in the corporatization of medical marijuana. Authorities would see a vast overreach of California's medical marijuana law.

Ebyam had streamed into Oakland in a silver Mercedes and with a shadowy business past. In 2005, at twenty-eight, he had accepted a plea bargain to serve twenty-two months of a thirty-month federal prison sentence for his role in a money-laundering conspiracy involving the resale of stolen Cisco and Sun Microsystems computer routers and servers worth more than $6 million. Federal authorities seized $480,000 from Ebyam's bank and cash holdings, plus his Cadillac Escalade. In Oakland, Ebyam, Hoffman, and another partner sold their first growing operation to investors. The investors soon complained, with attorneys asserting in a 2010 letter to Hoffman that they were wrongly promised a marijuana yield "well in excess of $1 million." The investors, who would later file a lawsuit, complained that actual proceeds were "significantly lower than $1 million" and that it had taken far longer to sell the pot yield to dispensaries than they were promised. Yan Ebyam moved on to grow marijuana in a huge, barn-shaped warehouse on Oakland's San Leandro Street—and earn a splash of fame. Marjyn Investments signed a labor contract with the Teamsters. The Associated Press distributed a national story and photos showing plant-tending marijuana gardeners of Alameda County's Teamsters Local 70 working in the new cannabis enterprise.

Lou Marchetti, business manager for Local 70, knew little about the quixotic cannabis CEO who dressed down in rumpled T-shirts and jeans. Ebyam told Marchetti he was organizing a hundred-thousand-square-foot marijuana farm and asked him to bring him all the workers he could. Marjyn Investments signed on thirty-eight employees, paying Teamster trimmers, gardeners, and maintenance workers twenty-five dollars an hour, plus health care and union pension benefits. Marchetti visited the warehouse filled with what looked like "half a football field of marijuana." But the facility was unlicensed by the city. Oakland's liberal marijuana policy allowed individual medical cannabis patients to grow up to 72 plants each and permitted groups of three patients to have 226 plants or a maximum growing space of ninety-six square feet per three-person group. When Oakland city inspectors came to the warehouse grow room, Ebyam told them he was only the master tenant. He said the plants were being grown by numerous medical marijuana patients under the city guidelines. The inspectors took his word for it.

Ebyam told Marchetti, a union official with considerable local political clout, he wanted in on one of Oakland's sanctioned commercial cannabis farms. Marchetti and Teamster representatives started schmoozing city officials on his behalf. "We spent a lot of time, lobbying people that this guy is good and should get one of the permits," Marchetti recalled. Ebyam peppered Marchetti about other cities and counties that might be receptive to marijuana cultivation. Marchetti took him to meet the mayor and city council members in the neighboring Alameda County city of San Leandro to inquire about growing marijuana in a shuttered Kellogg cereal plant. The town had a $3-million budget deficit. The Teamsters business manager sat at his side as Ebyam told the San Leandro officials he could grow enough tax-producing weed to make their deficit disappear. Later, as Oakland's cultivation plans sputtered in controversy, and mounting conflicts and challenges beset Marjyn Investments, Yan Ebyam disappeared from Oakland. Marchetti couldn't venture a yes, no, or maybe on where he went.

After the meeting with his friend from the Justice Department, John Russo wrote a report to the city council. He told council members of his informed legal opinion: they should get out of the marijuana cultivation business before it was too late. In the memo and personal discussions, Russo argued to council members that Proposition 19 lost and there was nothing in state law to support the city's plans and no plausible shield against federal action. He related the warnings from the Justice Department and the U.S. Attorney's Office in San Francisco. If Oakland opened its pot farms, Russo said, the feds were going to come down hard. Russo said the government was unlikely to stop at the marijuana warehouses. He predicted federal agents would target dispensaries, the vast California medical marijuana economy, and nearly every gain that cannabis-supportive Oakland had fought for since California voters approved Proposition 215. In a tense closed session attended by Russo, some on the city council expressed incredulity over his warnings, irked to the point of insult that the city attorney would seek to undercut Oakland's progress on medical marijuana. Russo saw them as "portraying themselves as crusaders in a righteous cause." He heard skeptical council members telling him they didn't believe him and directing him to ask the U.S. Justice Department specifically what its concerns were.

The council didn't take a vote on the matter. But Russo walked out of a closed meeting convinced he had been instructed to write the attorney general of the United States to ask his opinion of Oakland's pot farm idea. The city attorney drafted a letter to Eric Holder. He would later be ripped by cannabis advocates and the new mayor, Jean Quan, a council member in 2010 who sat in on sessions with Russo. Quan would claim afterward that the city attorney authored and sent the letter to Holder on his own volition, not on orders of the city. "The council told me to contact the feds," Russo would insist. "I am going to assert this until I die."

In early December, Alameda County's district attorney, Nancy O'Malley, wrote a letter congratulating Quan on her election, warmly opening: "I look forward to joining together in our work towards a safe and thriving Oakland in the New Year." The district attorney noted she was a cancer survivor who supported the rights of people benefiting from medical marijuana under California's Compassionate Use Act. Then O'Malley told the incoming mayor not to expect any support from the district attorney's office on its industrial cultivation ordinance or the legality of the cannabis farms. "The prosecuting agency in Alameda County is not providing any assurances that activities authorized by the Ordinance, but not authorized under state law or federal law, are permissible," she wrote, underlining for emphasis. "Persons should not rely solely upon pronouncements by city officials or enactment of the Ordinance as providing any legal or equitable defense to criminal prosecution." Finally, O'Malley suggested that city officials might have some personal legal concerns. "It remains an open question," she wrote, "whether public officers or public employees who aid and abet or conspire to violate state or federal laws in furtherance of a city ordinance are exempt from criminal liability."

Jeff Wilcox got a meeting with O'Malley. He came away unnerved by what she told him. Her admonitions rang in his ears about law enforcement's concerns about diversion of medical marijuana into illegal drug trafficking markets. Wilcox had convinced himself that his audacious industrial cultivation plan could work under state law. He had told himself and others he would form and run a medical marijuana "collective" as a closed organization of registered patients. Other cultivation or baking or laboratory operations in his cannabis business park would do the same. Then, the building executive figured, they would establish "reciprocal collective agreements" that would include memberships with California marijuana stores, other patient "collectives." After speaking with O'Malley, he ran it through his head. The legal conformity of the venture, with "collectives" doing business with "collectives," seemed like an illusion, like the magicians' trick of joining and separating closed metal rings, making them appear or vanish altogether.

Wilcox also started envisioning shipments of hundreds of pounds of marijuana from his factory farm disappearing as southbound drivers on deliveries to dispensaries in Los Angeles took sharp turns to the east for higher earnings in illicit out-of-state trafficking. "I was truly fearful it would end up in the East Coast and in the black market," he said. Paul Gallegos, the district attorney in Humboldt County, whom Wilcox had met in 2010, warned the wealthy building contractor over the perilous venture he was constructing. He told Wilcox, who had spent five hundred thousand dollars toward the $20 million he was prepared to invest in the cannabis warehouse development, that he could lose it all to the U.S. government. "I just want to let you know, you should read the federal seizure reports," Gallegos told him. "You're too big of a target."

Wilcox's final business plan, prepared in his bid for an Oakland industrial cultivation permit, was ready. But as he looked over Oakland's pot farm ordinance, introduced in July by city council president Larry Reid and at-large council member Rebecca Kaplan, Wilcox concluded the council had written "an illegal ordinance that didn't comply with state laws." He no longer thought it could work. In late December, a day before the applications were due, the city council abruptly suspended the licensing process. Yet despite warnings from Russo and the district attorney, the city wasn't giving up. Oakland was still determined to become a cannabis factory town. The council announced it would have a revised ordinance ready by February 1, 2011. Kaplan, long a key supporter of the medical marijuana community, said Oakland had been "the center of the medical cannabis movement since its inception," and it wasn't going to stop now. "We're not giving up," she asserted. We've always been a leader on this. This can be done well."

In late January 2011, as advocates at the California NORML chapter's Berkeley conference fretted over clarifying state law to regulate and protect

California's marijuana industry, Oakland City Council member Desley Brooks proclaimed the death of the city pot farms greatly exaggerated. Brooks was advancing a new ordinance to permit cultivation centers up to fifty thousand square feet that would operate under the control of marijuana dispensaries. She labeled fears of a federal crackdown as overblown.

The same month, Yan Ebyam took to exploiting new cannabis horizons. One hundred miles from Oakland, his silver Mercedes found its way to Rio Oso, a town of 350 residents and sprawling rice farms amid the cattails and wild blackberries of Sutter County, north of Sacramento, in California's Central Valley. Ebyam signed a deal to lease greenhouses from Thomas and David Jopson, fourth-generation farmers and former cattle ranchers who had earned national acclaim for their heirloom tomatoes. The two men, ages sixty-two and sixty, agreed to convert the greenhouses for commercial production of marijuana. Their attorneys would later say the brothers were convinced it was a legal business opportunity under California medical marijuana law. The Jopsons had planned to sell their adjoining family farms before retirement. They anticipated heading on to their golden years with leasing riches from gilded marijuana harvests.

The Sutter County cultivation operation was dubbed Black Horizon. And Yan Ebyam moved on to Sacramento County to start another greenhouse marijuana farm, called Blue Horizon, with rented space from a floral company known for its poinsettias.

On February 1, 2011, the day Brooks introduced her new industrial cultivation plan to the Oakland City Council, Melinda Haag, the United States Attorney in San Francisco, replied to John Russo's letter to Eric Holder. "The U.S. Department of Justice is familiar with the City's solicitation of applications for permits to operate 'industrial cannabis cultivation and manufacturing facilities,'" Haag wrote. "I have consulted with the Attorney General and the Deputy Attorney General. . . . This letter is written to ensure there is no confusion regarding the Department of Justice's view of such facilities." The U.S. Attorney made it clear federal authorities were "concerned" about the city's "licensing scheme"—and were prepared for a sweeping crackdown with "civil and criminal legal remedies" against those setting up or participating in the marijuana cultivation. Haag went on: "Others who knowingly facilitate the actions of the licensees, including property owners, landlords, and financiers, should also know that their conduct violates federal law."

Despite the implicit threat, Oakland wasn't surrendering on cannabis. The previous November, local voters had blessed the city with a 5 percent medical marijuana tax. The city council, still declining to announce the death of its pot farms, soon authorized four new dispensaries with allowable cultivation. A city staff report noted that Oakland's four existing dispensaries—and their $28 million in taxable marijuana transactions—left room in the marketplace for more marijuana stores and new tax revenues for the city.

But in East Oakland, there was trouble at Yan Ebyam's marijuana warehouse. Employees at Marjyn Investments reported to Oakland police a series of burglaries and the theft of more than a thousand plants. Though responding officers counted three thousand plants remaining, Marjyn Investments would lay off more than two-thirds of its Teamster workforce. City code enforcement officers, by now distrustful of the unlicensed operation's claim to be a haven for small groups of patient-growers, were contemplating what to do. After Melinda Haag's letter to Oakland, Nathan Hoffman, the L.A. lawyer in the partnership, suggested the venture wasn't going to get a city cultivation permit anytime soon. On February 18, 2011, he alluded to multiple problems, in an otherwise upbeat email to his new business associate Thomas Jopson, one of the Rio Oso tomato farmers.

"I'm in Oakland now dealing with the Marjyn investor/member meeting," Hoffman wrote. "As you can imagine [there are] a lot of disgruntled investors that the facility is not in the black yet and struggling with union labor issues. This is not an easy business . . . and now of course the City licensing and permitting process is indefinitely suspended as a result of the US Attys ominous public pronouncement . . . that any cultivation facility acting under a City permit would be immediately targeted by the Feds as crossing the proverbial 215 line in the sand."

And yet the lawyer told the tomato grower that their plan to convert the Jopson family greenhouses "to a model facility producing only 'pharmaceutical grade' cannabis has great merit." He cautioned that the operation "brings the chance the feds will target us no matter how much security and confidentially we achieve on paper." But the venture was going forward, despite the risk.

In John Russo's mind, so too was Oakland. Melinda Haag's letter provided little political vindication for the city attorney. He took umbrage over derision heaped on him by some city council members at their February 1, 2011, meeting, in which members pledged allegiance to furthering taxable cannabis commerce. Russo sent the council a follow-up memo. He said he was recusing himself from working with Oakland on its marijuana endeavors, citing professional standards that allowed a lawyer to refuse to represent a client that "seeks to pursue an illegal course of conduct." Russo soon resigned to take a job as the city manager in Alameda, a nearby town without the cannabis aspirations that stoked Oakland, several other cities and towns, and pot dreamers and schemers across the California landscape.

· · ·

Perhaps no place yearned for prosperity—or solvency—through marijuana more than the crawdad-fishing town of Isleton, a beleaguered municipality lost beyond the pear orchards and levies of the Sacramento River delta south of California's capital city. Isleton, with its faded Roaring Twenties Main Street and giant crawdad on the brick exterior of Isleton Joe's diner, was home to 840 residents, one police officer, and a town government in perpetual crisis. In 1995, as the then-Isleton police chief sought to rescue the city and refill city coffers by selling concealed-weapons permits to people streaming in from across Sacramento County, the county grand jury called for the town government to disband. Thirteen years later, the grand jury suggested Isleton should quit on itself once more because of its fiscal ineptitude and "state of perpetual crisis." The city's new residential development—its Village on the Delta, with raised model homes in splashy colors—was in foreclosure, abandoned. Even Isleton's famed crawdad festival had gone broke and left town.

But in 2010, a handsome young businessman, the nephew of legendary jazz pianist Dave Brubeck, strode into Isleton. He made an offer to restore the economic confidence of the town, once heralded as "the Little Paris of the Delta," by converting its empty subdivision lots into a seven-structure medical marijuana farm. Michael Brubeck, a former mortgage officer who worked with dispensaries in Los Angeles and marketed himself as a consultant to California cannabis businesses, dazzled the town council with a PowerPoint presentation for a not-for-profit medicinal cultivation enterprise to be insured by Lloyd's of London. He promised that his Delta Allied Growers, supplying dispensaries in Southern California, would employ fifty people and pay Isleton 3 percent of its gross revenues. Based on projections, the town anticipated a windfall of $350,000 in the first year alone—more than one-fourth of the city budget—and perhaps as much as $600,000.

Isleton had run off an unlicensed marijuana dispensary and rejected several cannabis-shop overtures because city council members didn't want the town overrun with pot smokers. But Brubeck pledged no local marijuana sales, just a professionally run complex that would make Isleton proud. The city signed off on his plan in November 2010, and he became a popular presence. He dropped by the fund-raiser at Rogelio's restaurant for the American Cancer Society relay event of Councilwoman Elizabeth Samano, who took office after the project was approved. He made a donation and eased her concerns about marijuana, describing emerging cannabis science and the new production of nonpsychoactive plants that helped seriously ill people without getting them high. Samano saw Brubeck as "healthy looking and well educated. He didn't look like a user. . . . He was a gorgeous man. I threw him questions and he never faltered."

Neither did Isleton, not even after word of Melinda Haag's scathing warning to Oakland. The town accepted legal advice that its project was proper under California law. As Delta Allied Growers began erecting greenhouses in March and April of 2011 and, unbeknownst to the city, storing marijuana plants in houses in the foreclosed subdivision, Isleton was cashing $150,000 in checks on the project. It was hiring a second police officer, with plans for two more.

Other municipalities were reaping proceeds from cannabis. The City of Sacramento brought in $1.2 million in permitting and licensing fees from cannabis dispensaries in the first six months of 2011. It counted on another $1 million in voter-approved annual marijuana taxes after declaring in 2010 that its thirty-eight pot stores could remain in place—even though nearly all violated distance requirements the city had set to keep dispensaries away from neighborhoods, schools, and parks. In Los Angeles, the city council may have been fighting a pitched, losing battle to close hundreds of marijuana stores, but L.A. officials also took steps to ensure the city got paid for its troubles, placing local Measure M—for *marijuana*—on the 2011 ballot to impose a 5 percent tax on local medical marijuana transactions. Proponents, including dispensaries that saw paying taxes as buying political protection, argued that the measure could generate $10 million for the city. In its first year after passage, Measure M brought in $2.5 million, because only 241 marijuana stores—one-half to one-third of the city's total—paid up. Yamileth Bolanos, fiery leader of the Greater Los Angeles Collective Association, refused to pay the tax, declaring it a punitive action against medical marijuana providers and a risk that could leave a paper trail for federal prosecution. "I already have to worry about the DEA coming in my door anyway without having to give [the city] a signed piece of paper saying I sold so much marijuana," she said.

Worried about local farmers getting frozen out of the market by Oakland's industrialization, medical cannabis grower and trimming-equipment salesman Joey Burger, of the Humboldt Growers Association, brought in Sacramento lobbyist Max Del Real to pitch a plan for county-licensed outdoor farms of up to forty thousand square feet. "The revolution is starting here," the pompadour-sporting Del Real declared at a conference in southern Humboldt County, rallying pot growers and political leaders for a plan he argued could generate $10 million in taxes and fees for the county. Humboldt supervisors went to work on a more measured cultivation-licensing program in hopes of distinguishing legitimate medicinal growers from illegal operators.

The State of California also sought to get its fair share of marijuana money. The Board of Equalization taxation agency stepped up audits of cannabis dispensaries, with officials suggesting California was getting shorted by tens of millions of dollars by marijuana stores failing to pay state sales taxes. The tax agency in 2011 ordered the Berkeley Patients Group, one of California's pioneering marijuana dispensaries, to pay $6.4 million in back taxes and interest on $51 million in cannabis sales between 2004 and 2007, a period in which the dispensary had argued medical marijuana wasn't legally taxable. Tax board member Betty Yee, estimating California's potential statewide haul in medical marijuana sales taxes at $400 million, urged the Berkeley Patients Group—which had paid sales taxes since 2007—to negotiate its previous debt through an "offer in compromise program." The state didn't want to lose its valued taxpayer.

The town of Isleton got no such respect. A top prosecutor from the Sacramento County District Attorney's Office called Isleton's city manager, Bruce Pope, telling him: "We have the authority to come down and arrest you and your City Council." The entire council, city manager, police chief, and city attorney were subpoenaed by a county grand jury after the district attorney's office suggested the town was illegally sanctioning a $10-million-a-year illegal commercial marijuana operation. District Attorney Jan Scully contacted federal prosecutors.

To the United States Attorney in Sacramento, Benjamin B. Wagner, Isleton was "exhibit A" among California cities and counties looking to taxable marijuana commerce to compensate for plummeting tax revenues in an economic recession. He briefed superiors in the Justice Department on his desire to make a declarative statement on the little town grabbing at a moneymaking opportunity. With department approval, Wagner sent a letter to

Isleton and Delta Allied Growers. He made clear the Justice Department's view of "municipal ordinances and state laws that purport to establish proposed marijuana cultivation or licensing programs." Warning of civil or criminal actions by the federal government, Wagner wrote, "The Department is concerned about the large-scale industrial marijuana cultivation and manufacturing operation contemplated in the City of Isleton as it would involve conduct contrary to federal law and threatens the government's efforts to regulate the possession, manufacturing and trafficking of controlled substances."

The Sacramento County Grand Jury said Delta Allied Growers "reportedly buried more than 1,000 marijuana plants" before abruptly leaving town. Federal prosecutors filed no charges. The county grand jury issued no indictment—just another scathing review of Isleton's civic performance. "The city allowed the community to be pushed into a project that is perched on the blurry edge of marijuana law without properly questioning the situation," wrote grand jury foreperson Donald Prange Sr. "It did so . . . because of the promise of money and jobs. They forgot the old saying, 'If it sounds too good to be true, it probably is.'"

The proverb would also come to apply to tomato growers Thomas and David Jopson after a Sutter County sheriff's deputy, Matthew Naples, came to visit the family's ranch on April 20, 2011. The Jopson brothers were respected sons of the former local fire chief. Within the community of heirloom tomato growers, they were legends—nationally renowned for producing premium greenhouse products retailing at more than four dollars a pound. "Tom Jopson has no regrets about becoming a greenhouse grower, and wishes anyone who makes a similar move all the success in the world," declared a glowing 2008 article in *American Vegetable Grower* magazine. "But he had some words of warning. It's not for the faint of heart." Now the brothers had a far bolder venture—signing with Yan Ebyam to produce marijuana that could retail for thirty-five hundred dollars a pound. Eventual federal criminal complaints would detail emails that Nathan Hoffman sent Thomas Jopson. The emails offered instructions on becoming a patient-member of a Southern California dispensary, New Age Canna in Garden Grove, and a grower producing up to six plants per dispensary member under the legal pretense of sick people cultivating for other sick people. When Deputy Naples asked Tom Jopson what was in his greenhouse, he hesitantly replied, "It's 215 or 420 stuff." Then, obligingly, he volunteered to give the deputy a tour and let him take photographs.

Naples would later report to a regional narcotics task force for Yuba and Sutter Counties that Tom Jopson told him there would be up to six crops a year, each with an estimated $4-million return. He said David Jopson suggested there were to be four growing cycles worth $2 million each, and that the brothers were due to receive $150,000 per cycle. Under either scenario, the younger Jopson told Deputy Naples, the brothers were to soon head off to "lead the good life" in retirement.

In May, narcotics officers interviewed a former Northern California general manager for Denny's restaurants. Thirty-year-old Aimee Sisco told them she was taking over the lease on the Jopsons' property from Yan Ebyam, who was moving on to start the Blue Horizon operation in Sacramento County. Sisco had some complaints. She said she had put $350,000 into the venture while Ebyam only invested $150,000. She expressed frustration over what she earned from a dispensary on the first marijuana yield. And she told officers that when Ebyam moved on to Sacramento County he left her with hundreds of plants on the Jopsons' ranch that were infected with mold. In the first meeting with Naples, Thomas Jopson had told the deputy that Yan Ebyam's behavior in the venture was making him nervous. He asked if the sheriff's department wouldn't mind stepping up patrols around his property.

Officers from the regional drug task force found Ebyam's silver Mercedes parked outside the greenhouses of the Cal-Nevada Florist in Sacramento County. They placed a global tracking device on the car. Soon a California Department of Justice airplane flew over, looking for marijuana plants through the translucent greenhouse roofs. In late June, local and state narcotics officers raided the properties, seizing 2,168 plants from the Jopson family ranch and 3,305 plants at the Sacramento County greenhouse. They called in federal authorities to take over. For Wagner, the Sacramento U.S. Attorney, the case wasn't the first time he had heard from local police or county district attorneys who were "apoplectic" over huge medical marijuana enterprises and begging the feds to intervene.

On June 29, 2011, James M. Cole, the deputy United States Attorney, issued a new memo seeking to clarify any confusion over the earlier Ogden memo, which was famously seen by dispensary operators, cultivators, and cannabis entrepreneurs as the green light for a green rush. Cole said the earlier memo was intended to declare that the federal government wouldn't focus resources on patients or people caring for "individuals with cancer or serious illnesses who use marijuana as part of a recommended treatment regimen consistent with applicable state law." Cole wrote, "The term 'caregiver' as used in the memorandum meant just that: individuals providing care to individuals with cancer or other serious illness, not commercial operations cultivating, selling or distributing marijuana." Medical marijuana advocates shuddered. They charged that the government was reversing course and imperiling the distribution of cannabis as medicine.

A day later, on June 30, Yan Ebyam, Thomas and David Jopson, Aimee Sisco, and five others were indicted by a federal grand jury in Sacramento on conspiracy and marijuana charges that carried minimum penalties of ten years in federal prison. Los Angeles attorney Nathan Hoffman and a Southern California dispensary operator, John Nguyen, were named in a criminal complaint the following October and indicted a year later.

To federal prosecutors, the cases represented criminal overreach and ava-rice of individuals using the cover of California's medical marijuana law. From cities looking to license commercial operations to unsanctioned culti-vators looking to cash in, the Justice Department saw a troubling pattern of excess. In September 2011, a federal grand jury in Sacramento indicted three purported medical marijuana farmers in Madera County on charges of traf-ficking marijuana in FedEx and United Parcel Service packages to Connecticut, Texas, and Massachusetts. The same month, the last of seven defendants pleaded guilty to federal trafficking charges for reaping $3,000 a pound in shipping California marijuana to drug dealers in Boston from a Fresno County farm that had more than four thousand plants arranged in plots—posted with physicians' recommendations for state-permitted medi-cal marijuana.

And while many California medical marijuana dispensaries maintained the appearance of compliant, compassionate, nonprofit providers, the feds saw unscrupulous operators on the fringes stuffing their pockets with cash. Narcotics officers in 2011 seized nearly $2.5 million in cash from an Orange County dispensary and another $390,000 from the home of its purported operator, John Melvin Walker. A fifty-six-year-old San Clemente beach com-munity resident known as "Pops," Walker personally reaped $25 million in six years from nine pot stores opened in Orange and Los Angeles Counties as healing collectives for medical marijuana patients. He would be indicted on drug-trafficking and tax evasion changes—and, two years later, net more than twenty-one years in federal prison. Another indictment, in September 2011, targeted employees and associates of the Sacramento R & R Wellness Collective dispensary, including its ambitious young operator, Bryan Smith, who was twenty-seven. Police found $256,000 in vacuum-sealed bags of cash at Smith's house, $16,700 in a backpack, and a reported audition tape for an MTV program, *True Life,* that featured a pot segment called "I'm in the Marijuana Business." Smith boasted on the tape that he was counting on $100,000 in earnings every forty to sixty days—and was sure glad Proposition 19 hadn't passed, because it would have driven the prices down. He would later plead guilty with five associates to a scheme involving multiple growing houses, stolen electricity, and pot distributed in San Diego, far from the Sacramento dispensary. Elsewhere, federal drug agents tracked email messages from the BlackBerry phones of operators of a North Hollywood dispensary. While purporting to serve patients coming in the front door, they were allegedly shipping hundreds of pounds of marijuana a month out the back door—and across America.

In late September 2011, California's four United States Attorneys began sending letters to owners of property on which marijuana was being cultivated and to landlords of dispensaries, including some of California's longest established and most reputable medical cannabis providers. The letters threatened seizure of land and buildings and prosecution under the federal Controlled Substances Act. The feds' medical marijuana truce in California was ending. All that was left was the official announcement.

THIRTEEN

Return of the Feds

On October 7, 2011, medical marijuana advocates and patients arrived early in the diamond-patterned granite plaza of the Robert T. Matsui United States Courthouse in Sacramento. They sensed the seismic nature of what was about to occur on the tenth floor of the federal building, where representatives for California's four United States Attorneys were meticulously checking credentials, refusing to admit anyone without an up-to-date press pass. A day earlier, the state's top federal prosecutors had put out a brief advisory saying that they were to issue a joint statement on the sale, distribution, and cultivation of marijuana.

The word was already out, spreading rapidly through the medical marijuana community, as advocates and cannabis business operators faxed each other letters from U.S. Attorneys received in recent days by landlords of scores of California dispensaries. They threatened federal property seizures if the establishments didn't stop selling marijuana within forty-five days. One letter, directed at the state's longest-operating dispensary, the Marin Alliance for Medical Marijuana, which had opened in the San Francisco Bay Area town of Fairfax before the 1996 passage of Proposition 215, threatened its landlord with prolonged prison time for drug dealing within a thousand feet of a park—a Little League field. "Violation of the federal law referenced above is a felony crime," the missive read, "and carries with it a penalty of up to 40 years in prison." Demonstrators at the Sacramento federal building waved signs—"Closing Collectives Harms Patients" and "By Legal Democratic Vote, Cannabis Is Medicine"—at passing traffic. As media members streamed inside, the protesters chanted, "We're healers! Not dealers!"

The host of the joint press conference, Benjamin Wagner, the Sacramento U.S. Attorney, was the first top federal prosecutor appointed in California by President Barack Obama, in November 2009. He had started in his office's Narcotics and Violent Crime Unit but made his name over nearly a decade as chief of the Special Prosecution Unit, targeting public corruption and financial and corporate fraud. Wagner would go on to assert he never sought to become the United States Attorney for the Eastern District of California "to launch a campaign against medical marijuana." Wagner preferred to be known for prosecuting perpetrators of mortgage fraud. His vast district, extending from the lower Central Valley to the Oregon and Nevada borders, included Sacramento and Stockton, two of the hardest-hit regions in the financial meltdown created by the marketing of subprime loans. Wagner had come to see in medical marijuana a similar confidence game. He saw the cover of providing cannabis for sick people as "a fig leaf" for big-money enterprises. His office was now preparing to prosecute a Los Angeles attorney, Nathan Hoffman, and a former Oakland cannabis businessman, Yan Ebyam, in the venture that had lured the two tomato growers in the small farming town of Rio Oso to register as medical marijuana patients and lease their greenhouses for marijuana. Wagner had seen pot farmers elsewhere amassing medical recommendations for California patients only to traffic out of state. He saw investment schemes, in cultivation and in dispensaries teeming with cash, being perpetrated by people who "know nothing about treating glaucoma and cancer" and who were encouraging others to join in cannabis business endeavors "because they had skin in the game—a lot of skin in the game."

Wagner had convened with fellow U.S. Attorneys and midlevel Justice Department officials a week after the defeat of Proposition 19 in a prescheduled meeting at the Drug Enforcement Administration offices in Sacramento. It was then that they began discussing a coordinated response to California's burgeoning industry. Over the ensuing months in 2011, Wagner, one of fifteen U.S. Attorneys on the Attorney General's Advisory Committee assembled by Eric Holder, participated in roundtable discussions in Washington, D.C., with America's top law-enforcement officer and his chief deputy. He circulated, with other U.S. Attorneys, drafts of the eventual letter in which Deputy Attorney General James Cole declaratively spelled out the government's opposition to commercial cannabis operations. Over time, Wagner let Justice Department officials at the roundtables know that "federal law is totally being flouted here in California and we have to respond." Weeks before the Sacramento media event, he informed his superiors that California's U.S. Attorneys were to declare ongoing and sweeping actions against purported medical marijuana profiteers. The Justice Department signed off on the announcement.

As reporters and camera crews crowded the tenth-floor conference room, Wagner started with a qualifier. He declared that federal authorities weren't "focusing on backyard grows with small amounts of marijuana for use by seriously ill people." Then he cut briskly to the crackdown that was under way and would unfold for many more months to come. "We are targeting money-making commercial growers and distributors who use the trappings of state law as cover," Wagner said. He went on: "Today, we put to rest the notion that large marijuana businesses can shelter themselves under state law and operate freely without fear of federal enforcement."

André Birotte Jr., the U.S. Attorney in Los Angeles appointed by President Obama in March 2010, held aloft a pot magazine, *Mota,* that featured a cover with a marijuana leaf and reams of cash to make his point about an excess of "brick and mortar Costco/Wal-Mart dispensaries" turning huge profits "in a new California Gold Rush" and violating both state and federal law. Birotte unveiled a forfeiture lawsuit filed in order to seize a single property leasing space to seven marijuana stores in the Orange County city of Lake Forest. And he announced the indictment of seven people in what he depicted as an egregious case of drug trafficking under anyone's law. The indictment alleged that defendants from the NoHo Caregivers dispensary in North Hollywood used nicknames—"Pimpin," "Chuckles," "Egypt," "T. W.," "Phats," "Audi," and "OC"—as they sent BlackBerry messages exulting over the $194,000 a month each expected to earn. The operation took in nearly $15 million in eight months, allegedly spurning sick people in California to ship six hundred to seven hundred pounds of marijuana a month to dealers in New York and Pennsylvania.

Laura E. Duffy, the U.S. Attorney in San Diego, brought in multiple props as she announced indictments against two dispensaries for marijuana distribution and letters warning forfeiture actions against dozens more. In so doing, she issued a moral indictment, declaring that medical marijuana stores were marketing to young adult customers most likely to provide pot to minors. The Obama appointee in the state's conservative Southern District held aloft a ziplock bag full of pharmaceutical vials with cannabis leaf logos. She said they were given to her by a mother of a teenager. "When she talked to her son about these, what he told her is, 'Mom, this is how kids are buying marijuana now,'" Duffy said. "They get it at the stores." She pulled out a bag for a dispensary's marijuana-laced cotton candy. It bore the face of a clown.

"This is not a marketing campaign aimed at people under the supervision of a doctor," she asserted.

The enduring sound bite was delivered by Melinda Haag, the U.S. Attorney in San Francisco. Appointed by the president in August 2010, she was a veteran trial lawyer and federal prosecutor who had specialized in white collar crime, environmental abuses, civil rights offenses, and child exploitation. Haag, a product of the University of California, Berkeley School of Law, presided in the Northern District of California, the progressive coastal region, where the medical marijuana movement was born during the San Francisco AIDS crisis, where cannabis growing became a regional art in Mendocino and Humboldt Counties, and where Oakland—and Oaksterdam—emerged as the political and intellectual nerve center for a sanctioned marijuana economy. On this day, Haag took direct aim at people exploiting the 1996 Proposition 215 medical marijuana initiative championed in the name of AIDS and cancer patients.

"The California Compassionate Use Act was intended to help seriously ill people," Haag said with a steely gaze. "But the law has been hijacked by profiteers who are motivated not by compassion but by money."

Haag announced she was immediately targeting dispensaries "that sell marijuana very close to schools, parks and other places where children learn and play." She was sending letters to landlords and lienholders, threatening property seizures and federal prison if they didn't cease sales of marijuana "in close proximity to children … [, to] playgrounds and schools and Little League fields."

Over the ensuing weeks and months, agents for the Drug Enforcement Administration, the Internal Revenue Service, and the U.S. Marshall's Service in Haag's district would go after medical marijuana operations and icons of the California marijuana movement. More than any other U.S. Attorney, Haag—the top prosecutor in the state's most liberal federal district—would be depicted by cannabis advocates as waging war on medical marijuana.

．　．　．

Six days after the U.S. Attorneys' announcement, an armored-vehicle caravan—carrying heavily armed DEA agents in camouflage—rumbled over winding roads in southern Mendocino County. The caravan passed wine grapes and grazing cattle and barreled beyond a gate marked "Member,

Mendocino Farm Bureau." The drug agents brought a battering ram to the country home and front door of Matt Cohen. "You don't have to knock it down," Cohen pleaded. "I'll open it. And please don't shoot the dogs."

In Mendocino County, Cohen had been the golden boy for a great medical marijuana regulatory experiment in a region with a long, illicit cannabis history. He was the earnest public figure who worked with Mendocino supervisors and the sheriff to establish Ordinance 9.31. It allowed marijuana growers with confirmation of providing medicine for dispensaries or networks of patients to cultivate up to ninety-nine plants, tagged with zip ties and regularly inspected by the sheriff's department. The Mendocino cannabis accord bought Cohen and the sheriff, Tom Allman, national attention in a *Frontline* documentary. And four weeks before DEA agents arrived at Cohen's house, a county supervisor and sheriff's sergeant had testified in neighboring Sonoma County on behalf of two of Cohen's drivers, who had been arrested while driving his Northstone Organics "farm direct" marijuana to people with medical recommendations. As he was pressed against an exterior wall and handcuffed outside his door, Cohen tried to impress upon the agents that he was a Mendocino County–approved, regulated, and supervised cannabis grower. "It's a sham," one of the agents answered. Crews with chain saws set off to hack down the ninety-nine plants in his fenced, video-monitored garden.

No federal criminal charges followed, and local charges were later dropped against Cohen's drivers in Sonoma County. But the federal raid put Cohen out of business, bigfooted the Mendocino County sheriff, and frightened the Mendocino Board of Supervisors into repealing the county's tagging and oversight program. Sheriff Allman had never personally visited Cohen's marijuana garden—he left that to his medical cannabis inspections sergeant—but he saw Cohen as a model for local compliance and adherence to California medical marijuana law. "I think Matt Cohen's reputation as a cooperative operator snowballed into somebody at the federal level saying we need to make an example of this guy," the sheriff complained. Allman now wanted the matter "to go all the way to the nine justices." He wanted the United States Supreme Court to tell him what to do about making sense of the marijuana mess in his county. And he wanted the State of California to step in and finally set clear rules and regulations for medical marijuana. Allman had been burned. He didn't want his sheriff's department "to be the plant inspector" anymore.

Two weeks after the Mendocino County raid, medical marijuana advocates and a supportive state lawmaker gathered in a hotel conference room near where President Obama was due to appear for a fund-raiser in San Francisco. What was supposed to be a media event decrying the Obama Justice Department's assault on medical marijuana resembled an anxious encounter session. California's marijuana dispensaries were already closing in fear of federal actions. After its warning letter, the government was pursuing a forfeiture suit against the Marin Alliance for Medical Marijuana. The dispensary would soon surrender and close its doors. The movement-revered Berkeley Patients Group dispensary was also targeted—threatened with property seizure and prosecution for distributing medical marijuana within a thousand feet of a French language school and a school for the deaf—and would also succumb and shutter. (It would later reopen at a new location, only to be targeted again in a federal forfeiture lawsuit in 2013.) As worry and anger consumed the October 24, 2011, gathering, San Francisco Assemblyman Tom Ammiano opened the press conference by saying, "Everybody take a deep breath. Everybody inhale." He paused, and then continued: "Look, this is getting a little Kafkaesque for my blood."

The assembly Democrat, along with Dan Rush of the United Food and Commercial Workers Union, Oaksterdam University chancellor Dale Sky Jones, and Dale Gieringer, the California director of the National Organization for the Reform of Marijuana Laws, went on to say that state medical marijuana law needed to be fortified in the face of ongoing federal incursions. They announced they were drafting a 2012 ballot initiative to impose California medical marijuana industry oversight—"and a robust system of statewide regulation," Jones vowed—in the hopes of calming the feds. The U.S. Attorneys had announced prosecutions against huge commercial cultivators and people trafficking out of state. Now advocates saw some of California's most compliant operators getting targeted. "They stated they were conducting this campaign because California's medical marijuana law had been hijacked by profiteers," said Steve DeAngelo of Oakland's Harborside Health Center, excoriating the government for going after organizations that were "one hundred percent compliant and have not diverted medical marijuana anywhere." DeAngelo protested that the feds "should either learn how to aim or learn how to tell the truth."

For much of the previous year, DeAngelo had been followed by a documentary crew filming a four-part Discovery Channel series called *Weed Wars*. It was to focus on Harborside Health Center, its founders—DeAngelo and peace activist Dave Wedding Dress—and DeAngelo's brother, Andrew, who became general manager in 2010. It was to tell of the cultivation trials of

Harborside's patient marijuana growers and the tribulations of its medical clients, including a father, Jason David, who went to the dispensary for a nonpsychoactive cannabis tincture to quell the unrelenting seizures of his five-year-old son, Jayden. Episodes of the documentary series would open with the voice of Harborside's executive director: "I'm Steve DeAngelo. I've dedicated my entire life to the cannabis plant. And today, my family and I run the largest cannabis dispensary on the entire planet. By selling the amount of cannabis I've sold, I'm now eligible for three federal death penalties. But I believe in this plant. I believe in what it can do for people."

Adding new drama to the documentary series, Harborside was facing a $2.4-million tax-deficiency demand from the Internal Revenue Service on its 2007 and 2008 federal tax returns. An ongoing audit targeted subsequent tax years. Under IRS Section 280E, an obscure tax code approved by Congress in 1982 to prevent illegal drug dealers from deducting business expenses, the IRS was refusing to let Harborside take tax deductions for executive and employee salaries, patient services ranging from counseling to chiropractic care, utility payments, rent, and other expenses. Ironically, the IRS allowed Harborside to declare its inventory costs for a federally prohibited narcotic, marijuana. In Oakland, DeAngelo staged a public event, presenting the city with a giant check for one-third of the $1.1 million Harborside paid in total local medical marijuana taxes for 2011. Harborside, which also paid over $2 million in state sales taxes, was one of Oakland's largest taxpayers. But the IRS's refusal to budge on routine deductions, DeAngelo declared, could put Harborside and medical marijuana dispensaries across California out of business.

DeAngelo—the former yippie who once chained himself to the White House fence in pro-marijuana protests, who now ran a California collective that handled $22 million in annual cannabis transactions in Oakland and another $8-million at a dispensary in San Jose—became the most visible defender of an industry under siege. Two weeks after advocates announced in San Francisco their push for a state-regulated—and, they hoped, protected—medical marijuana market, DeAngelo led a demonstration outside the Sacramento courthouse where the U.S. Attorneys had announced their enforcement actions. Surrounded by people hoisting placards reading "Marijuana is medicine. Let states regulate!" he stood on the courthouse steps in his black fedora, signature pigtails, black narrow-lapelled suit, and skinny red tie. DeAngelo evoked a past champion, martyr, and heroine for medical marijuana. He saluted the partner of a victim of AIDS in San

Francisco who led the political campaign for medical use. He grieved for the doctor in the Sierra Nevada who recommended medical marijuana and went to prison for providing it. He hailed the caregiver in the Santa Cruz community of seriously and terminally ill patients raided for cultivating cannabis.

"People like Dennis Peron and Mollie Fry and Valerie Corral made it possible for the first time in modern history for medical cannabis patients to get their medicine, to get access to the medicine they need safely and affordably in an environment of respect and kindness," DeAngelo said, building to an emotional roar. "It was not easy then. It's not easy now. Ever since we passed Proposition 215, we've been threatened and we've been slandered and we've been raided and prosecuted and, in too many cases, thrown into darkness and prison."

He finished with a crescendo: "We want to know, Mr. Holder. We want to know, U.S. Attorneys. How many more need to suffer before you do the decent thing and surrender this campaign of terror and intimidation?"

In some cities and counties that had long fought the presence of marijuana dispensaries, the federal crackdown was exceedingly effective. For nearly two years, code enforcement officers in Sacramento County had sent out nuisance abatement notices, levied fines, and gone to court to close marijuana stores that county supervisors said weren't permitted under local zoning laws. The number of marijuana stores only surged, from a dozen to nearly a hundred. And then, as numerous landlords received federal prosecution threats and forfeiture threats, they all closed in a matter of weeks. One of the last holdouts, the Magnolia Wellness Center in the community of Orangevale, went out with a flourish, offering free grams of marijuana and heavy discounts on strains ranging from Lemon Wreck to Violator Kush. Hundreds of people, from feeble patients in wheelchairs to college kids with a bounce in their step, encircled the building like a Depression-era breadline.

In the city of Sacramento, where local regulations had grandfathered in numerous stores that failed to meet local requirements regarding their distance from schools and parks, letters from the U.S. Attorney led to their closure. Lino Catabran, who went from running a waterbed warehouse to selling Porsches and, later, recreational vehicles before converting his Sacramento dealership into a marijuana store, saw the end when federal authorities seized his bank account. A criminal complaint charged that his One Love Wellness dispensary illegally structured deposits in amounts under ten thousand dollars to avoid IRS reporting requirements. Catabran, who once revealed that—unlike in the car business—there were "very few unhappy customers" with pot, closed the dispensary with a New Year's Eve party. He advertised it with the headline "Feds Closing Sacramento Collectives."

The city attorney in San Diego, Jan Goldsmith, suing to shutter local dispensaries, got a major boost when U.S. Attorney Laura Duffy sent out property-seizure letters to landlords. Duffy declared, "United States law takes precedence over state law. . . . Accordingly, it is not a defense . . . that the dispensary is providing 'medical marijuana.'" Goldsmith exulted, hailing federal "asset forfeiture" as "a devastating tool." Within months, nearly two hundred dispensaries in the city would close. By mid-2012, one marijuana store remained open in the unincorporated region of San Diego County, prompting local Democratic congressman Bob Filner to write Duffy, requesting a stay in seizing the property of the county's lone licensed dispensary. "This threat is a form of unwarranted intimidation that the My Mother Earth Co-op doesn't deserve," Filner wrote, continuing: "I understand you have a duty to enforce federal law but I hope you keep in mind the will of the voters of California." The Mother Earth dispensary later closed voluntarily. Elsewhere in California, operators of medical marijuana stores that resisted or ignored federal warnings did so at their own peril. Federal drug agents raided a holdout Sacramento store, the El Camino Wellness Center, and seized its bank accounts. They served search warrants and brought marijuana trafficking charges against operators of a Southern California dispensary chain, G3 Holistic stores, netting guilty pleas and convictions for its operators in 2012.

The preferred enforcement tactic of U.S. Attorney Melinda Haag proved maddening to dispensary operators in the densely packed urban tapestry of San Francisco. Haag's pronouncement that she would protect children by targeting medical marijuana sales near parks and schools led to a forfeiture order against the Divinity Tree dispensary in the city's Tenderloin District because it was within one thousand feet of a playground. The dispensary was on a different street, out of view of the swings and wooden climbing train of tiny Sgt. John Macaulay Park. Directly across from the street-corner playground was a strip club with flashing lights advertising "Live Nude Shows." People walking around the block to the dispensary would encounter a massage parlor, a porn theater, four liquor stores, and a tobacco and head shop. But none of those were against federal law. Operators Charlie Pappas, a quadriplegic after a robbery and shooting three decades earlier, and fellow medical marijuana advocate Raymond Gamley closed the Divinity Tree rather than face the wrath of the feds. "I can't tell you how bad it feels, what they did to us," Gamley said. The way he saw it, there was virtually no place in San Francisco that wasn't within a thousand feet of some sensitive use that would offend the government. Al Shawa, the former fashion industry executive who remade his Mission District store into an upscale marijuana dispensary with buds that glistened like jewels in lighted displays, also gave up after a landlord notice from Haag threatened forty years in prison for "operating within prohibited distance" of another playground. Shawa had spent $250,000 to open the Shambhala Healing Center. He found it hard to fathom that he was quitting over a federal letter that cost forty-four cents to mail.

Catherine Smith, a former Bangor, Maine, police officer who ran the HopeNet Co-op dispensary south of San Francisco's Market Street, refused to close just because, three years earlier, a private Mandarin immersion school for youths opened blocks from her establishment. Inside one of the few city dispensaries that allowed patients to smoke marijuana on-site, Smith seethed in the aromatic air: "I'm not a drug dealer. I'm permitted and regulated. It seems to me California voted for this overwhelmingly. And I don't sell to kids." The dispensary displayed a framed letter from the former San Francisco District Attorney Kamala Harris, now California's attorney general. It read, "My office will not compromise in supporting the rights for our loved ones who are sick and need medical marijuana." But within a few months, Smith and operators of another San Francisco dispensary, the Vapor Room, surrendered in spectacular fashion. They staged a funeral procession to the federal building with a blaring brass band, coffins adorned with "Marijuana Is Medicine" signs, and a marching twelve-foot puppet—a giant caricature of Melinda Haag.

The federal crackdown emboldened local drug cops in their ongoing actions. In the Los Angeles Police Department's Devonshire Division, home of the LAPD narcotics squad, officers making undercover buys and raiding marijuana stores closed thirty-seven dispensaries in 2011 and 2012. And six years after police black-and-whites had stopped in disbelief and then driven on from the 2 A.M. Dispensary in the adult entertainment complex of Brad Barnes, narcotics officers raided the marijuana store staffed by strippers in booty shorts. They went next door to the featured business of the former porn star Brick Majors. They burst into Barnes's Xposed nude juice bar, busted an interior door and opened a safe packed with more than $550,000 in cash. Officers seized the money as drug proceeds. Barnes asserted it was properly earned from nonmedicinal pleasures, from his Private Moments sex toys emporium, Wet Spot bikini bar, and the all-nude club. He insisted none of the money came from the medical marijuana collective, for which he said he was only a patient-member who didn't even use pot. All charges against him, including money laundering and maintaining a place for selling controlled substances, were dismissed a year later. He began legal efforts to get his cash back.

While marijuana dispensaries all but vanished from some California communities, they still flourished in others. In Los Angeles, neither LAPD raids nor federal enforcement efforts seemed to make a dent in a resilient pot store population. As scores closed, new ones opened. And after the city council in the summer of 2012 passed its "gentle ban," limiting marijuana distribution to groups of three patients or fewer in hopes of shuttering at least 762 listed dispensaries and as many as 1,000, medical cannabis advocates trumped the council's action. They raised more than fifty thousand signatures to place a referendum—to overturn the ban—on the ballot for the 2013 city elections, when eight city council members would have to face the voters. The upbraided city council voted to rescind the ban.

And, after having roiled the feds with its industrial cultivation plans, the City of Oakland declared itself unfazed by federal actions against California marijuana stores. In 2012, it granted four new dispensary permits in hopes of bringing in another $1.7 million in marijuana tax revenue. "The expansion of the medical cannabis permits is a natural extension . . . to provide patients suffering from serious illness and pain with a safe and reliable source of medical marijuana," proclaimed Mayor Jean Quan. "I am proud that Oakland has long been at the forefront of the compassionate movement." Yet one of the suitors the city selected for a dispensary permit, Dhar Mann, the politically connected founder of Oakland's "Walmart of Weed" hydroponics store, was soon disqualified. Alameda County prosecutors charged him with thirteen felonies, including grand theft and forgery, for allegedly defrauding a city development-grant program. And another dispensary permit recipient, Jeff Wilcox, the wealthy building contractor who stirred Oakland's dreams of commercial cultivation, came to realize he wanted no part of the marijuana business. Wilcox was unnerved by the federal crackdown and had an epiphany—he began to worry that his twenty-year-old son was smoking too much marijuana. "This isn't me," Wilcox finally announced to his fiancée, making his decision to walk away. "I'm not a pot dealer."

· · ·

At 6:30 A.M. on April 2, 2012, agents from the DEA, the IRS, and the U.S. Marshals Service entered an apartment building overlooking Oakland's Lake

Merritt. They ascended to a third-floor apartment, yelling to the president of Oaksterdam University and chief funder and architect of the Proposition 19 marijuana legalization campaign to open his door. Richard Lee pushed himself out of bed and into his wheelchair. He recalled instructions of attorneys who lectured on cannabis law at his marijuana trades school: Don't let the cops in—that can be seen as consenting to a search by officers who may not have a warrant. So Lee waited for the federal officers to break down his door. He greeted them after they burst in.

The agents, serving five search warrants, demanded keys for Oaksterdam University and storefronts he leased, including his Coffee Shop Blue Sky dispensary location. Lee had only recently moved the dispensary after a letter from U.S. Attorney Haag warned of its proximity to a school that had opened years after the dispensary. Lee had renamed the dispensary "Oaksterdam Blue Sky" and moved it to a space directly behind his Oaksterdam University hemp-and-cannabis-prohibition museum, which featured hemp product exhibits and a display of turn-of-the-century cannabis medicine bottles, called "Marijuana before the Drug War."

For more than a year, Lee had been quietly negotiating with the Internal Revenue Service. He had agreed to a payment schedule for additional taxes after the IRS had, under its 280E antidrug trafficking statute, refused deductions for Coffee Shop Blue Sky and audited the books of the university and his other S.K. Seymour enterprises that helped bankroll the Proposition 19 campaign. The IRS was seeking increased payments. Lee thought they were working it out. He asked the federal agents in his apartment if he were under arrest. They told him no. They didn't handcuff him. Lee appreciated that at least "they were pretty nice about it and weren't trashing the place and throwing things around."

But anger erupted on the streets of Oakland as word of the raid got out and federal agents swarmed into Oaksterdam University and the Oaksterdam Blue Sky dispensary. They handcuffed university employees, broke doors, and hauled out instructional marijuana plants—marked with stickers calling for jury nullification in marijuana cases. An angry crowd gathered on Broadway outside the university. Protesters screamed at flak-jacketed federal agents who blocked the entrance to the Princeton of Pot. Agents hauled out a safe containing nearly $100,000—including $90,000 Lee had set aside to pay medical marijuana taxes and licensing fees to the city of Oakland. Finally, the agents stripped bare the Oaksterdam nursery, taking Lee's beloved mother plants used to clone designer cannabis strains.

People in the street screamed, "Shame on you!" "DEA go away!" and "Fuck the DEA!"

Steve DeAngelo delivered a sidewalk message to the media. "What a sad day it is to see American agents going in and raiding a university," he said. "They didn't distribute cannabis at this university. They distributed knowledge." He went on, "It's not a coincidence they went after Richard. They are trying to silence him. . . . The federal government has turned against the lead organizer and fundraiser for Proposition 19, which very nearly legalized cannabis in the state of California. This is not about justice. This is about revenge."

Nate Bradley, a former police officer from the Central Valley town of Wheatland who had joined the Proposition 19 campaign as a spokesman for the group Law Enforcement Against Prohibition, took a loudspeaker to berate the federal officers who stared back through dark sunglasses. "Anyone who is seen here today is an embarrassment to anyone who ever wore the badge," Bradley declared, going hoarse as he repeated the damning word. "This is an embarrassment! You guys are standing here when there are people being kidnapped, when there are crimes to be investigated. And you're standing here threatening somebody for a ground-up herb!"

The Oaksterdam raid soon took on a surreal quality as some media members bailed upon word that Oakland police SWAT teams were responding to a mass shooting elsewhere in Oakland. A gunman had opened fire at a small Christian college, Oikos University, killing seven people and injuring three others. Oakland City Council member Rebecca Kaplan, who showed up at Oaksterdam to deliver a tribute to Richard Lee for his work in promoting a compliant, taxed, and regulated local marijuana industry, wound up decrying gun violence, declaring that it should be the priority for police.

As the federal convoy, including an unmarked truck filled with seized plants and property, prepared to move out, Matthew Witemyre lay in front of it wearing the yellow jacket of the United Food and Commercial Workers. Witemyre had gone to work for the union after quitting his partnership in the joint-rolling and -packaging factory Medi-Cone not long before the company, fearing a federal raid, announced its closure. He lit up a joint and waited to see if the government trucks would run him over. The exiting vehicles easily whipped around and past Witemyre—but not the wheelchair of Mira Ingram, a forty-four-year-old advocate for Americans for Safe Access who used marijuana for nerve damage from diabetes. Ingram angled her chair to cut off the first government truck. When the heavy pickup backed up, she shifted the motorized chair in reverse and then zoomed forward again when it tried to advance. This time it got past her. The rest of the caravan followed.

Richard Lee, who had watched the unfolding raids and street drama on television from his apartment, went to retrieve his mail that afternoon. There was a letter from the civil division of the IRS. It was to confirm a meeting at the end of the month to discuss resolving his tax debt. He read it incredulously. "It was like they were reaching out and shaking your hand with one hand," Lee thought, "and then punching you in the face with the other."

The next morning, at a prescheduled San Francisco rally to protest federal threats against dispensaries in that city, Oaksterdam chancellor Dale Sky Jones took the microphone on the steps of San Francisco City Hall. She offered a tribute to the victims of the mass shooting at Oikos University who died while federal authorities were raiding Oaksterdam. Lee looked on from a distance. He followed in his wheelchair as the procession marched to the San Francisco federal building, as the crowd chanted, "Stop the war on Oakland!" He conceded to reporters that he could be indicted or arrested at any time. Days later, Lee announced he was liquidating his cannabis businesses. He was giving up the Blue Sky dispensary and resigning as president of Oaksterdam University. "Hopefully, our misfortune will end cannabis prohibition sooner," he said. Richard Lee, the celebrated mayor of Oaksterdam, was stepping down.

. . .

Tom Ammiano, the San Francisco state assembly member, went to see his United States Attorney, Melinda Haag, to find out what state legislation to regulate the medical marijuana industry might satisfy the feds and ease the crackdown. He came away frustrated. When asked directly, Haag and the other U.S. Attorneys were not going to guide California lawmakers on how to violate federal marijuana law. Yet Colorado, with its heavily regulated cannabis industry, with state-licensed marijuana workers, with a state medical-cannabis-policing agency and video surveillance of cultivation, transportation, and sales, wasn't drawing anywhere near the heat that California was. John Walsh, Colorado's U.S. Attorney, sent a few dozen letters to dispensaries operating near schools; many merely moved and reopened with neither fear nor recrimination. And in interviews and public remarks, Benjamin Wagner, the Sacramento U.S. Attorney, dropped some heady hints for legislative action. He told the Sacramento Press Club that "what we saw as U.S. Attorneys was an unregulated free-for-all in California."

Marijuana advocates came up with a regulation plan for California that seemed determined to satisfy every movement constituency. The Medical Marijuana Regulation, Control and Taxation Act ballot initiative called for a twenty-one-member commission, under the state Department of Consumer Affairs, to license and govern operators in the California medical marijuana industry. At least fourteen of the commission members were to come from cannabis interests, including two medical marijuana advocates, two cannabis patients, one member "with extensive experience in the scientific or therapeutic research on medical marijuana," one marijuana industry union member, two marijuana policy specialists, and six members experienced in "dispensary operations, infused product manufacturing, cultivation practices or lab testing." Law enforcement lobbyist John Lovell, representing the California police chiefs and narcotics officers associations, gleefully mocked the proposed ballot measure. "To say this board will be regulating marijuana," he scoffed, "is like saying the tobacco industry will form a commission to look at health issues involving cigarette smoking." Backers, including the United Food and Commercial Workers, Americans for Safe Access, and the California chapter of NORML, abandoned the initiative effort after they couldn't get sufficient financial pledges from national drug policy groups or California medical marijuana operators to fund the signature drive to place the measure on the November 2012 ballot.

Regulation fell onto the shoulders of Ammiano, who introduced Assembly Bill 2312. It called for a nine-member oversight commission, still weighted toward cannabis interests, that would impose licensing fees on marijuana businesses to create a medical marijuana policing agency. Under pressure from the California League of Cities, Ammiano dropped language that would have prohibited cities and counties with more than fifty thousand residents from banning marijuana dispensaries without the consent of local voters. The bill, purporting to regulate medical marijuana from seed to sales, included none of Colorado's strict provisions. Ammiano and marijuana advocates wanted the new state medical cannabis commission to set the rules. Anxious Democrats, many from communities that had been overrun with dispensaries, weren't embracing the bill. And Republicans were eager to ridicule it when it reached the assembly floor. "Medical marijuana is a phrase that is meaningless," argued Fresno Republican Linda Halderman. "This is about whether people should be able to legally get high and, as far as that being a public debate, that's where it belongs."

Ammiano held the vote open, trying to rally "ayes" from lawmakers who wandered in and out of the chambers feeling little urgency. "People want to preserve the chaos and confusion to say that medical marijuana has failed or is a sham," he pointedly informed the body. The openly gay lawmaker told of his having "sat by way too many death beds" of AIDS patients whose suffering was alleviated by cannabis. "It is obvious that a great deal of education, particularly in this chamber, is needed," he said. After hours of chasing votes, Ammiano got the minimum—forty-one, all Democrats—for the bill to clear the eighty-member assembly. But three weeks later, he pulled the bill out of committee in the state senate, effectively killing it for the legislative session. In the state that was the first to legalize medical marijuana, that spawned the nation's largest cannabis economy and influenced the politics of pot in states across America, Ammiano couldn't muster enough votes to bring medical marijuana regulation to the senate floor.

On Monday, July 9, 2012, employees at Harborside Health Center in Oakland and its sister dispensary in San Jose arrived to find posted notices. U.S. Attorney Melinda Haag had filed civil lawsuits to seize the dispensaries. Earlier, Haag had pledged to use her office's "limited resources" to target dispensaries near schools, parks, and playgrounds. Even though it was nowhere near such sites, Haag now noted the awesome scale of Harborside in Oakland. "I now find the need to consider actions regarding marijuana superstores such as Harborside," she said in a statement. "The larger the operation, the greater the likelihood that there will be abuse of the state's medical marijuana laws, and marijuana in the hands of individuals who do not have a demonstrated medical need."

Steve DeAngelo, medical cannabis advocates, and city officials packed a news conference inside Oakland City Hall to declare their outrage. "This attack, if it's successful, is going to return many thousands of patients to the illegal market. Street drug sales and law enforcement costs in Oakland are immediately going to rise when $22 million worth of cannabis sales goes back on the streets," DeAngelo protested. "Over three million dollars in tax revenues is going to be destroyed."

Harborside refused to close. On October 20, 2012, the City of Oakland sued Attorney General Eric Holder, Melinda Haag, and the United States Justice Department to stop the forfeiture action. "This property is vital to the safe and affordable distribution of medical cannabis to patients suffering from chronic and acute pain, life threatening and severe illnesses, diseases and injuries," the city declared. "Oakland has a broad public interest in promoting the health, safety and welfare of its citizens, in protecting the regulatory framework it adopted in compliance with the laws of the State of California." Oakland, which years earlier had declared a public health emergency and filed amicus briefs as the Oakland Cannabis Buyers Cooperative brought a medical marijuana case to the U.S. Supreme Court, now embraced a legal crusade for Harborside. Federal law wasn't on the side of the city or its prized dispensary. Yet Steve DeAngelo took to speaking of the Freedom Riders and Rosa Parks and quoting Dr. Martin Luther King's recitation "The arc of the moral universe is long but it bends towards justice." He saw himself in a struggle that could settle "a constitutional crisis between local, state, and federal distribution of power." He insisted the moral universe now bent toward medical cannabis—and the largest marijuana dispensary on the planet. And the City of Oakland had his back.

FOURTEEN

Back to the Garden

Before the explosion of the California medical marijuana market, before the world's largest dispensary in Oakland and the glut of pot stores in Los Angeles, before the medicinal kush rush in the Emerald Triangle and carnival barkers leading passersby to the Medical Kush Doctor in Venice Beach, before 420 Nurses and stripper-staffed pot bars, before Proposition 19 and civic dreams of cannabis industrialization, there was a group of sick and dying people tending to a communal marijuana garden in the Santa Cruz Mountains. After it all, there still was.

The Wo/Men's Alliance for Medical Marijuana, the "socialist organization trying to exist in a capitalist world" of cannabis commerce, continued on as it always had. Long after the September 5, 2002, raid by Drug Enforcement Administration agents on the terraced garden of Mike and Valerie Corral, of wheelchair patients and people with cancer, AIDS, seizures, and searing pain, WAMM members continued raising seedlings before the first full moon in spring, planting before the summer solstice, and reaping and sharing the fall harvest. The raid by federal drug agents and the resulting standoff with medical marijuana patients, who locked the gate to trap the agents' vehicles inside, stirred national compassion for seriously and terminally ill people alleviating their suffering through cannabis. Eight years later, the settlement of WAMM's long legal challenge to the government was sealed after the United States Justice Department promised it wouldn't prosecute patients and caregivers in compliance with state medical marijuana laws. The famous Ogden memo was attached to the settlement in the WAMM case, proof of the government's pledge not to target sick people such as those who had faced heavily armed agents raiding their garden and medicinal and spiritual refuge.

And yet that same government pledge was widely interpreted as the green light for accelerating a lucrative cannabis industry that bloomed in the name of compassionate care for the sick and, in numerous cases, hardly resembled the healing fellowship found at the Wo/Men's Alliance for Medical Marijuana. The feds returned in a calculated fury directed at curtailing the exuberance of the medical marijuana economy and reasserting their authority under the 1970 Controlled Substances Act. They aimed a vast crackdown at commercial cannabis operations in California, at cash-reaping cultivators and retail stores, at overreaching speculators, and, in egregious cases, rogue drug traffickers exploiting the cover of medical marijuana. And yet the federal actions also swept over people seen as models of local compliance, over some of the state's longest established and most respected medical cannabis providers, over icons of marijuana politics and activism.

Through it all, the people of WAMM continued sharing their medicine and distributing it at weekly meetings for free or based on ability to pay. The organization of 200 to 250 people at any given time, the truest of true medical marijuana collectives, continued soothing the sick. With photo tributes blanketing the walls of its downtown Santa Cruz offices, and painted memorial stones and ashes scattered along the crescent ridge above its garden refuge, the community kept on honoring its dead as still more members made their final passages.

Years after the DEA raid of 2002, Don Ivey continued arising in the early morning light two mornings a week to drive to the mountain garden. After stretching his muscles and quieting his shooting paints by sharing a joint with WAMM companions, he scaled the terraces. With his functioning right hand, he plucked away yellowish leaves to promote the plants' vitality, stuffing the excess leaves into his left hand that was permanently balled into a fist. Ivey had seen death "face-to-face" many times, diagnosed with AIDS and hepatitis C years earlier, surviving a stabbing and a scuba diving accident years before that, and later crashing a motorcycle and winding up paralyzed on his left side. He had lived life as a competitive in-line skater, as a carpenter, and now, as a partially disabled pottery maker. He wasn't about to spend his remaining days shopping for heavily marketed designer marijuana strains in California cannabis stores. Ivey found purpose amid the WAMM community and its lush cultivation.

Sometimes, Ivey was joined in the garden by Seth Prettol, who had become a paraplegic after falling from a rope swing near Yosemite. Prettol had just enough use of his hands to grind marijuana leaves for medicinal tinctures, skin creams, and baked goods. Sometimes they were joined by Solbeatriz Posada, a Colombian-born, former local hotel manager who had been HIV-positive for two decades. She was flirty and flip, demanding and contemplative. One moment, she was heaping good-natured abuse on her fellow gardeners, the next she was quoting the Dalai Lama.

Mike Corral, who had founded WAMM with Valerie after discovering that cannabis alleviated her wrenching seizures, came away deeply affected by his encounter with DEA agents. Well afterward, Corral was at a beach resort in Mexico, eating prawns and sipping beer when the ocean before him seemed to disappear. "All of a sudden, I'm in the raid," he recalled. "I'm not in Mexico anymore. I'm handcuffed. I've got guns at my head." He sought counseling for posttraumatic stress, and continued.

After a federal judge's protective order barring government raids on the collective expired in 2005, the WAMM garden lay barren until the community's fear of another incursion subsided. During that time, Mike Corral offered guidance to a handful of members who cultivated at home to produce medicine for the group. Eventually, as WAMM's legal challenge advanced, Corral returned to oversee the replanted garden, joining with ill and physically challenged medical-marijuana patients who worked its terraced rows in a harmony of healing.

Suzanne Pfeil, the polio patient who was rousted from her bed by federal agents, and who later alerted WAMM members and the media about the raid, afterward went to Washington for Senate confirmation hearings for then-new DEA administrator Karen Tandy. She chased Tandy down in the hallway in a motorized wheelchair bearing a sticker, "Stop Raids on Medical Marijuana Patients," and presented a letter calling for an end to federal targeting of medical marijuana collectives such as WAMM. The DEA administrator accepted it and winked at her. Pfeil interpreted the wink as saying, "You got me—but I can get you."

Valerie Corral, brushing off the title "the Mother Teresa of medical marijuana" that others bestowed on her, came away from the DEA raid convinced she had made a lasting impression on the supervising officer and, ultimately, the U.S. Justice Department about the uniqueness of the WAMM garden they were destroying and the environment of compassion they were invading. She didn't believe there were "too many people who have gone face-to-face with the DEA," who sued the government and were "still growing pot, giving it away, and embracing people in a very intimate time" of illness and approaching death. In 2013, Valerie and Mike divorced after twenty-five years of marriage and two decades of running WAMM. Valerie stayed on. Mike left the stewardship of the garden to others.

Agent Patrick Kelly, who led the DEA operation at the medicinal sanctuary, believed then and afterward that the raid was both appropriate under federal law and professionally carried out. He remained surprised "at the amount of media attention it garnered," having never fathomed "it was going to be as politicized as it ended up becoming." By 2011, Kelly would be targeting something altogether different—a Southern California dispensary chain with an industrial-scale grow room and operators pulling out more than $3 million in bank withdrawals in a matter of months. Despite his insistence in 2002 that he wouldn't remember, he forgot neither WAMM nor, especially, Valerie Corral.

From the depths of the San Francisco AIDS epidemic, which inspired passage of Proposition 215 and breakthrough state-funded clinical research into the therapeutic benefits of cannabis, California created a massive medical marijuana market that operated largely without rules. Despite public acceptance of marijuana as medicine, the splintered California cannabis movement, along with state lawmakers unwilling or unable to reconcile with pot, stumbled in trying to enact a plan for oversight and distribution, leaving it to Colorado to sanction America's first regulated marijuana industry. California inspired nineteen other states and the District of Columbia to legalize marijuana for medical use. In November 2012, two of those states, Colorado and Washington, passed voter initiatives to legalize marijuana purely as an adult recreational pleasure, raising landmark new challenges to federal marijuana prohibition.

Richard Lee, the father of Proposition 19 and now the retired "mayor of Oaksterdam," took satisfaction in tracking the Colorado and Washington votes on his smartphone in the cannabis-scented student union of his former school of pot, Oaksterdam University, where he now served as professor emeritus for cannabis politics. Lee, whose personal "suicide mission" was to make it through each year without being jailed for marijuana, had survived another year with neither arrest nor charges in the raids on Oaksterdam University and his cannabis enterprises. He still faced continued tax demands from the Internal Revenue Service. Yet the man who drew worldwide attention for Proposition 19 and nearly pulled it off felt rejuvenated by the legalization votes his initiative had birthed elsewhere. He romanticized about coming out of retirement.

Lee's Proposition 19 coproponent, Jeff Jones, deeply disappointed by the initiative's defeat, would much later celebrate over how the campaign forced

Governor Arnold Schwarzenegger's hand in signing a critical marijuana decriminalization bill. As a result of the legislation, Senate Bill 1449, misdemeanor marijuana arrests in California fell from 54,849 in 2010 to 7,764 in 2011, even as the feds began targeting the medical marijuana industry.

Proposition 19 had a ripple effect. Backers of two victorious marijuana legalization measures, Colorado's Amendment 64 and Washington State's Initiative Measure 502, meticulously studied and built upon the California initiative. Noting the rift that Proposition 19 created in California's medical marijuana community, Colorado advocates wrote in specific protections for medical cannabis patients and dispensaries in their measure that legalized possession and cultivation of marijuana for recreational use and directed the state to regulate retail sales of pot for pleasure. In the Washington initiative, calling for the state liquor control board to tax and regulate recreational marijuana for adults over twenty-one, advocates addressed Proposition 19 opponents' warnings of stoned drivers. Washington's legalization measure created America's first state standard—a blood measure of pot's psychoactive property, THC—for driving while high.

In 2010, retired heads of the federal Drug Enforcement Administration had urgently written Attorney General Eric Holder, imploring him to stand against Proposition 19 in California. Then, Holder famously declared he would "vigorously enforce" federal law in California if voters passed the initiative. But two years later, the attorney general stayed silent after the retired DEA administrators implored him to speak out on Colorado and Washington State. Notably, Colorado was a swing state in the 2012 presidential election. President Barack Obama won the state with 51 percent of the vote. Legal pot won with 55 percent—the same margin as in Washington State. In April 2013, for the first time in polling history, a Pew Research Poll said a majority of Americans—a 52 to 45 percent margin—supported legalization of marijuana. Sixty percent of respondents said the federal government shouldn't enforce federal marijuana law in states that legalized pot for medical or recreational use. Yet that same month, the White House Office of National Drug Control Policy signaled it wasn't standing down on marijuana and enforcement of the Controlled Substances Act. "No state, no executive, can nullify a statute that's been passed by Congress," announced director R. Gil Kerlikowske in a Washington, D.C., address.

In early 2013, California marijuana advocates gathered in a cavernous hall at Fort Mason in San Francisco. They invited representatives from the Washington and Colorado campaigns for inspiration as state and national drug policy groups announced plans to fund a new California legalization measure in 2016, the next presidential election cycle. As the crowd celebrated the Colorado and Washington results, Richard Lee, the former concert roadie that many in the movement had once tried to dismiss, was given a Pioneer of Marijuana Reform award and a standing ovation. With federal actions continuing against California cannabis businesses, state legislators remained skittish about regulating the existing medical marijuana industry. Two more bills to license and oversee California medicinal cannabis businesses would fail in mid-2013 in the face of intense law-enforcement opposition. And yet Assemblyman Tom Ammiano of San Francisco announced at the Fort Mason gathering that he fully planned to introduce implementation legislation to support a 2016 legalization initiative for recreational use. "I do believe Richard Lee is a hero of all heroes," the lawmaker proclaimed to the crowd. "He really put himself out there. There is hope. Yes we cannabis."

During the federal crackdown, Stephen Gasparas, the cannabis seeker from suburban Chicago whose marijuana journeys led him to a wonderland of weed in the Emerald Triangle, closed his Arcata marijuana dispensary after a bitter permitting battle with the city and a property forfeiture letter from the U.S. Attorney. Gasparas, who had once trekked to marijuana fields in the Himalayas of India, bought an Indian restaurant in the town of Eureka. He moved on from selling kushes to serving curries.

In nearby Mendocino County, the board of supervisors sued to block a sweeping 2012 federal subpoena demanding county records on every marijuana farmer who had participated in Mendocino's unprecedented licensing program, in which the sheriff affixed zip ties on plants to certify local medicinal growers. In a 2013 settlement with the government, the county agreed to give the feds paperwork on fees it collected before canceling the program—but not a word on identities of local pot growers who participated.

Dr. Donald Abrams, the San Francisco AIDS and cancer doctor who battled government agencies to win approval for clinical research that showed that cannabis didn't interfere with protease inhibitor drugs and—by the way—also boosted the weight of people with AIDS and HIV, continued submitting new research protocols for federal approval. The process and politics of approving and funding medical marijuana research remained frustrating. "As I've said for almost twenty years now, I don't think science drives the train here," Abrams reflected.

California researchers, in unprecedented state clinical trials, demonstrated measurable benefits from cannabis. They didn't call it a "miracle drug" or "God's medicine" but concluded it was a promising medical treatment that indeed had therapeutic value and merited more study. Armed with the California findings, Americans for Safe Access sued the Drug Enforcement Administration over marijuana's forty-two-year-long classification as a Schedule I drug with no accepted medical use.

On January 22, 2013, the United States Court of Appeals for the District of Columbia Circuit in Washington, D.C., sided with the DEA. "There is serious debate in the United States over the efficacy of marijuana for medical uses," wrote senior circuit judge Harry T. Edwards, ruling for the DEA in the court's majority opinion. He said "substantial evidence" supported the government claim that studies affirming accepted medical use of marijuana "do not exist." Following the California clinical studies involving more than three hundred research subjects, the government didn't sanction larger, comprehensive Food and Drug Administration–approved trials on marijuana that could have led to the drug's consideration as a prescription medication and rescheduling under federal law. Thus, to the D.C. circuit court, it was as if the California clinical trials never happened.

Despite federal actions against cannabis dispensaries, California marijuana doctors continued writing many thousands of recommendations for people wanting medicinal relief and safe passage to legal marijuana.

Dr. David Allen, the Mississippi cardiothoracic surgeon who became a medical marijuana physician in California only to be brought back to his home state, locked up for fourteen months, and put on trial over a small amount of pot, became a fixture at pro-cannabis events. He stood with Steve DeAngelo at Oakland City Hall, decrying the government's effort to seize the Harborside Health Center and endorsing the continuing legal challenges to save America's most famous dispensary. As the fight for Harborside stretched on, with DeAngelo and the city of Oakland refusing to submit to federal authority, Dr. Allen donned his surgeon's coat at the federal building in Sacramento to condemn a DEA raid on another cannabis store in California's capital. "I'm a better surgeon than I am a public speaker," Allen said in an uncertain drawl. "And I'm stepping out of my comfort zone because I need to stop this war." The heart-doc-turned-pot-doc then declared his evolution into "a cannabis activist until I die."

Dragonfly de la Luz, the ganja princess celebrating cannabis culture and pot pleasures in her "Getting High with Dragonfly" weed reviews, penned an article on a medicinal strain, Harlequin, bred for elevated cannabidiol (CBD), a therapeutic marijuana constituent that doesn't get you stoned. She hailed the "functional high" and the "musky, sweet, sugar loaf pineapple taste" of "one of the most alluring strains to hit the market." She touted its medical applications with a disclaimer: "I'm not a doctor. I'm a stoner."

After a referendum drive by cannabis advocates caused Los Angeles City Council members to junk their attempted ban on marijuana dispensaries in 2012, Yamileth Bolanos kept raging for a sensible solution permitting medical marijuana providers. Quadriplegic marijuana patient Carlos Kruschewsky continued his visits to her dispensary. He kept up his samba dancing, using his chin to spin his motorized wheelchair to the music. She promised him, "I'm going to take care of you as long as I'm alive." In May 2013, with an estimated 850 dispensaries in the city, Los Angeles voters overwhelmingly approved a ballot measure allowing Yami's Pure Life Alternative Wellness Center and about 130 other medical marijuana establishments in business by 2007 to continue operating. Voters rejected a rival measure that would have permitted unlimited marijuana stores. After L.A.'s elected officials failed in 2007, 2010, and 2012 to rein in and regulate the city's wild dispensary market, voters seemingly took it upon themselves to bring sanity to the L.A. excess.

The California Supreme Court in 2013 upheld the rights of cities and counties to ban marijuana dispensaries under local nuisance laws. But tough-on-pot local politicians didn't fare well. Carmen Trutanich, Los Angeles' pugnacious city attorney in the city's cannabis club battles, finished third in a 2012 primary for district attorney, then was voted out of his city attorney job a year later. Bonnie Dumanis, the district attorney who prosecuted San Diego's Operation Green Rx campaign against medical marijuana businesses, lost in the primary election for mayor of San Diego as former marijuana defendant Eugene Davidovich and his local chapter of Americans for Safe Access waged a social media campaign against her.

San Diego ASA members went on to perpetrate a hoax on the local U.S. Attorney, Laura Duffy, creating a press release on her letterhead warning of federal forfeiture actions against pharmacies doling out prescription drugs in "a pervasive for-profit industry" in a spoof of the feds' medical marijuana crackdown. Some news outlets picked up on the phony story. Duffy, not amused, issued a clarification.

Davidovich, whose self-generated media campaign had courted compassion over his prosecution for distributing medical marijuana, put out a press release on October 24, 2012, announcing the reversal of the conviction of Jovan Jackson, a fellow sailor and dispensary operator also targeted in Operation Green Rx. In his second trial, California's Fourth Appellate District Court of

Appeal ruled Jackson was improperly denied a medical marijuana defense under California law. The court also rejected the trial judge's ruling that California law required patient members of dispensaries or collectives to directly participate in growing marijuana. They all didn't have to be like WAMM. Still, determined San Diego prosecutors brought a third trial, convicting Jackson on three marijuana felonies in November 2013.

Years after refusing a plea deal in their long-running medical marijuana saga, Dr. Mollie Fry and her husband, Dale Schafer, completed their second of five years in federal prison in July 2013 at California correctional institutions in Dublin and Taft, respectively. Their son, Geoffrey Schafer, just fourteen when he was detained at gunpoint as authorities raided the cannabis-providing doctor and lawyer in 2001, became the family spokesman. He portrayed his parents as people who were motivated by caring and who were not the drug dealers the government depicted. Geoffrey also went to work at the Christian-run Canna Care dispensary in Sacramento, where a large poster bearing his parents' photos called for their freedom with the slogan "Wanted by the Federal Government to serve five years for providing compassionate relief to the sick and dying."

Benjamin Wagner, the United States Attorney in Sacramento who informed Justice Department superiors in Washington, D.C., that federal law was being flouted by the commercial cannabis industry in California, insisted there was "not a command from Washington" to "slay the marijuana enterprises." Despite the cannabis movement's portrayal of a calculated federal assault on medical marijuana providers and patients, Wagner contended it was U.S. Attorneys in the state who initiated the enforcement actions to make a stand—and a statement—against a profiteering industry "surprising in its scale and audacity." Wagner hoped there would be fewer marijuana cases in coming years. As long as federal marijuana law remained unchanged, he suggested, the feds were likely to bring some future actions "just to remind people it's still against the law; yes, we're still here; and yes, we're still enforcing it." Yet he saw no federal interest in raiding sick people and their gardens.

On August 29, 2013, the United States Justice Department offered nuanced—yet potentially historic—terms of concession. Responding to votes legalizing marijuana beyond medical use in Colorado and Washington State, a directive was sent out to U.S. Attorneys. In the new memo, Deputy Attorney General James Cole suggested the feds wouldn't intervene in states legalizing pot—either for medicinal or pleasurable pursuits—if the states enacted "robust controls" regulating marijuana sales and distribution. National associations for narcotics officers, police chiefs, and sheriffs sent

Attorney General Holder a furious protest letter, assailing the Justice Department for offering "an open invitation to other states to legalize marijuana in defiance of federal law."

The feds weren't surrendering on pot. The Cole memo directed U.S. Attorneys to target operations using the cover of state laws to traffic marijuana into illicit markets, to minors, or into states where cannabis use remained illegal. Yet, emboldened by the new federal memo, Ammiano and supportive lawmakers rushed forth still another marijuana bill in the closing days of the 2013 California legislative session. Their Senate Bill 604 stood to enact sweeping regulations by placing the Golden State's teeming marijuana industry under the authority of the California Department of Alcoholic Beverage Control and mandating state licensing and oversight of all medical cannabis cultivation, transportation, and sales. But the effort was shelved for another year.

So eleven years after DEA agents surged past the "Love Grows Here" sign to take chain saws to the garden of the Wo/Men's Alliance for Medical Marijuana, federal enforcement actions went on and the politics of pot remained unsettled. Yet this haven in the mountains above Santa Cruz had endured.

After the feds' raid on WAMM, Hal Margolin, the only member to get inside to personally witness the destruction of the garden, suffered a second heart attack and became ill with leukemia. The retired Santa Cruz clothing manufacturer, once wary about associating with "a bunch of potheads," found his life lifted in WAMM. He told Marcia, his wife of fifty-eight years, that he was proud to have been a plaintiff in the lawsuit challenging the government's authority to target the community again.

After the raid, Margolin was given marijuana seedlings to grow at home. The first year that he brought his harvest to Mike Corral, the WAMM master gardener gently told him not to bother. Corral assured him the community would take care of providing for him. But Margolin had served in Korea. He wasn't going to be defeated by a plant. After the raid depleted WAMM's medicinal reserves, Margolin had learned to regulate his marijuana doses. He found he could alleviate his pain from back surgery with less. He came to enjoy not feeling stoned. And he kept growing, determined to get it right. He talked to his plants, every day. By his second year, he boasted, his homegrown cannabis was "pretty damn good." By the third year, he brought his bounty to share. He was affirmed. Fellow patients said it was the best homegrown medicine in the collective.

Margolin joined Valerie Corral in developing the group's Design for Dying hospice program. It was there for him when his time came. With his wife at his side and an around-the-clock vigil of WAMM members supporting him in his passage, he died in 2011 at seventy-eight. "Even as illness ravaged his body," Valerie Corral said in his eulogy, "as his mobility became more compromised, Hal explored his mind with grace and agility and always with humor."

The Wo/Men's Alliance for Medical Marijuana lived on, unchanged amid tectonic events that triggered unimagined marijuana commerce, stirred a new social dynamic for pot, riled the United States Justice Department, and spurred voter support of broader legalization and new challenges to federal authority. For many years after the siege of September 5, 2002, ended, when he cut the locked chain off the gate to enable the convoy of DEA agents and their U-Haul of seized marijuana to pass, Danny Rodrigues would return to the road traveled by the government vehicles. The former San Francisco barkeep, the AIDS patient who also survived quadruple-bypass heart surgery, would whack away the weeds by the gate and sweep the route up to the garden. Only when his work was done would he take time to medicate there, to rest and reflect on his life and on fellow WAMM members who had passed away. He would think about "my most important things—my friends and my loved ones." He often concluded: "My gosh, we don't have much time left on this earth."

A dramatic arc of history in California inalterably changed the marijuana landscape in the state, and in America. A multigenerational social, political, and legal clash over marijuana prohibition, over marijuana medicine, over pot culture and cannabis capitalism was moving on to its new, uncharted phase. Yet in the marijuana garden of the Wo/Men's Alliance for Medical Marijuana, Rodrigues and his fellow members found far more personal matters to contemplate.

ACKNOWLEDGMENTS

I thank the more than fifty individuals, from diverse stations along the fault lines of America's marijuana epicenter, who were interviewed for this book, many of whom tirelessly shared their time to help make it a reality. I also acknowledge the editors of *The Sacramento Bee,* who recognized that an unfolding phenomenon in California and beyond merited an unusual news assignment: the marijuana reporter. I would like to recognize the scores of people encountered during that coverage, including many whose accounts are told, and cited, in this book. I especially thank Kim Robinson, the social science publisher and regional editor at University of California Press, who saw the potential of this project and—with a talented editing and production team—guided it to fruition. I thank literary agent Jeff Gerecke for shepherding the *Weed Land* proposal and finding this home for the book. I additionally thank my wife, journalist Cynthia Halleen Craft, and my colleagues and friends, who supported and encouraged this journey.

NOTES

1. THE WAY IT WAS SUPPOSED TO BE

Corral, Mike. Interviews by author. 2010, 2012.

Corral, Valerie. Interviews by author. 2010, 2012.

County of Santa Cruz et al. v. Eric Holder, Jr. Joint Stipulation of Dismissal without Prejudice. U.S. District Court. No. 503-CV-0182-JF. January 21, 2010, WAMM website, www.wamm.org/legal/scvholderstipulation.pdf.

Hecht, Peter. "Harvest of Compassion: Collective True to Its Roots as Pot Trade Booms." *Sacramento Bee,* September 19, 2010.

Kelly, Patrick. Interview by author. 2012.

Leff, Arnold. Interview by author. 2010.

Margolin, Harold. Interview by author. 2010.

Mintz, Howard. "Medicinal Pot Wins Round: Judge Allows Marijuana Growing for Sick and Dying." *San Jose Mercury News,* April 22, 2004.

Ogden, David W. "Memorandum for Selected United States Attorneys." *The Justice Blog.* U.S. Department of Justice, October 19, 2009. http://blogs.justice.gov /main/archives/192.

Pfeil, Suzanne. Interview by author. 2012.

Ritter, John. "Pot Raid Angers State, Patients." *USA Today,* September, 16, 2002.

Rodrigues, Danny. Interview by author. 2010.

Senate Bill 420, introduced by Senator John Vasconcellos, February 20, 2003, and signed into law by Governor Gray Davis, October 12, 2003, Legislative Counsel, State of California, website, www.leginfo.ca.gov/pub/03–04/bill/sen/sb_0401– 0450/sb_420_bill_20031012_chaptered.html.

U.S. Department of Justice. "Attorney General Announces Formal Medical Marijuana Guidelines" (press release). October 19, 2009, www.justice.gov/opa /pr/2009/October/09-ag-1119.html.

Vasconcellos, John. Interview by author. 2010.

Waiting to Inhale. Jed Riffe Film + Electronic Media, Berkeley, CA. Documentary, 2005, www.waitingtoinhale.org/jed.htm.

Bobb, Robert C., Oakland city manager, letter to Jeff Jones designating Oakland Cannabis Buyers Cooperative as administrator of the city's medical cannabis distribution program. Patient ID Center website. August 11, 1998, www.rxcbc.org/legal/Legal/US_District_Court/2002–03–08_25_Oakland_Designates_Dispensary.pdf.

Bock, Alan. *Waiting to Inhale: The Politics of Medical Marijuana.* Santa Ana, CA: Seven Locks Press, 2000.

DeAngelo, Steve. Interviews by author. 2010, 2011, 2012.

"Findings of Fact, Conclusions of Law and Decision of Administrative Law Judge." Drug Enforcement Administration, Marijuana Rescheduling Petition. Docket No. 86–22, Francis L. Young, September 6, 1988, www.ukcia.org/pollaw/lawlibrary/young.php.

Hecht, Peter. "Bay Pot Center Is Touted as Model, Bigger Is Better, Advocate Says." *Sacramento Bee,* April 14, 2010.

———. "Dispensary's Growers Develop Pot Strain That's Not for Stoners." *Sacramento Bee, Weed Wars* blog, April 14, 2010.

———. "Man behind Pot Initiative Is a Force in 'Oaksterdam.'" *Sacramento Bee,* May 4, 2010.

———. "Oakland Tax Stokes Push for Pot Levies." *Sacramento Bee,* August 2, 2009.

———. "Pot Lab Weeds Out Bad Batches." *Sacramento Bee,* April 5, 2010.

———. "World's Largest Dispensary Offers Bonus for Marijuana Activism." *Sacramento Bee, Weed Wars* blog, April 7, 2010.

Herer, Jack. *The Emperor Wears No Clothes.* Van Nuys, CA: AH HA Publishing, 2007.

Jones, Jeff. Interviews by author. 2011, 2012.

Lee, Richard. Interviews by author. 2009, 2010, 2011, 2012.

Measure F, Ordinance Amending the City of Oakland's Business Tax to Establish a New Tax Rate for "Cannabis Businesses." 2009, http://smartvoter.org/2009/07/21/ca/alm/meas/F/.

Measure Z, Oakland Cannabis Regulation and Revenue Ordinance. 2004, http://smartvoter.org/2004/11/02/ca/alm/meas/Z/.

Oakland City Council Resolution No. 74618, declaring public health emergency with respect to safe and affordable access to medical cannabis. October 27, 1998. A summary of this resolution can be found at http://clerkwebsvr1.oaklandnet.com/attachments/10571.pdf.

Oakland City Council Resolution No. 79258, renewing the city council's declaration of a local public health emergency. July 7, 2005, http://clerkwebsvr1.oaklandnet.com/attachments/10571.pdf.

Peron, Dennis. Interview by author. 2012.

United States v. Oakland Cannabis Buyers' Cooperative. Appeal from the U.S. District Court for Northern California, U.S. Court of Appeals for the Ninth Circuit. Opinion. September 13, 1999, https://bulk.resource.org/courts.gov/c/F3/190/190.F3d.1109.98–17137.98–17044.98–16950.html.

United States v. Oakland Cannabis Buyers' Cooperative. U.S. Supreme Court. No. 00–151. Argued March 28, 2001; decided May 14, 2001, http://caselaw.lp.findlaw. com/cgi-bin/getcase.pl?court=US&navby=case&vol=000&invol=00–151.

Walker, Thaai. "Oakland Deputizes Pot Club." *San Francisco Chronicle,* August 14, 1998.

Walsh, Denny. "Medical Pot Use Backer Gets Jail." *Sacramento Bee,* February 28, 2003.

———. "Plea Cuts Prison Term for Medical Pot Seller Brian Epis." *Sacramento Bee,* July 25, 2012.

———. "Pot Activist's Prison Term Is Thrown Out." *Sacramento Bee,* March 4, 2003.

3. KUSH RUSH

Allman, Tom. Interview by author. 2012.

Blake, Tim. Interview by author. 2010.

Brown, Ben. "6772 Plants and 800 Lbs. Pot Seized." *Ukiah Daily Journal,* July 18, 2008.

Budwig, Jennifer. "Business Sense: The Impact of Potential Legalization of Marijuana on the Humboldt Economy, Part I: Estimating the Size of the Underground Economy." *Eureka Times-Standard,* December 4, 2011.

———. "Business Sense: The Impact of Potential Legalization of Marijuana on the Humboldt Economy, Part II: When and How It Is Legalized Will Have Short- and Long-Term Implications." *Eureka Times-Standard,* December 11, 2011.

Burger, Joey. Interview by author. 2010.

Cohen, Matt. Interview by author. 2011.

Du Bois, Lelehnia. Interviews by author. 2010, 2012.

Gallegos, Paul. Interview by author. 2010.

Gasparas, Stephen. Interviews by author. 2009, 2010, 2012.

Gravois, John. "The Closing of the Marijuana Frontier." *Washington Monthly,* November–December 2010.

Greenson, Thadeus. "Garberville Developer Sentenced to Six Years for Pot Operation." *Eureka Times-Standard,* October 31, 2009.

———. "Humboldt's $400 Million Question; Banking Thesis Quantifies Impact of Pot on Local Economy." *Eureka Times-Standard,* December 4, 2011.

———. "Pot Lobbying Group to Host Gallegos Fundraiser; Sacramento Soiree for DA Charges $250 a Plate and More." *Eureka Times-Standard,* June 27, 2011.

Hecht, Peter. "Accidental Pot Grower Ponders the Future in Humboldt County." *Sacramento Bee, Weed Wars* blog, November 29, 2010.

———. "Best of Pot Winners Proud but Shy at Mendocino's Emerald Cup." *Sacramento Bee, Weed Wars* blog, December 16, 2010.

———. "Feds' Raid Had Mendocino Riled, Local Pact with Growers Called Real Target." *Sacramento Bee,* October 30, 2011.

———. "Humboldt's Growth Industry, Lax Laws Stoke Some, Irk Others." *Sacramento Bee,* December 14, 2009.

———. "Identity Crisis in the Land of Weed, Boom in Medical Pot Fuels Bid to Go Legit." *Sacramento Bee,* November 28, 2010.

———. "Mendocino County—Pot Initiative Challenges Long-Standing Way of Life." *Sacramento Bee,* April 25, 2010.

———. "Mendocino's Area 101 Strives to Be the 'Learning Center' of Pot." *Sacramento Bee, Weed Wars* blog, April 26, 2010.

———. "Mexican Growers Boldly Operate in California." *Sacramento Bee,* September 20, 2009.

Humboldt County District Attorney's Health and Safety Code §§11357–11360, Prosecution Guidelines. County of Humboldt, Office of the District Attorney.

Humboldt State University. "Schatz Lab Finds Indoor Grows Use Huge Amounts of Power" (press release). November 13, 2011.

Medical Marijuana: Cultivation and Dispensing. City of Arcata Code 9.42.105. City of Arcata.

Medical Marijuana Cultivation Regulation. Mendocino County Code, chapter 9.31. County of Mendocino.

"The Pot Republic, Inside the Country's Oldest, Largest and Most Wide-Open Marijuana Market." *Frontline,* PBS, 2011. Documentary, www.pbs.org/wgbh /pages/frontline/the-pot-republic/.

Turner, Tony. Interview by author. 2009.

United States v. David Winkle. Criminal complaint. U.S. District Court for the Western District of New York. No. 6:11-MJ-04085-MWP. August 26, 2011.

U.S. Attorney's Office, Northern District of California. "Garberville Resident Sentenced to Six Years in Prison for Marijuana Cultivating Operation" (press release). October 30, 2009.

———. "Humboldt County Marijuana Grower Indicted for Murder" (press release). March 1, 2010.

Williams, Linda. "Nearly One-Third of Mendocino County Economy Is Underground." *Ukiah Daily Journal,* April 14, 2012.

4. REEFER RESEARCH

Abrams, Donald I. Interviews by author. 2010, 2012.

———. "Medical Marijuana: Tribulations and Trials." *Journal of Psychoactive Drugs* 30, no. 2 (April–June 1998): 163–69.

Abrams, Donald, et al. "Antihyperlipidemic Effects of *Pleurotus ostreatus* (Oyster Mushrooms) in H.I.V.-Infected Individuals Taking Antiretroviral Therapy." *BMC Complementary and Alternative Medicine* 11, no. 60 (2011): 258–67.

———. "Cannabinoid-Opioid Interaction in Chronic Pain." *Clinical Pharmacology and Therapeutics* 90, no. 6 (December, 2011): 844–51.

———. "Cannabis in Painful HIV-Associated Sensory Neuropathy." *Neurology* 68 (February 13, 2007).

———. "Short-Term Effects of Cannabinoids in Patients with HIV-1 Infection." *Annals of Internal Medicine* 139, no. 4 (August 19, 2003): 515–21.

Center for Medicinal Cannabis Research. *Report to the Legislature and Governor of the State of California.* San Diego: University of California, San Diego, Health Sciences, February 11, 2010, www.cmcr.ucsd.edu/images/pdfs/CMCR_REPORT_FEB17.pdf.

Corey-Bloom, Jody, et al. "Smoked Cannabis for Spasticity in Multiple Sclerosis: A Randomized, Placebo-Controlled Trial." *Canadian Medical Association Journal* 184, no. 10 (July 10, 2012): 1143–50.

DeRienzo, Paul. "Dennis Peron: The Marijuana Mouse That Roared." *High Times,* August 1998.

"Despite Marijuana Furor, 8 Users Get Drug from the Government." *New York Times,* December 1, 1996.

Doblin, Rick. Interview by author. 2012.

Doheny, Kathleen. "Pot Might Help Ease Multiple Sclerosis Symptoms." *Health-Day,* May 14, 2012, http://consumer.healthday.com/printer.asp?AID=664706.

Ellis, Ron. Interview by author. 2012.

Ellis, Ronald, et al. "Smoked Medicinal Cannabis for Neuropathic Pain in HIV: A Randomized, Crossover Clinical Trial." *Neuropsychopharmacology* 34 (2009): 672–80, published online August 6, 2008.

Grant, Igor. Interview by author. 2012.

Grant, Igor, and B. Rael Cahn. "Cannabis and Endocannabinoid Modulators: Therapeutic Promises and Challenges." *Clinical Neuroscience Research* (September 19, 2008): 185–99.

Hatfield, Larry D. "Mary Rathbun—Brownie Mary." *San Francisco Examiner,* April 12, 1999, www.sfgate.com/news/article/Mary-Rathbun-Brownie-Mary-3088870.php.*.

Hecht, Peter. "California Pot Research Backs Therapeutic Claims." *Sacramento Bee,* July 21, 2012.

———. "Research Offers Contrasting Views of Marijuana." *Sacramento Bee,* May 16, 2010.

———. "Study: Pot Can Be Pain Reliever." *Sacramento Bee,* February 18, 2010.

Larson, Troy. Interview by author. 2012.

"Marijuana Abuse." National Institute on Drug Abuse research report series, National Institute on Drug Abuse website, 2010, http://drugabuse.gov/publications/research-reports/marijuana-abuse.

Marine, Craig. "The Good Doctor: He's Been in on the AIDS Battle since the Beginning, but It's the Feds Donald Abrams Fights When It Comes to Scoring Marijuana." *San Francisco Chronicle Magazine,* April 12, 2001.

Miller, Talea. "Essay: Treating the Earliest Cases of AIDS." *PBS NewsHour,* June 6, 2011, www.pbs.org/newshour/updates/health/jan-june11/volberding_06–06.html.

Murphy, Gene. Interview by author. 2012.

Russo, Ethan, et al. "Chronic Cannabis Use in the Compassionate Investigational New Drug Program: An Examination of Benefits and Adverse Effects of Legal Clinical Cannabis." *Journal of Cannabis Therapeutics* 2, no. 1 (2002): 3–57.

Vasconcellos, John. Interview by author. 2012.

Wallace, Mark. Interview by author. 2012.

Wallace, Mark, et al. "Dose-Dependent Effects of Smoked Cannabis on Capsaicin-Induced Pain and Hyperalgesia in Healthy Volunteers," *Anesthesiology* 107, no. 5 (November 2007): 785–96.

Werner, Clint. *Marijuana Gateway to Health.* San Francisco: Dachstar Press, 2011.

Wilsey, Barth. Interviews by author. 2010, 2012.

Wilsey, Barth, et al. "A Randomized Placebo-Controlled, Crossover Trial of Cannabis Cigarettes in Neuropathic Pain." *Journal of Pain* 9, no. 6 (June 2008): 506–21.

Woo, Elaine. "'Brownie Mary' Rathbun Dies; Advocated Medical Marijuana." *Los Angeles Times,* April 13, 1999.

5. THE POT DOCS

Allen, David. Interviews by author. 2009, 2012.

Conant, Marcus. Interview by author. 2012.

Conant HIV AIDS v. Walters DEA. U.S. Court of Appeals for the Ninth Circuit. No. 11–17222. Argued and submitted April 8, 2002. Filed October 29, 2002, www.erowid.org/plants/cannabis/cannabis_medical_9thcircuit_firstamendment_nov2002.pdf.

Conant v. McCaffrey. Class Action Complaint for Declaratory and Injunctive Relief. U.S. District Court of Northern California. No. C-97–00139-WHA. January 14, 1997.

Conant v. McCaffrey. Ruling, U.S. District Judge William Alsup. September 7, 2000, www.aclu.org/FilesPDFs/conant_courtdecision.pdf.

Dr. Tod: The Story of Dr. Tod Mikuriya and the Medical Marijuana Movement. LG5 Films, Spring 2011. Online documentary excerpts, http://DrTod.com/movie.html.

Fox, Margalit. "Tod H. Mikuriya, 73, Dies; Backed Medical Marijuana." *New York Times,* May 29, 2007.

Fry, Marion P. Interview by author. 2011.

Gardner, Fred. "Doctor of Last Resort." *Counterpunch,* May 24, 2007.

Havens, April M. "This Long Nightmare Is Over." *Mississippi Press,* January 11, 2012.

Hecht, Peter. "Judge Sending Medical Pot User to Jail." *Sacramento Bee,* April 9, 2010.

———. "Patients Flock to Doctors Practicing Pot Medicine." *Sacramento Bee,* November 8, 2009.

———. "Pot of Gold: As Medical Marijuana Dispensaries Proliferate, Some Argue the State Should Get a Cut of the Action." *Sacramento Bee,* January 1, 2010.

———. "Sacramento Pot Physician in Deep Legal Weeds in Mississippi." *Sacramento Bee, Weed Wars* blog, March 19, 2010.

Hopkins, Milan. Interview by author. 2012.

"How to Get a Medical Marijuana Recommendation." Hash Bar TV, March 23, 2011, http://hashbar.tv/2011/03/23.

Lucas, Reed. "Boardwalk Hempire: The Rise and Fall of the Medical Beach Kush Club." PRNewswire, April 13, 2012, www.prnewswire.com/news-releases /tommy-chong-rob-van-dam-seek-to-free-kush-with-new-documentary.

Lucido, Frank. Interviews by author. 2009, 2012.

Lucido, Frank H., with Mariavittoria Mangini. "Implementation of the Compassionate Use Act in a Family Medical Practice." *O'Shaughnessy's Journal of the California Cannabis Research Group* (Spring 2004).

Lyman, Donald. Interview by author. 2012.

Medical Board of California. Accusation against Marion Fry, MD, November 4, 2004. Medical Board of California, Central File Room, Sacramento.

———. Accusation against Milan L. Hopkins, MD, March 30, 2010. Medical Board of California, www2.mbc.ca.gov/LicenseLookupSystem/PhysicianSurgeon/ document.aspx?path=\DIDOCS\20120329\DMRAAADE42\&did=AA ADE120329173049046.DID&licenseType=C&licenseNumber=34406#page=1.

———. Accusations against Milan Lewis Hopkins, MD, September 12, 1979, and May 6, 1998. Medical Board of California, Central File Room, Sacramento.

———. Accusation against Tod Mikuriya, MD, January 30, 2004. Factual Findings. Medical Board of California, Central File Room, Sacramento.

———. Decision and Order in Accusations against William Stuart Weil, MD, March 23, 2012, and January 11, 2013. Medical Board of California, www2.mbc. ca.gov/LicenseLookupSystem/PhysicianSurgeon/document.aspx?path=\ DIDOCS\20130109\DMRAAAEC1\&did=AAAEC130109233014839.DID& licenseType=G&licenseNumber=7720#page=1.

———. Stipulated Settlement and Disciplinary Order for Marion Fry, MD, July 22, 2009, and Accusation against Marion Fry, MD, February 29, 2008. Medical Board of California, www2.mbc.ca.gov/LicenseLookupSystem/PhysicianSurgeon /document.aspx?path=\DIDOCS\20090721\DMRAAABI1\&did=AA ABI090721225509953.DID&licenseType=G&licenseNumber=57771#page=1.

Medical Board of California. "Medical Board Reaffirms Its Commitment to Physicians Who Recommend Medical Marijuana" (press release). May 13, 2004.

"MED/RX'C Is Seeking Physicians—You Can Earn up to $16,000 per month!" Web advertisement. 2011, http://222.medrxc.com/physicians.php.

Mikuriya, Tod H. "Chronic Conditions Treated with Cannabis Reported to California Doctors between 1900 and 2004." *O'Shaughnessy's Journal of the California Cannabis Research Group* (Autumn 2005), http://cannabisclinicians.org /wp-content/uploads/2012/02/Tod_SCC-IC-ICD9list-2005.pdf.

———. Untitled speech delivered at "Hempstalk 2006." Portland, Oregon, 2006. YouTube video. Uploaded January 21, 2009, www.youtube.com/watch?v= q1Ri1lIKFc4.

People of California v. Sean Cardillo and Andrew Stephen Cettei. Arraignment hearing and charges, Los Angeles County Superior Court. No. BA 389476. July 6, 2012.

People v. Superior Court of Los Angeles County, Respondent Sean Cardillo et al. California Second District Court of Appeal. No. B246745. July 31, 2013, www.courts.ca.gov/opinions/documents/B246745.pdf.

"Prosecutors Drop Charges against Miss. Heart Surgeon." *Huntsville Times,* January 12, 2012.

Sullum, Jacob. "Pot Shots—Governmental Resistance to Medical Marijuana Represents a Triumph of Ideology over Science." *Reason,* August 11, 1997.

Wilkinson, Kaija. "Witnesses Describe High-Tech Grow Room." *Mississippi Press,* February 10, 2011.

6. L.A. EXCESS

Baeder, Ben, and Thomas Himes. "D.A. Targeting Over-the-Counter Pot Sales." *San Gabriel Valley Tribune,* October 8, 2009.

Barnes, Brad. Interview by author. 2012.

Berens, Brian. Interview by author. 2012.

Bolanos, Yamileth. Interviews by author. 2010, 2012.

"Brick Majors Porn Star" (biography). Excaliburfilms.com. N.d., www.excaliburfilms.com/pornlist/malepgs/Brick_Majors.htm.

Brown, Edmund G., Jr. "Guidelines for the Security and Non-diversion of Marijuana Grown for Medical Use." Office of the Attorney General. August 2008, http://ag.ca.gov/cms_attachments/press/pdfs/n1601_medicalmarijuanaguidelines.pdf.

Carmen A. Trutanich v. Jeffrey Joseph. Court of California, Second Appellate District, Division Two. Opinion filed. No. B232248. March 25, 2012.

"Carmen Trutanich Outburst at City Council Meeting, 2009." YouTube video. Published June 4, 2012, www.youtube.com/watch?v=On2eUX6JZGs.

Esposito, Joseph. Interview by author. 2012.

Hecht, Peter. "A Hollyweed Story: Portrait of a Budding Actress." *Sacramento Bee, Weed Wars* blog, February 26, 2010.

———. "L.A. Dispensary Case Stirs Probe of Toxic Buds." *Sacramento Bee, Weed Wars* blog, March 1, 2010.

———. "L.A. Rolls Out Law That Targets Flood of New Pot Dispensaries." *Sacramento Bee,* February 15, 2010.

———. "Smoke Never Settles in L.A. Fight over Pot Shops." *Sacramento Bee,* August 7, 2012.

Hoeffel, John. "D.A. Chides L.A. Council, Says He'll Target Pot Stores." *Los Angeles Times,* November 18, 2009.

———. "L.A. County Charges Medical Marijuana Distributor with 24 Felonies." February 23, 2010.

———. "Once-Popular Venice-Area Medical Marijuana Dispensary Is Barred from Reopening." *Los Angeles Times,* March 10, 2011.

"Jeff Joseph—Organica Medical Cannabis Collective Operator" (responding to raid). YouTube video. Uploaded November 16, 2009, www.youtube.com/watch?gl=NG&feature=relmfu&hl=en-GB&v=AtYK2qKsHRg.

"Jeff Joseph Speaks before LA City Council on Medical Marijuana ..." YouTube video. Uploaded November 24, 2009, www.youtube.com/watch?v=UAcxsP8NVxs.

Kramer, Barry. Interview by author. 2012.

Kruschewsky, Carlos. Interviews by author. 2010, 2012.

Los Angeles Collective Association and Westside Green Oasis v. City of Los Angeles. Ex Parte Application for Temporary Restraining Order. No. BC422214. September 22, 2009.

Los Angeles Collective Association and Westside Green Oasis v. City of Los Angeles. Preliminary Injunction. No. BC422214. October 19, 2009.

Los Angeles County District Attorney Steve Cooley. "Dispensary Owner Sentenced" (press release). September 26, 2011.

People v. Hemp Factory V et al. Tentative Decision on OSC re: Preliminary Injunction Granted. Los Angeles Superior Court, Judge James C. Chalfant. No. BC424881. January 29, 2010.

Thicke, Brennan. Interview by author. 2012.

Zine, Dennis. Interview by author. 2010.

7. WAFTING WIDELY

Ammiano, Tom. "State Board of Equalization Staff Legislative Bill Analysis," for Assembly Bill 390, February 23, 2009, California State Board of Equalization, www.boe.ca.gov/legdiv/pdf/ab0390–1dw.pdf.

Davies, Bryan. Interview by author. 2012.

Davies, Lanette. Interview by author. 2012.

Davis, Glenn. "TV Reporter at World Series: There's 'People Smoking Weed over There!'" Sportsgrid.com, October 28, 2010, with video: www.sportsgrid.com/mlb/newy-scruggs-nbc-weed-video/.

De la Luz, Dragonfly. Interview by author. 2012.

Estrada, Dania. Interview by author. 2012.

Field Research Corporation. *Tabulations from a Survey of California Registered Voters about Marijuana.* Prepared for *Sacramento Bee.* San Francisco: Field Research Corporation, July 2010.

Gaura, Maria Alicia. "Stoner Chic Traces Origin to San Rafael; Snickering High Schoolers Brought '420' into Lexicon." *San Francisco Chronicle,* April 20, 2000.

Hecht, Peter. "Brownie Baker Tests for Safe Weed, but Pot Treats Can Be Potent." *Sacramento Bee, Weed Wars* blog, April 6, 2010.

———. "Builders Offer Home Accessory: A Pot-Growing 'Time Machine.'" *Sacramento Bee, Weed Wars* blog, April 21, 2010.

———. "Dragonfly, the 'Weedly World Traveler,' Reviews the High Life." *Sacramento Bee, Weed Wars* blog, June 24, 2010.

———. "420—Number's Mystique Lights Up Pot Parties across U.S. Today." *Sacramento Bee,* April 20, 2010.

———. "Marijuana Trading Cards Pitch the 'Sweet and Exotic' to Pot Fans." *Sacramento Bee, Weed Wars* blog, August 23, 2010.

———. "Salesman Pitched RV Fun, Now Offers 'Wellness' and Medical Pot.'" *Sacramento Bee, Weed Wars* blog, August 3, 2010.

———. "Sexy Pot Ads Provoke Debate." *Sacramento Bee,* November 28, 2011.

———. "Weed Goes Mainstream: As Big Vote Nears, New Poll Finds Who's Using Pot in State and Why." *Sacramento Bee,* August 8, 2010. (Includes *Sacramento Bee*/Field Poll survey interviews with Robert Girvetz, Steve Keegan, Kyle Printz, Ryan Issaco, Dawn Sanford, Annette Drennan, John Wade, 2010.)

King, George A., and Mike Puma. "Pot Doesn't Get Josh Out of Joint." *New York Post,* October 28, 2010.

Lambert, Diana. "Sacramento School Alert: Beware of Pot-Laced Brownies." *Sacramento Bee,* February 27, 2011.

Mills, Evan. *Energy up in Smoke: The Carbon Footprint of Indoor Cannabis Production.* Self-published, April 5, 2011, http://evan-mills.com/energy-associates/Indoor.html.

Nunberg, Helen, et al. "An Analysis of Applicants Presenting to a Medical Marijuana Specialty Practice in California." *Journal of Drug Policy Analysis* 4, no. 1 (February 2011): 1.

Sahagun, Vanessa [ChaCha VaVoom]. Interview by author. 2012.

"State Estimates of Substance Use and Mental Disorders." 2008–2009 National Survey on Drug Use and Health. 2011, store.samhas.gov/product/State-Estimates-of-Substance-Use-and-Mental-Disorders-from-the-2008–2009-National-Survey-on-Drug-Use-and Health-NSDUH-/SMA11–4641.

8. COURTING COMPASSION

City of Garden Grove v. Superior Court of Orange County (Felix Kha, Real Party in Interest). Opinion of the Court of Appeal of the State of California, Fourth Appellate District, Division Three. No. G036250. November 28, 2007.

Davidovich, Eugene. Interview by author. 2012.

Davis, Charles. "Why Won't the Government Let James Stacy Tell the Truth?" *Change.org News,* September 16, 2010.

Duncan, Don. Interviews by author. 2011, 2012.

Elford, Joe. Interviews by author. 2011, 2012.

"Eugene Davidovich." Eugene Davidovich's channel, YouTube, www.youtube.com/EugeneDavidovich.

Friends of Charles C. Lynch website, www.friendsofccl.com.

Green Screen: Operation Green Rx v. Eugene Davidovich (trial footage). Nosuchproductions and Broken Eulogy Productions, director's cut. 2010. Documentary. YouTube, http://www.youtube.com/watch?v=dJZ2WQONLbY.

Hecht, Peter. "San Diego DA Has a Losing Streak with Medical Marijuana Prosecutions." *Sacramento Bee, Weed Wars* blog, April 5, 2010.

————. "San Diego Marijuana Defendant Covering His Own Trial." *Sacramento Bee, Weed Wars* blog, March 15, 2010.

Hermes, Kris. "San Diego Dispensary Operator Sentenced, Advocates Vow to Appeal" (press release). San Diego Chapter of Americans for Safe Access, December 18, 2010.

Kelly, Patrick Kevin. Interview by author. 2012.

Lynch, Charles. Interview by author. 2012.

Moran, Greg. "Manager of Medical Pot Dispensary Is Acquitted." *San Diego Union-Tribune,* December 2, 2009.

————. "Man Convicted in Medical Marijuana Case Will Appeal." *San Diego Union-Tribune,* September 28, 2010.

Murphy, Dean E. "Jurors Who Convicted Marijuana Grower Seek New Trial." *New York Times,* February 5, 2003.

————. "Marijuana Grower Sentenced to Day in Prison." *New York Times,* June 5, 2003.

Operation Green Rx: "Navigating the Serpentine Roadmap." Eugene Davidovich blog, http://operationgreenrx.blogspot.com.

People of the State of California v. Jovan Jackson. Appellant's Opening Brief. State of California Fourth Appellate District, Division One. No. DO58988. November 21, 2011.

People v. Davidovich, Eugene Davidovich trial website, https://sites.google.com/site/peoplevdavidovich/.

People v. Patrick K. Kelly. Opinion of the Supreme Court of California. No. S164830. January 21, 2010.

Raiding California. Reason TV, 2008. Documentary, http://reason.com/reasontv/2008/06/10/raiding-california.

Stacy, James. Interview by author. 2012.

United States of America v. Edward Rosenthal. Appeal from the United States District Court for the Northern District of California, Charles R. Breyer, District Judge. U.S. Court of Appeals for the Ninth Circuit. Opinion. No. 03–10370. April 26, 2006.

United States of America v. Edward Rosenthal. Notice of Motion to Dismiss on Grounds of Vindictive Prosecution. U.S. District Court for the Northern District of California. No. CR 02–0053 CRB. February 20, 2007.

United States of America v. Edward Rosenthal. Order Granting Motion to Dismiss for Vindictive Prosecution. U.S. District Court for the Northern District of California, Judge Charles R. Breyer. No. CR 02–0053 CRB. March 14, 2007.

United States of America v. Edward Rosenthal. Sentencing Memorandum. U.S. District Court for the Northern District of California, Judge Charles R. Breyer. No. CR 02–0053 CRB. June 9, 2003.

United States of America v. James Dean Stacy. Sentencing transcript. U.S. District Court for the Southern District of California. No. 09cr3695. January 7, 2011.

United States v. Charles C. Lynch. Sentencing Memorandum. U.S. District Court for the Central District of California, Judge George H. Wu. No. CR 07–0689-GW. April 29, 2010.

9. MARTYRDOM FOR THE MISSIONARIES

Ashworth, Robert. Interview by author. 2011.

Eisenberg, Bobby. "Cool Couple Hopes for Jury Nullification" (press release). Fry /Schafer Defense Committee, August 11, 2007.

Fry, Marion P. Interview by author. 2011.

Gardner, Fred. "Why Did the Feds Target Mollie Fry, MD, and Dale Schafer?" Counterpunch, May 6–8, 2011, www.counterpunch.org/2011/05/06 /why-did-the-feds-target-mollie-fry-md-and-dale-schafer/.

Garvin, Cosmo. "Cali-Nullification." Sacramento News and Review, August 27, 2007.

Hecht, Peter. "Ex-ally One of El Dorado DA's Foes." Sacramento Bee, February 25, 2002.

———. "Martyrs, Pot Dealers . . . or Possibly Both?" Sacramento Bee, May 1, 2011.

———. "Pot Couple's Surrender a Rallying Cry." Sacramento Bee, May 3, 2011.

Hermes, Kris. "Clemency Sought for Medical Marijuana Patient, Cancer Survivor Sentenced to 5 Years in Prison" (press release). Americans for Safe Access, April 20, 2011.

Schafer, Dale. Interview by author. 2011.

Undercover Folsom police officer, meeting with Dr. Marion Fry, February 15, 2001. Transcript provided to author.

United States v. Dale Schafer and Marion Fry. Trial transcripts. U.S. District Court, Sacramento, California. No. CR-00238FCD. August 2, 2007–March 20, 2008.

United States v. Dale Schafer and United States v. Marion P. Fry. Appeal from the United States District Court. Ruling by Court of Appeals for the Ninth Circuit. No. 08–10167. Argued and submitted August 31, 2010, filed November 8, 2010.

Walsh, Denny. "Couple Found Guilty in Pot Case." Sacramento Bee, August 7, 2007.

10. CAMPAIGN FOR CANNABIS

Corral, Valerie. Interviews by author. 2010, 2012.

De la Luz, Dragonfly. Interview by author. 2012.

———. "Why Pro-Pot Activists Oppose Prop. 19: 19 Reasons to Vote Know." Ston-ers Against the Prop. 19 Tax Cannabis Initiative blog. July 10, 2010, http://votetax

cannabis2010.blogspot.com/2010/07/why-pro-pot-activists-oppose-2010-tax.
html.

Drug Enforcement Administration former administrators, letter to Eric Holder,
attorney general, August 24, 2010, www.govexec.com/pdfs/0917on1.pdf.

Holder, Eric, attorney general, letter to Drug Enforcement Administration former
administrators, October 13, 2010, www.scribd.com/doc/39415470
/Holder-letter-on-California-Pot-Prop-19.

Gasparas, Stephen. Interviews by author. 2010, 2012.

Hecht, Peter. "Big Tobacco Snuffs Out Rumors of California Marijuana Interest."
Sacramento Bee, Weed Wars blog, September 27, 2010.

———. "California NAACP Backing of Pot Legalization Outrages Minister." *Sacramento Bee,* June 29, 2010.

———. "Capitol Marijuana Debate Offers Parallel Universes for Proposition 19."
Sacramento Bee, Weed Wars blog, September 21, 2010.

———. "Governor Signs Bill to Soften Pot Crime." *Sacramento Bee,* October 3, 2010.

———. "Head of Medical Marijuana Physicians Network Decries Prop 19." *Sacramento Bee, Weed Wars* blog, October 1, 2010.

———. "Legal Pot a Threat to Cartels Only If Exported." *Sacramento Bee,* October
13, 2010.

———. "Medical Marijuana Pioneer Protests Cash Cow Pot Stores." *Sacramento
Bee, Weed Wars* blog, August 12, 2010.

———. "Months after Death, Legendary Pot Activist Stokes Prop. 19 Debate."
Sacramento Bee, Weed Wars blog, August 25, 2010.

———. "Pot Initiative Challenges Long-Standing Way of Life." *Sacramento Bee,*
April 25, 2010.

———. "Pot Mecca Bid in Limbo." *Sacramento Bee,* October 3, 2010.

———. "Prop 19 Trailing by 7 Points in Poll." *Sacramento Bee,* October 31, 2010.

———. "Some Medical Pot Providers Fight Proposition 19." *Sacramento Bee,*
August 25, 2010.

———. "Stephen Colbert: Prop. 19 'Most Popular Candidate in California.'" *Sacramento Bee, Weed Wars* blog, October 8, 2010.

———. "Study: Legal Weed Cheap, but State's Tax Haul Iffy." *Sacramento Bee,* July
8, 2010.

———. "Unions Reach Out to Weed Workers." *Sacramento Bee,* October 3, 2010.

———. "While Proposition 19 Loses, Nine Cities Okay Levy for Local Dispensaries." *Sacramento Bee,* November 4, 2010.

Hoeffel, John. "Marijuana Activist Jack Herer Dies at 70." *Los Angeles Times,* April
23, 2010.

Jones, Dale Sky. Interviews by author. 2010, 2012.

Jones, Jeff. Interviews by author. 2010, 2012.

Kilmer, Beau, Jonathan P. Caulkins, Brittany M. Bond, and Peter H. Reuter. *Reducing Drug Trafficking Revenues and Violence in Mexico: Would Legalizing Marijuana in California Help?* Occasional paper. Santa Monica, CA: Rand International Programs and Drug Policy Research Center, 2010.

Lee, Richard. Interviews by author. 2010, 2012.

Legalize It. Produced by Daniel Katzir and Ravit Markus. Los Angeles: New Love Films, 2012. Documentary, www.legalizeitmovie.com.

Levine, Harry G., Jon B. Gettman, and Loren Siegel. *Targeting Blacks for Marijuana: Possession Arrests of African Americans in California, 2004–08.* Los Angeles: Drug Policy Alliance, 2010.

Lillis, Ryan, and Peter Hecht. "Pot Tax, Hike in Business Levy May Go before Voters." *Sacramento Bee,* June, 19, 2010.

Peron, Dennis. Interview by author. 2012.

Proposition 19: The Regulate, Control and Tax Cannabis Act of 2010, ag.ca.gov /cms_attachments/initiatives/pdfs/i821_initiative_09-0024_amdt_1-s.pdf.

Rush, Dan. Interviews by author. 2010, 2012.

Sims, Hank. "General Lee: Can Oaksterdam Weed Magnate Richard Lee Push Legalization over the Top?" *Journal* (Humboldt County), July 29, 2010.

"Snoop Dogg Cosigns Prop 19—VOTE NOVEMBER 2nd!!" YouTube video. Uploaded October 28, 2010, www.youtube.com/watch?v=RX_QASE_sII.

Wilcox, Jeff. Interviews by author. 2010, 2012.

Witemyre, Matthew. Interview by author. 2012.

11. A MILE HIGH AND BEYOND

Burke, Anita. "Dispensaries Will Further Abuse, Police Believe." *Medford (OR) Mail Tribune,* October 4, 2010.

"Cal. NORML Estimates 750,000–1,125,000 Medical Marijuana Patients in California Retail Medical Market Is $1.5–$4.5 Billion per Year." California NORML, May 31, 2011, http://canorml.org/news/cbcsurvey2011.html.

Carrol, Rick. "Man Replaces Pot with Yoga, Gets Probation." *Aspen Times,* May 6, 2012, www.aspentimes.com/article/20120306/NEWS/120309910.

Colorado Department of Revenue, Marijuana Enforcement Division. "Laws and Regulations." Colorado: The Official State Web Portal, www.colorado.gov/cs /Satellite/Rev-MMJ/CBON/1251592984795.

Cook, Matt. Interviews by author. 2011, 2012.

Craig, Tim. "6 D.C. Firms Will Grow Marijuana." *Washington Post,* March 30, 2012.

Duncan, Don. Interview by author. 2012.

Durrah, Scott. Interview by author. 2011.

Gieringer, Dale. Interviews by author. 2011, 2012.

Hagengruber, Matt, and Angela Brandt. "Raids Target Medical Marijuana Shops." *Billings Gazette,* March 15, 2011.

Hecht, Peter. "Pot Raids Spur Call for Statewide Rules." *Sacramento Bee,* February 13, 2011.

———. "Rocky Mountain High, Colorado Allows—and Strictly Regulates—a For-Profit Cannabis Industry." *Sacramento Bee,* August 14, 2011.

———. "'Stonerville, USA,' Townsfolk Chafe at Colorado's Regulation of Established Pot Trade." *Sacramento Bee,* August 15, 2011.

Hood, Grace. "UFCW Vows to Continue Fighting for Medical Marijuana." KUNC Community Radio for Northern Colorado, November 2, 2011, http://kunc.org /post/ufcw-vows-continue-fighting-medical-marijuana.

Hoover, Tim. "Ritter Turns to Medical-Marijuana Fund to Help Balance Colorado Budget." *Denver Post,* August 24, 2010.

James, Wanda. Interviews by author. 2011, 2012.

Kamin, Sam. "Medical Marijuana Regulation in Colorado and the Future of Medical Marijuana Regulation in the United States." *McGeorge Law Review* 43 (2012): 147.

King, Bonnie. "Oregon Governor Signs Marijuana Dispensary Bill into Law." Salem-News.com, August 14, 2013, www.salem-news.com/articles/august142013 /oregon-marijuana-dispensariesbk.php.

Mitchell, Kirk, and Ryan Parker. "Colorado's Medical Pot Industry Fuels Illegal Trade, Review Shows." *Denver Post,* August 2, 2012.

National Cannabis Industry Association. *The Colorado Cannabis Industry: A Tale of Ten Cities.* Washington, DC, National Cannabis Industry Association, 2011, http://thecannabisindustry.org/The-Colorado-Cannabis-Industry-A-Tale-of-Ten-Cities.pdf.

Rogers, Dan. Interviews by author. 2011, 2012.

Rush, Dan. Interview by author. 2012.

Senate Bill 420, introduced by Senator John Vasconcellos, February 20, 2003, and signed into law by Governor Gray Davis, October 12, 2003. Legislative Counsel, State of California, website, www.leginfo.ca.gov/pub/03–04/bill/sen/sb_0401-0450/sb_420_bill_20031012_chaptered.html.

Shepherd, Michael. "Maine Marijuana Dispensary Operator Settles Lawsuit." *Maine Sunday Telegraph,* September 30, 2012.

Spellman, Jim. "Colorado's Green Rush: Medical Marijuana." CNN, December 14, 2009, www.cnn.com/2009/US/12/14/colorado.medical.marijuana/.

"State Sen. Nicholas Scutari Says New Jersey Has the Most Restrictive Medical Marijuana Program in the U.S." Politifact.com, August 14, 2010, www.politifact.com /new-jersey/statements/2011/aug/14/nicholas-scutari/state-sen-nicholas-scutari-says-new-jersey-has-mos/.

Sterling-Nichols, Alison. Interview by author. 2012.

Substance Abuse and Mental Health Administration. "National Survey Shows a Rise in Illicit Drug Use from 2008 to 2010" (press release). September 8, 2011, www.samhsa.gov/newsroom/advisories/1109075503.aspx.

Taylor, Ted. "Will Medical Pot Inspire?" *Eugene Weekly,* October 28, 2010.

Warner, Joel. "Ganjapreneurs Are Cashing In on Colorado's Booming Medical Pot Business." *Westword,* September 9, 2009, http://westword.com/2009–09–10 /news/medical-marijuana-is-a-pot-of-gold-for-dispensaries/.

Wyatt, Kristen. "AP News Break: Pot Regulators Slashed in Colorado." *Denver Post,* April 3, 2012, www.denverpost.com/news/marijuana/ci_20316774 /apnewsbreak-pot-regulators-slashed-co#ixzz27UUT3GX.

"Another Defendant Sentenced to 30 Months Imprisonment; Forfeiture of Hundreds of Thousands of Dollars and a Cadillac Escalade" (press release). Law Fuel News Network. August 24, 2005, www.lawfuel.com/show-release. asp?ID=3993.

Bolanos, Yamileth. Interview by author. 2012.

Bulwa, Demian, and Matthai Kuruvila. "Pot Business Owner Charged in Scam on City." *San Francisco Chronicle,* May 18, 2012.

City of Isleton and Delta Allied Growers: Trouble in River City. Sacramento County Grand Jury Report, Superior Court of California, June 27, 2011, www.sacgrand jury.org/reports/10–11/Revised-Report-Trouble-In-Isleton.pdf.

City of Oakland Ordinance No. C.M.S. "Pertaining to Medical Cannabis Cultivation Facility Permitting." Office of the City Clerk, Oakland. July 15, 2010, clerk websvr1.oaklandnet.com/attachments/25511.pdf.

Eddy, David. "Diving In, California Grower Makes Abrupt Switch to Hydroponics." Web version of an article published in *American Vegetable Grower,* November 1, 2008, www.growingproduce.com/article/14908/how-hydroponics-helped.

Elinson, Zusha. "Entrepreneur's Ambitious Plans Go Up in Smoke." *New York Times,* May 21, 2011.

———. "Indicted Oakland Pot Entrepreneur Leaned on Political Relationships." *Bay Citizen,* September 6, 2012, http://californiawatch.org/money-and-politics /indicted-oakland-pot-entrepreneur-leaned-on-political-relationships-17869.

Hecht, Peter. "Farm's Switch to Pot Brings Arrests." *Sacramento Bee,* July 2, 2011.

———. "Isleton Vows to Stonewall DA's Probe of Pot Farm." *Sacramento Bee,* April 20, 2011.

———. "Pot Seller May Pay High Price." *Sacramento Bee,* September 25, 2011.

———. "Pot Shops Told to Pay Up." *Sacramento Bee,* March 10, 2011.

———. "Prop 19 Defeat Forces City to Suspend Plan." *Sacramento Bee,* December 27, 2010.

———. "Weed Lovers Welcome weGrow." *Sacramento Bee,* February 27, 2011.

Industrial Medical Cannabis Cultivation and Manufacturing Facility, Economic Analysis, City of Oakland, Alameda County. Report prepared for AgraMed. Santa Rosa, CA: Brion and Associates, March 2010.

Kaplan, Rebecca. Interviews by author. 2010, 2011.

Kuruvila, Matthai. "City Attorney Won't Advise on Pot Farms." *San Francisco Chronicle,* February 8, 2011.

———. "Oakland Talks Break Down; Layoffs for 80 Cops." *San Francisco Chronicle,* July 14, 2010, www.sfgate.com/bayarea/article/Oakland-talks-break-down-layoffs-for-80-cops-3182095.php.

Marchetti, Lou. Interview by author. 2012.

Medical Cannabis Industrial Cultivation and Processing Facility Request for Permit Applications, Special Permits Division, City of Oakland Office of the City Administrator, draft, November 9, 2010.

Ogden, David W. "Memorandum for Selected United States Attorneys." *The Justice Blog.* Office of the Deputy Attorney General. October 19, 2009, http://blogs. justice.gov/main/archives/192.

Richman, Josh. "Guilty Plea, Sentencing in Computer Theft Plot." *Inside Bay Area,* August 24, 2005, www.insidebayarea.com/dailyreview/localnews/ci_2968288.

Russo, John. Interview by author. 2012.

Samano, Elizabeth. Interview by author. 2012.

Stanton, Sam. "DA Probes Isleton Pot Farm." *Sacramento Bee,* April 15, 2011.

Stanton, Sam, and Peter Hecht. "Isleton Grilled about Pot Farm." *Sacramento Bee,* April 28, 2011.

United States of America v. Nathan Hoffman, Hung Cao Nguyen. Criminal complaint. Affidavit of Internal Revenue Service Special Agent Lisa Ulrikson, signed by U.S. Magistrate Kendall J. Newman. No. 2:11-mj-00312-KJN. October 4, 2011.

United States v. Bryan Smith, Kelly Smith, Daniel Goldsmith, Bruce Goldsmith, Robert Klaus, and Ryder Phillips. Criminal complaint. Signed by U.S. Magistrate Gregory G. Hollows. No. 2:11-mj-00288-GGH. September 12, 2011.

United States v. Yan Ebyam. Criminal complaint. Affidavit of Drug Enforcement Administration Special Agent Robert Marchi, signed by U.S. Magistrate Edmund F. Brennan. No. 2:11-mj-00177-EFR. June 22, 2011.

United States v. Yan Ebyam, Thomas Wesley Jopson, David Eldon Jopson, Jesus Bruse, Aimee Kristine Sisco, Pablo Omar Vasquez, Dolf Fred Podva, Donald William Fried, and Thomas Marrs. Indictment. U.S. District Court for the Eastern District of California. No. 2:11-cr-00275-JAM. June 30, 2011.

U.S. Attorney Benjamin B. Wagner, Eastern District of California. "Marijuana Enforcement Actions in the Eastern District of California" (press release). October 7, 2011.

U.S. Attorney's Office, Central District of California. "Owner of Nine Marijuana Stores in Orange and Los Angeles Counties Sentenced to 262 Months for Drug Trafficking and Tax Evasion" (press release). July 22, 2013, www.justice.gov/usao /cac/Pressroom/2013/096.html.

U.S. Department of Justice. "Attorney General Announces Formal Medical Marijuana Guidelines" (press release). October 19, 2009, www.justice.gov/opa /pr/2009/October/09-ag-1119.html.

Wagner, Benjamin B. Interview by author. 2012.

Wilcox, Jeff. Interview by author. 2012.

13. RETURN OF THE FEDS

Allman, Tom. Interviews by author. 2011, 2012.

Assembly Bill 2312. Introduced by Assembly Member Tom Ammiano, February 24, 2012, Legislative Counsel, State of California, website, http://leginfo.ca.gov /pub/11–12/bill/asm/ab_2301–2350/ab_2312_bill_20120224_introduced.html.

Banks, Sandy. "A Compassionless Crackdown." *Los Angeles Times,* February 4, 2012.

Bulwa, Demian, and Matthai Kuruvila. "Pot Business Owner Charged in Scam on City." *San Francisco Chronicle,* May 18, 2012.

City of Oakland. "City of Oakland Announces the Selection of Four Medical Cannabis Permit Applicants" (press release). March 14, 2012, www2.oaklandnet.com /oakca/groups/cityadministrator/documents/pressrelease/oak034119.pdf.

City of Oakland v. Eric Holder. Complaint for Declaratory and Injunctive Relief. October 20, 2012. Oakland City Attorney, www.oaklandcityattorney.org/PDFS /Fed%20med%20cannabis%20complaint%20Oct.%2010%202012.pdf.

Cohen, Matt. Interview by author. 2011.

DeAngelo, Steve. Interviews by author. 2011, 2012.

Filner, Bob, letter to Laura E. Duffy. *San Diego Reader,* July 13, 2012, www .sandiegoreader.com/documents/2012/jul/23/bob-filners-letter-laura-duffy/.

Hecht, Peter. "Bill to Oversee Pot Sales Passes." *Sacramento Bee,* June 1, 2012.

———. "Feds Charge Growers, Pot Shops." *Sacramento Bee,* October 8, 2011.

———. "Feds' Raid Had Mendocino Riled." *Sacramento Bee,* October 30, 2011.

———. "Feds Raid Home, Firms of Oakland Pot Advocate." *Sacramento Bee,* April 3, 2012.

———. "Feds Target Pot Dispensers." *Sacramento Bee,* October 7, 2011.

———. "IRS Probes Tax Returns of Oakland Dispensary." *Sacramento Bee,* February 18, 2011.

———. "Medical Pot Backers Seek Regulatory Ballot Initiative." *Sacramento Bee,* October 25, 2011.

———. "Oakland Dispensary Vows to Fight Seizure Order." *Sacramento Bee,* July 13, 2012.

———. "Pot College Founder Pulls Back after Raid." *Sacramento Bee,* April 7, 2012.

———. "Pot Forces Look to the Ballot." *Sacramento Bee,* February 6, 2012.

———. "Pot Shop Crackdown All about Location." *Sacramento Bee,* April 15, 2012.

———. "Sacramento County Pot Store Closes with a Flourish—and a Vow to Fight Back." *Sacramento Bee,* December 17, 2011.

———. "San Francisco Leaders Fight Dispensary Closure Efforts." *Sacramento Bee,* April 4, 2012.

———. "Troubled Pot Dispensary to Close New Year's Eve." *Sacramento Bee,* December 30, 2011.

Lee, Henry K., Stephanie Lee, Demian Bulwa, and Justin Berton. "Deadly Rampage, 7 Killed, 3 Injured at Small Oakland College." *San Francisco Chronicle,* April 3, 2012.

Lee, Richard. Interview by author. 2012.

Linthicum, Kate. "L.A. Repeals Its Ban on Pot Stores." *Los Angeles Times,* October 2, 2012.

Medical Marijuana Regulation Control and Taxation Act, proposed initiative, December 2011, Office of the Attorney General, http://ag.ca.gov/cms_attach ments/initiatives/pdfs/i1043_11-0098a1s_%7Bmedical_marijuana%7D.pdf.

Patients Mutual Assistance Collective Corporation d.b.a. Harborside Health Center v. Commissioner of Internal Revenue. U.S. Tax Court case documents, www.ustaxcourt.gov/USTCDockInq/DocketSheet.aspx?DocketNo= 11029212.

United States of America v. Paul Montoya, Noah Kleinman, Kathy Thabet, James Stanley, Terrence Smith, Bryant Watson, and Casey Wheat. First Superseding Indictment. CR No. 11–893(A)-ODW. June 2011.

United States of America v. Real Property Located in Lake Forest, California (H&H) Investments, LP). Complaint for Forfeiture. No. SACV11–01545. October 6, 2011.

Van Oot, Tory. "Push for Pot Regulation Stalls." *Sacramento Bee,* June 26, 2012.

Wagner, Benjamin B. Interview by author. 2012.

Weed Wars. Discovery Channel, 2011. Documentary, http://dsc.discovery.com/tv /weed-wars/.

Wilcox, Jeff. Interview by author. 2012.

14. BACK TO THE GARDEN

Abrams, Donald. Interview by author. 2012.

Allen, David. Interview by author. 2012.

Americans for Safe Access. "Medical Marijuana Patients Get Their Day in Federal Court with the Obama Administration" (press release). July 30, 2012, www. safeaccessnow.org/article.php?id=7260.

Americans for Safe Access v. Drug Enforcement Administration. On Petition for Review of a Final Order of the U.S. Drug Enforcement Administration, U.S. Court of Appeals for the District of Columbia Circuit. No. 11–1265. Opinion. January 22, 2013.

Assembly Bill 604. Introduced by Assembly Member Tom Ammiano, February 20, 2013, and amended in Senate with principal coauthors, Senator Darrell Steinberg and Senator Mark Leno, September 11, 2013. Legislative Counsel, State of California, 2013, www.leginfo.ca.gov/pub/13–14/bill/asm/ab_0601–0650/ab_604_ bill_20130911_amended_sen_v95.html.

Bolanos, Yamileth. Interview by author. 2012.

Cole, James M. "Memorandum for All United States Attorneys." U.S. Department of Justice, August 29, 2013. www.justice.gov/iso/opa/resources/ 3052013829132756857467.pdf.

Corral, Mike. Interview by author. 2012.

Corral, Valerie. Interview by author. 2012.

Davidovich, Eugene. "Duffy Hoax Revealed—Medical Marijuana Advocates Tell All." San Diego Chapter of Americans for Safe Access. August 10, 2012, www. safeaccesssd.org/2012/08/duffyhoax-revealed-medical-marijuana.html.

———. "Dumanis Continues Raiding While Court of Appeals Tells Her She Is Wrong." San Diego Chapter of Americans for Safe Access. October 25,

2012, www.safeaccesssd.org/2012/10/dumanis-continues-raiding-while-court.
html.

———. Interview by author. 2012.

De la Luz, Dragonfly. "How CBD Is Revolutionizing Medical Marijuana."
Kush Magazine, July 15, 2011, www.kushmagazine.com/index.php?option
=com_content&view=article&id=147:how-cbd-is-revolutionizing-medical-
marijuana-by-dragonfly-de-la-luz&catid=35:latest-news.

———. Interview by author. 2012.

Gasparas, Stephen. Interview by author. 2012.

Hecht, Peter. "County Fights Pot Subpoena." *Sacramento Bee,* January 4, 2013.

———. "Harvest of Compassion, Collective True to Its Roots as Pot Trade Booms."
Sacramento Bee, September 19, 2010.

Hotakainen, Rob. "Drug Czar Gil Kerlikowske Talks Tough on Marijuana as Pressure Grows." McClatchy Newspapers, April 24, 2013, www.mcclatchydc.
com/2013/04/24/189578/drug-czar-gil-kerlikowske-talks.html.

Ivey, Don. Interview by author. 2010.

Kelly, Patrick Kevin. Interview by author. 2012.

Lee, Richard. Interview by author. 2012.

"Majority Now Supports Legalizing Marijuana." Pew Research Center for the People and the Press, April 4, 2013, www.people-press.org/2013/04/04
/majority-now-supports-legalizing-marijuana/.

Margolin, Harold. Interview by author. 2010.

Margolin, Marcia. Interview by author. 2012.

People v. Jovan Jackson. Appeal from a Judgment of the Superior Court of San
Diego County, California, Court of Appeal, Fourth Appellate District reversal.
No. D058988. October 24, 2012.

Rodrigues, Danny. Interview by author. 2010.

Schafer, Geoffrey. Interview by author. 2012.

Stanek, Richard W., Michael H. Leidholt, Robert McConnell, Craig T. Steckler,
Charles H. Ramsey, Bob Bushman, and Chuck Wexler to Eric H. Holder (sher-
iffs, police chiefs, and narcotics officers' associations letter to the Attorney Gen-
eral of the United States). International Association of Chiefs of Police website,
August 30, 2013, www.theiacp.org/portals/0/pdfs/FINALLawEnforcement-
GroupLetteronDOJMarijuanaPolicy.pdf.

State of Colorado, Amendment 64: The Regulate Marijuana like Alcohol Act
of 2012, Campaign to Regulate Marijuana like Alcohol, 2012, www.regulate
marijuana.org/s/regulate-marijuana-alcohol-act-2012.

State of Washington, Initiative Measure 502, filed July 8, 2011, Washington Secretary of State, http://sos.wa.gov/_assets/elections/initiatives/i502.pdf.

United States v. the Premises Known as 3412 Amberwood Avenue. Search Warrant
Affidavit by S. A. Patrick Kelly, signed by U.S. Magistrate Andrew J. Wistrich.
No. 11–2586M. October 28, 2011.

U.S. Attorney's Office, Central District of California. "Six People Associated with
Inland Empire Marijuana Operation That Ran Three Stores Arrested on Fed-

eral Drug Trafficking Charges" (press release). www.justice.gov/usao/cac
/Pressroom/2012/077.html.

U.S. Department of Justice. "Justice Department Announces Update to Marijuana
Enforcement Policy" (press release). August 29, 2013, www.justice.gov/opa
/pr/2013/August/13-opa-974.html.

Wagner, Benjamin B. Interview by author. 2012.

INDEX

Abatin Wellness Center (Washington, DC), 164

Abrams, Donald: AIDS patients of, 45–47; bureaucratic obstacles encountered by, 51–53; clinical trials of, 51, 53–55; marijuana research by, 49–51, 57–58, 61, 131; post-crackdown career of, 208; publications of, 54–55; relationship with Henry, 45, 46–47, 55

ACT UP (AIDS Coalition To Unleash Power), 47, 53

AgraMed (planned Oakland marijuana factory), 172

AIDS/HIV: antiretroviral medications, 47; first appearances of, 45–46; first inpatient ward, 46; marijuana as treatment for, 48–55; San Francisco epidemic, 46, 47, 131, 206

Alameda County (CA), 173, 174

Alameda County District Attorney's Office, 175–76, 196

Alaska, 165

Albertus, Megan, 84

Allen, David, 64–66, 77–78, 209

Allen, Harold, 5

Allen, Ron, 147

Allman, Tom, 37–38, 40–41, 190

Alsup, William, 69

American Alliance of Medical Cannabis, 126

American Civil Liberties Union (ACLU), 67

Americans for Safe Access: as advocacy group for marijuana patients, 8, 116;

budget of, 116; California medical marijuana regulations efforts and, 200; California medical marijuana taxation opposed by, 167; Davidovich as San Diego director of, 110, 111, 119–20, 210; Davidovich defense and, 109, 112; federal crackdown protested by, 198–99; Fry/Schafer arrests and, 136; Jackson decision appealed by, 120; litigation by, 88, 209; media campaigns of, 210; Proposition 19 and, 150; Rosenthal defense and, 115, 116; WAMM raid and, 8

American Vegetable Grower (magazine), 182

Ammiano, Tom, 146, 167, 191, 199–201, 208, 212

Amsterdam (Netherlands), 17, 23, 49

Annals of Internal Medicine of the American College of Physicians, 54–55

Ansari, Bahar, 112

Answerdam Alternative Care (San Diego, CA), 110

antiretroviral medications, 52

Apothecary of Colorado (Denver), 160

Arbelaez, Norton, 162

Arcata (CA), 32, 33, 34, 44, 208

Area 101 (Mendocino County, CA), 42–43, 151

Arizona, 165

Arts & Entertainment Network, 34

Ashworth, Robert, 124–26, 128, 129, 130, 133, 136

aspergillus, 42

Associated Press, 9, 173
AZT (AIDS drug), 47

Bakersfield (CA), 82
Barnes, Brad, 85–87, 100, 195–96
baseball World Series (2010), 98–99
Beat Club (Washington, DC), 25
Beck, Owen, 117
Berens, Brian, 83–84, 87, 91
Berkeley (CA), 155, 165–66, 167, 176–77
Berkeley Patients Group, 115, 164, 181, 191
Bevan, George, 116
Big Book of Buds (Rosenthal), 114
Big Tobacco, 150
Birotte, André, Jr., 188
Black Horizon (Sutter County, CA), 177
Blake, Tim, 42–43, 151
Blueberry Kush (marijuana strain), 94
Blue Dream (marijuana strain), 92
"Blue Hole" estate (MS), 64, 66
Blue Horizon (Sacramento County, CA), 177, 183
Blue Lady (marijuana strain), 104
Blue Lake (CA), 38
Blue Lake Fishing Products, 38
Bolanos, Yamileth ("Yami"), 79–81, 85, 87–88, 90, 91, 180, 210
Bollinger, Jody, 133
Bomia, Brent, 65
Bonner, Robert, 153
Boulder (CO), 156
Bradley, Nate, 198
Breyer, Charles R., 21, 115, 116
Bronze Horizon (Oakland, CA), 173
Brooks, Desley, 177
Brown, Jerry, 82, 145
Brownie Mary Day (San Francisco, CA), 49
Brownie Mary's Marijuana Cookbook and Dennis Peron's Recipe for Social Change (Rathbun and Peron), 48
Brubeck, Michael, 179–80
Brulte, Jim, 56–57
Bryant, Betty, 90
Budwig, Jennifer, 36–37
Bulldog (Oakland, CA), 22
Burger, Joey, 35–36, 151, 181
Bush, George W., 69

Cali Chronic X (magazine), 100
California: fiscal deficit in, 145; local marijuana taxes passed in, 155; marijuana consumption statistics, 92–93, 94–95, 99–100; marijuana economy in, 31, 44, 136–37, 155, 166, 173, 206; marijuana entrepreneurs from, in Colorado, 158; marijuana legalization initiatives in, 18, 207–8; marijuana possession decriminalized in, 152–53, 207; medical marijuana clinical trials in, 47; medical marijuana corporatization potential in, 173; medical marijuana regulation efforts in, 200–202; medical marijuana tax revenues in, 4–5; other states' emulation of, 164–65, 206, 207. *See also* California medical marijuana dispensaries *entries*
California Alcoholic Beverage Control Department, 212
California Assembly Bill 2312, 200–201
California Cannabis Association, 149
California Cannabis Business League, 168
California Chamber of Commerce, 138, 154
California Consumer Affairs Department, 200
California District Attorneys Association, 140
California Equalization Board, 146, 181
California Fourth Appellate District Court, 117, 210–11
California League of Cities, 200
California legislature, 113–14, 118, 145
California marijuana pop culture, 100–104
California Medical Association, 76–77
California Medical Board, 67, 70–71, 123
California medical marijuana dispensaries: advocacy group for, 149; California economy and, 104–5; Christian-themed, 103, 211; commercialization of, 136–37, 204, 211; defined, 4–5; Emerald Triangle suppliers of, 36; federal law concerning, 123; local bans on, 27; Proposition 19 and, 138–39; state regulation efforts, 122–23, 159, 200–202, 212; tax revenues from, 5, 155, 167.

See also Harborside Health Center (Oakland, CA); Los Angeles medical marijuana dispensaries; Oakland Cannabis Buyers Cooperative; San Francisco Cannabis Buyers Club; *specific dispensaries*

California medical marijuana dispensaries, federal crackdown on: initial cases, 181–85; locally compliant providers caught up in, 190, 204; in Los Angeles, 195–96; in Mendocino County, 189–90; in Oakland, 196–99; press conference announcing, 186–89; protests against, 191, 192–93, 197–99; in Sacramento, 193–94; in Sacramento County, 193; in San Diego, 194; in San Francisco, 194–95; state regulation efforts following, 200–202, 212; USDOJ warnings of, 170–72, 174–75, 177–79

California Medical Marijuana Program Act, 12, 172

California Medical Marijuana Regulation, Control and Taxation Act initiative, 200

California Narcotic Officers' Association, 82

Californians for Drug Free Youth, 97

California Organic Collective (Los Angeles, CA), 80

California Patients Alliance (Los Angeles, CA), 84

California Proposition 19, 28; campaign against, 138, 147–52, 153; campaign for, 138, 139–40, 154–55, 197, 198; coproponents of, 28, 138, 198; defeat of, 155, 157, 170, 185; federal opposition to, 153–54, 207; impact on Emerald Triangle farming, 43–44; language of, 150; legislative impact of, 155, 165, 206–7; marijuana movement divisions caused by, 138–39, 145, 147–52, 207; media coverage of, 154, 155; NAACP support of, 146–47; polling on, 140, 154; public support of, 152–53, 154; tax revenues from, 144–45, 146, 153–54, 167; union support of, 140–44, 145–46

California Proposition 215: AIDS epidemic as inspiration for, 206; architects of, 166; guidelines for, 125; Jones and, 19; as legal defense, 90, 108,

115, 120, 131; legislative impact of, 164–65; marijuana as federal offense despite, 7, 189, 193; medical marijuana prosecutions and, 113; Oakland marijuana industrialization plans and, 172; passage of (1996), 4, 7, 19, 48, 52, 67, 113, 206; San Francisco Measure P and, 48; values of, 100

California Public Health Department, 77

California Public Policy Institute, 140

California Second Appellate District Court, 90

California Secretary of State, 141

California Senate Bill 420, 12, 13, 108, 118–19, 159, 166, 168, 172

California Senate Bill 604, 212

California Senate Bill 847, 56–57

California Senate Bill 1449, 152–53, 207

California State Board of Equalization, 4–5

California Supreme Court, 75, 118–19, 154, 210

Campaign Against Marijuana Planting, 35

cannabidiol (CBD), 25, 63, 209

cannabinoid receptors, 56

cannabinoids, 54

Cannabis Action Network, 19

Cannabis Culture (magazine), 93, 94

Cannabis indica, 19, 20, 73

Cannabis sativa, 19, 73

Canna Care (Sacramento, CA), 103–4, 149, 211

CannBe, 158

Cardillo, Sean, 73–74

Carey, Drew, 117

Carpenters Union, 143

Catabran, Lino, 104–5, 193–94

Center for Medicinal Cannabis Research, 131

Center for Narcotics and Drug Abuse (NIMH), 69

Central Coast Compassionate Caregivers (Morro Bay, CA), 117

Chalfant, James C., 82, 87

CHAMPS (Cannabis Helping Alleviate Medical Problems; San Francisco, CA), 20

chemotherapy, 61–62, 122

Chico (CA), 166

Chippi, Kathleen, 167–68
Christine Craft Show, The (radio show), 131–32
Clinton, Bill, 52, 67
CNN, 147, 159
Coffee Shop Blue Sky (Oakland, CA), 22, 142, 147, 156, 197
Coggins, Tracy, 126–27
Cohen, Gloria, 118
Cohen, Matt, 40–42, 151, 190
Colbert, Stephen, 152
Colbert Report (TV program), 152
Cole, James M., 183–84, 187, 211–12
Colorado: federal overlooking of, 199; illicit California marijuana trade in, 158; marijuana economy in, 156, 158–59, 162; marijuana legalized in, 211; regulated medical marijuana industry in, 159–63, 167–69, 199, 206
Colorado Amendment 20, 156
Colorado Amendment 64, 207
Colorado Drug Investigators Association, 159
Colorado House Bill 1284, 159
Colorado Medical Marijuana Code (2010), 159
Colorado Medical Marijuana Enforcement Division, 160, 162–63, 169
Colorado Revenue Department, 159, 162, 168
Colusa County (CA), 38
Comedy Central, 152
Compassionate Caregivers (Los Angeles, CA), 80
Compassionate Investigational New Drug program (FDA), 51, 135
Compassionate Use Medical Marijuana Act (NJ), 165
Compassion Center (Eugene, OR), 164
Conant, Marcus, 67–69, 123
Conant v. McCaffrey, 68–69
Conant v. Walters, 69
Conlan, Jamie. *See* Henderson, Scott
Connecticut, 165
Conrad, Chris, 145, 151–52
Cook, Matt, 159, 160, 168
Cooley, Steve, 82, 89, 108
Cool Madness, 122, 127

Corey-Bloom, Jody, 57, 59
Corral, Mike: arrest of, 9–10; during DEA raid (2002), 1–4; divorce of, 205–6; as marijuana activist, 3, 11; marriage of, 2; PTSD suffered by, 205; as WAMM cofounder, 3, 16, 123, 213
Corral, Valerie, 193; arrest of, 9–10; during DEA raid (2002), 1–2, 6–7; divorce of, 205–6; head trauma suffered by, 2–3; lawsuits involving, 68; as marijuana activist, 3, 6, 11, 13–14; marriage of, 2; Proposition 19 as viewed by, 148; as WAMM cofounder, 3, 5, 16, 123, 213
Cotter, Michelle, 35
Covelo (CA), 39–40
Cow Palace (San Francisco, CA), 28–29
Cowpens, USS, 106
Craft, Christine, 131–32
Craig, Marney, 115–16
Crescent City (CA), 31
Crusaders for Patients' Rights, 103, 149
Culver City (CA) Police Department, 89

Damrell, Frank C., Jr., 131, 132, 135, 136
"Dancing with the Feds" (memoir; Blake), 42
Daschle, Tom, 18–19
Dave Wedding Dress, 26, 191
David, Jason, 192
David, Jayden, 192
Davidovich, Eugene: acquittal of, 112–13, 119; arrest of, 106–7; as ASA San Diego director, 110, 119–20, 210; background of, 106, 108; defense efforts of, 109–10; media coverage of, 106–7, 111; medical marijuana delivery service of, 106, 107, 109; as medical marijuana patient, 108–9; trial of (2010), 106, 111–12
Davies, Brittany, 104
Davies, Bryan, 103–4
Davies, Lanette, 102–4, 149
Davis, Gray, 56
DEA. *See* United States Drug Enforcement Administration (DEA)
DeAngelo, Andrew, 191
DeAngelo, Steve: appearance of, 24; background of, 25; California Proposition 19 supported by, 28; federal

crackdown protested by, 198, 201, 202, 209; as Harborside cofounder, 26; as Harborside media/marketing face, 23–24, 96–97, 143; illicit California marijuana trade feared by, 97; Lee and, 26–27; as marijuana activist, 25–26, 48, 192–93; media coverage of, 191–92. *See also* Harborside Health Center (Oakland, CA)

De la Luz, Dragonfly, 92–94, 103, 139, 149, 151–52, 209–10

Delaware, 165

Del Carpio, Francesca, 102

Del Real, Max, 168, 181

Delta Allied Growers, 179, 180, 182

Democratic Party, 139, 200–201

Denver (CO), 156, 158–59, 160, 163, 168–69

Devries, Don, 105

Dias, Dianne, 5

Discovery Channel, 191–92

Divinity Tree (San Francisco, CA), 194–95

Doblin, Rick, 49–50, 51

Domestic Cannabis Eradication/ Suppression Program (DEA), 2

Drennan, Annette, 96

Drug Enforcement Administration. *See* United States Drug Enforcement Administration (DEA)

Drug Policy Alliance, 67, 146, 166

Dr. Walker's Daze (marijuana strain), 94

Du Bois, Carole, 34

Du Bois, Lelehnia, 34, 35

Duffy, Laura E., 188–89, 194, 210

Dumanis, Bonnie, 107, 108, 119, 210

Duncan, Don, 109, 115, 136, 158

DuPont Chemical, 25

Durrah, Scott, 160–61, 168–69

Ebyam, Yan, 172–74, 177, 182, 183, 184, 187

Ecolution, 25–26

Ed Rosenthal's Marijuana Grower's Handbook (Rosenthal), 114

Edwards, Harry T., 209

8 Rivers Restaurant (Denver, CO), 160

Eisenberg, Bobby, 132

El Camino Wellness Center (Sacramento, CA), 194

El Dorado County (CA), 121

El Dorado County District Attorney's Office, 122, 130

El Dorado County Sheriff's Department, 124–26, 128–29

electricity use, 33–34, 35, 43, 93

Elford, Joe, 116

Ellis, Ron, 57–58

Emerald Cup (Mendocino County, CA), 42–43, 151

Emerald Growers Association, 168

Emerald Triangle, 30–31. *See also* Humboldt County (CA); Mendocino County (CA); Trinity County (CA)

Emerald Triangle marijuana farming: annual festival celebrating, 42–43, 151; Colorado-style regulation opposed by, 168; crime associated with, 38–40; economy of, 31, 36–37; farmer competition, 35; federal crackdown on, 189–90; Gasparas and, 31–33; indoor, and electricity use, 33–34, 35, 43; local regulations, 33, 37, 40–42, 75; marijuana legalization as threat to, 43–44, 139, 150–52; marijuana prices, 42, 43; media coverage of, 34; native vs. outside, 35–36; traditional culture of, 30–31, 35, 41

Emperor Wears No Clothes, The (Herer), 25, 148

employment drug tests, 154

endocannabinoids, 56, 65

environmentalists, 32

Epis, Brian, 27–28

Esposito, Joseph, 89

Estrada, Dania, 102

Etheridge, Melissa, 117

Eugene (OR), 164

Eugene Weekly, 164

Eureka (CA), 31–32, 33, 34, 208

Excalibur Films, 85

Fairfax (CA), 186

Farr, Sam, 113–14

FedEx, 184

Field Guide to California Agriculture, 93

Field Poll, 92–93, 94–96, 98, 140

Filner, Bob, 194

Flint (MI), 23

Flynn, Sean, 132–33
Fogel, Jeremy, 12
Folsom (CA) Police Department, 128–29
Fort Collins (CO), 163–64
420 legend, 100–101
420 Nurses, 101
Fox News, 147
Frontline (TV program), 190
Fry, Caroline, 121
Fry, Marion P. ("Mollie"), 70, 193; arrest/
trial of, 131–35; as cancer survivor,
121–22, 123–24; as cannabis celebrity,
126; conviction/sentencing of, 135–36;
family background of, 121;
imprisonment of, 211; as marijuana
doctor, 122–24, 125; marriage of, 122; as
martyr, 135–36; media coverage of,
131–32; as medical marijuana activist,
123; openness with local police, 124–25;
undercover investigations of, 127–29.
See also Whole Health Medical
Marijuana Research Center
(Placerville, CA)
Frye, Andrea, 101
Fry/Schafer Defense Committee, 132

Galaxy Gallery (Los Angeles, CA), 84
Gallegos, Paul, 36, 39–40, 168, 176
Gamley, Raymond, 194–95
Garcia, Maria Lucinda ("Lucy"), 5
Garcia, Shana Conte, 5
Garden Grove (CA) Police Department,
117
Gasparas, Stephen, 30–33, 44, 48, 150, 208
Genzlinger, Jarron, 105
George County Regional Correctional
Facility (Lucedale, MS), 77
"Getting High with Dragonfly" (review
column; *West Coast Cannabis*), 92
Gieringer, Dale, 8, 27, 166–67, 191
Girvetz, Robert, 95
Glenn County (CA), 38
Golden Gate State Park (San Francisco,
CA), 101
Goldsmith, Jan, 194
Gordnier, John, 20
Grace, Sativa, 101
Grant, Igor, 55–56, 57, 62–63

Grass Party, 148
Grateful Meds (Los Angeles, CA), 100
Grateful Meds (Nederland, CO), 168
Greater Los Angeles Collective
Association (GLACA), 81, 85, 86, 180
Green Crack (marijuana strain), 103–4
Green Doctor (Los Angeles, CA), 76
Green Oasis (Los Angeles, CA), 84, 87, 91
Greenwerkz marijuana store (Denver,
CO), 158
growing kits, 127
growing rooms, 105, 161
G3 Holistic stores, 194
gubernatorial election (1998), 56

Haag, Melinda, 177, 178, 180, 189, 194, 195,
197, 199, 201–2
Halderman, Linda, 200–201
Hamilton, Anna, 151
Hamilton, Josh, 98
Harborside Health Center (Oakland,
CA), 170; Colorado operations of, 158;
DeAngelo as media/marketing face of,
23–24, 96–97; federal crackdown on,
209; founding of, 26; media coverage
of, 158, 191–92; Oakland lawsuit to keep
open, 201–2; services offered at, 24–25,
156; as world's largest medical
marijuana dispensary, 24, 143
Harborside Management Consultants, 158
Harlequin (marijuana strain), 209–10
Harm Reduction Center (San Francisco,
CA), 7, 114
Harrelson, Woody, 84
Harris, Kamala, 195
Harvey, Michael, 121, 124, 127, 130, 133, 134
hash, 43
Hash Bar TV, 73, 74
Hawaii, 165
Headwaters Forest, 32
Hearst, William Randolph, 25
HempCon (San Jose, CA), 100, 101
Hemp Factory V (Los Angeles, CA), 82–83
Hempilation 1 and 2 (procannabis
compilation records), 25
Hempstalk Festival (Portland, OR; 2009),
149
Hemp Times, 16

Henderson, Scott, 110, 111
Henry, Mark, 45, 46–47, 50
Herer, Dan, 152
Herer, Jack, 25–26, 55, 148–49, 152
Hickenlooper, John, 161
High Times (magazine), 114, 126
HIV, 46, 47. *See also* AIDS/HIV
HIV wasting syndrome, 50
Hoffman, Nathan, 172–73, 178, 182, 184, 187
Holder, Eric, 193; Attorney General's
    Advisory Committee assembled by,
    187; Cole memo and, 211–12; Oakland
    lawsuit against, 201–2; Ogden memo as
    explained by, 12, 171; Proposition 19
    opposed by, 153–54, 207; Russo's letter
    to, 175, 177
Home Health Horticulture, 127, 129
homicides, 39–40
HopeNet Co-op (San Francisco, CA), 195
Hopkins, Milan, 74–75
Houston (TX), 16–17
Huffman, Alice, 146–47
Huizar, Jose, 90, 91
Humboldt Collective, 35
Humboldt County (CA), 13, 30–31;
    Colorado-style regulation opposed in,
    167; crime in, 39; environmental
    activism in, 32; indoor marijuana
    growing in, 33–34, 35; marijuana
    economy in, 31, 36–37; as marijuana
    tourism hub, 151; medical marijuana
    dispensaries in, 35; medical marijuana
    regulations in, 31, 33; native vs. outside
    farmers in, 35–36; Proposition 19
    impact in, 139. *See also* Emerald
    Triangle marijuana farming
Humboldt County District Attorney's
    Office, 176
Humboldt Growers Association, 36, 151, 181
Humboldt State University (Arcata, CA),
    32, 33
Hummingbird Healing Center (Eureka,
    CA), 34
Hutchinson, Asa, 11, 115
hydroponics stores, 105

iCenter (Arcata, CA), 33
iGrow (Oakland, CA), 172

Illinois, 165
"Implementation of the Compassionate
    Use Act in a Family Medical Practice"
    (Lucido), 71
Ingram, Mira, 198–99
Initiative 59 (Washington, DC), 26
Internal Revenue Service, 27, 189, 192,
    196–97, 199
International Conference on AIDS
    (Amsterdam; 1992), 49
International Conference on AIDS (San
    Francisco, CA; 1990), 47
International Faith-Based Coalition, 147
Island Mountain (CA), 39
Isleton (CA), 179–80, 181–82
Issaco, Ryan, 96
Ivey, Don, 204–5

J & J Earthmoving Company, 39
Jackson, Jovan, 110–11, 119–20, 210–11
Jackson County (MS) Narcotics Task
    Force, 66
Jamaican Café (Santa Monica, CA), 160
James, Wanda, 160–61, 168–69
Jeffries, Jessie, 39
Jezebel's (Denver, CO), 160
John S. McCain, USS, 106, 108
Jones, Dale Sky, 139–40, 142, 154, 166, 191,
    199
Jones, Jeff: background of, 18; Epis trial
    disrupted by, 27–28; influences on, 18;
    Lee and, 17–18, 19–20, 27–28, 138; as
    marijuana activist, 18–19; marijuana
    legalization promoted by, 43–44, 92; as
    OCBC founder, 19, 114; Patient I.D.
    Centers opened by, 139; post-
    crackdown career of, 206–7; as
    Proposition 19 coproponent, 138, 139,
    150, 153
Jones, Wayne, 18
Jopson, David, 177, 182, 184, 187
Jopson, Thomas, 177, 178, 182–83, 184, 187
Joseph, Jeffrey, 89–90
Journal (Humboldt County newspaper),
    151
Journal of Drug Policy Analysis, 99
*Journal of the American Medical
    Association,* 54

Kaiser Foundation Hospital (San Francisco, CA), 45
Kaplan, Rebecca, 176, 198
Kaposi's sarcoma, 45–46
Katzir, Dan, 154
Keefe, Brian, 127
Keegan, Steve, 96
Kelly, Patrick, 2, 6–7, 9, 206
Kelly, Patrick Kevin, 118–19
Kerlikowske, R. Gil, 153, 165, 207
Kha, Felix, 117
Khalsa, Jag, 53
Kitzhaber, John, 164
Knight, Pete, 56–57
Kramer, Barry, 84, 85
Kruschewsky, Carlos, 79–80, 90, 210
Kush (magazine), 94
Kush, Sean. See Cardillo, Sean
Kush Clubhouse (Los Angeles, CA), 73, 74
Kush Expo Medical Marijuana Show (Anaheim, CA), 76, 101–2

L.A. Confidential (marijuana strain), 84
Lacy, Gary, 125, 128, 130
Lake County (CA), 38, 74–75
Lake Forest (CA), 188
Lancet (journal), 54
Larson, Troy, 62
Law Enforcement Against Prohibition, 198
Lawrence, Tony, 78
Lawrence Berkeley National Laboratory, 93
Lee, Ann, 15
Lee, Bob, 15
Lee, Richard, 48; awards received by, 208; background of, 15; federal crackdown on, 196–99; Houston hemp store of, 16–17; Jones and, 17–18, 19–20, 27–28, 138; as marijuana activist, 16; marijuana legalization promoted by, 26–29, 43–44, 92; media coverage of, 154; Oakland marijuana network of, 22–23; as Oaksterdam founder, 23, 27, 28; opposition to, 27; paralyzing accident suffered by, 15–16; Peron and, 147; post-crackdown career of, 206; as Proposition 19 coproponent, 138, 139, 144, 147, 151, 154, 155, 198; resignation as Oaksterdam president, 199

Leff, Arnold, 11
Legal Marijuana—the Hemp Store (Houston, TX), 16–17
Leno, Mark, 152
Leshner, Alan I., 51–53
Leslie, Tim, 56–57
Lester, Frank, 150
licensing programs, 41–42, 162–63, 167, 170, 176
Lichter, Lawrence, 132
Lindberg, Chris, 119–20
Linney, Douglas, 142, 145
Lloyd, Bill, 146
Lockheed Corporation, 22
Lockyer, Bill, 11, 125
Long Beach (CA), 144–45
Los Angeles (CA): federal crackdown in, 7, 195–96; marijuana market in, 13; medical marijuana tax revenues in, 180; Oaksterdam University satellite campus in, 23. See also Los Angeles medical marijuana dispensaries; Venice Beach (Los Angeles, CA)
Los Angeles City Council, 79, 80, 87–88, 89, 90–91, 180, 196, 210
Los Angeles County (CA), 184
Los Angeles District Attorney's Office, 74, 82–83, 89
Los Angeles medical marijuana dispensaries: accreditation of, 85; city campaign against, 82–83; collective associations, 81, 85; crime associated with, 89; federal crackdown on, 195–96; Hollywood authors/actors associated with, 83–85; prices at, 87; proliferation of, 80, 82, 90, 91; regulation efforts, 80, 87–91, 196, 210; tax revenues from, 180
Los Angeles Patient I.D. Center, 139
Los Angeles Police Department, 86, 195–96
Los Angeles Police Protective League, 87
Lovell, John, 200
Lucido, Frank, 71–72
Lungren, Dan, 20, 56
Lyman, Donald, 77
Lynch, Charles, 117–18

Madera County (CA), 184
Maggy, Paul, 126–27, 129, 133–34
Magnolia Wellness Center (Orangevale,
    CA), 193
Maine, 164
Majors, Brick. *See* Barnes, Brad
Malverde, Jesus, 38
Mango OG (marijuana strain), 24–25
Mann, Dhar, 172, 196
Marchetti, Lou, 173–74
Margolin, Harold ("Hal"), 8–9, 12,
    212–13
marijuana: analgesic properties of, 25,
    60–61; California consumption of,
    92–93; clinical studies on effects
    of, 13; commercialization of, 22;
    decriminalization of, 152–53, 207;
    federal legal classification of, 18, 53,
    62, 67, 209; legalization initiatives,
    28, 92, 206, 207–8, 211–12; price of,
    42, 43; psychoactive substances
    in (*see* cannabidiol (CBD);
    tetrahydrocannabinol (THC));
    tax revenues from, 26, 144–45.
    See also medical marijuana
marijuana doctors: arrests of, 66, 77–78;
    California investigation of, 70–71;
    DEA distrust of, 123; federal legal
    threats to, 67; lawsuits allowing
    marijuana recommendations, 68–69;
    medical establishment opposition to,
    76–77; in medical marijuana economy,
    63; networks, 75–76, 99–100, 149;
    out-of-staters as, 64–66, 77–78; "paper
    mill" clinics, 72–76; police raids on,
    74; prices charged by, 72, 76, 123;
    Proposition 19 and, 139;
    "recommendations" written by, 66–67,
    69–70, 71–72, 76, 123. *See also* Fry,
    Marion P. ("Mollie")
marijuana edibles, 98, 129, 160–61
Marijuana Gateway to Health (Werner), 55
Marijuana Inc. (TV documentary), 34
Marijuana: Medical Papers, 1839–1972 (ed.
    Mikuriya), 69
Marijuana Policy Project, 67, 142
marijuana prohibition, conspiracy alleged
    behind, 25

"Marijuana Reform: Next Steps for
    California" conference (Berkeley, CA;
    2011), 165–66, 167
Marijuana Stamp Act (1937), 25
Marijuana USA (TV documentary), 161
Marin Alliance for Medical Marijuana,
    186, 191
Marinol, 50, 54
Marjyn Investments, 172–74, 178
Massachusetts, 165
Massey, Tom, 159
Maxim (magazine), 102
McCabe, Michael, 110, 112
McCaffrey, Barry, 67, 68
McClellan, Jim, 19
McCowen, John, 37
McNamara, Joseph, 155
McNulty, Timothy, 125, 128, 136
Measure B (Mendocino County, CA), 37
Measure F (Oakland, CA), 26
Measure G (Mendocino County, CA), 37
Measure M (Los Angeles, CA), 180
Measure P (San Francisco, CA), 48, 49
Measure Z (Oakland, CA), 22
Medical Cannabis Safety Council, 98
Medical Kush Beach Club dispensary
    (Los Angeles, CA), 73, 74
Medical Kush Doctor (Los Angeles, CA),
    73–74
medical marijuana: amounts allowed,
    118–19; California legalization of, 19,
    99; demographics of, 92–93, 94–96,
    99–100; diversion of, into illegal drug
    trafficking, 175–76; economy of, 66,
    166; efficacy of, 47; federal authority to
    prosecute, 130–31; federal legal
    classification of, 67, 122–23; Humboldt
    County (CA) regulations, 31; pesticides
    in, 82–83; political/legal acceptance of
    unresolved, 106; price of, 87, 151, 163,
    185; profitability of, 157; Proposition 19
    and, 150; sexual marketing of, 80,
    100–102, 103; state-permitted
    commerce in, 13; tax revenues from,
    167; trade shows, 100, 101–2
medical marijuana dispensaries, 4–5. *See
    also* California medical marijuana
    dispensaries; Los Angeles medical

medical marijuana dispensaries *(continued)*
marijuana dispensaries; *specific
dispensaries*
Medical Marijuana Program Act, 108
medical marijuana research: on analgesic
effects, 56–63; bureaucratic obstacles,
50–52; clinical trials, 53–55, 208–9;
legal impact of, 209; on long-term use
and brain dysfunction, 55–56; on
marijuana as AIDS treatment, 49–55;
state funding of, 55. *See also* Abrams,
Donald
Medical Use of Marijuana Act (Colorado;
2000), 156
MediCann (marijuana doctors' network),
75–76, 99–100, 149
Medi-Cone (marijuana-processing
factory), 143, 198
Med/Rx'C (marijuana doctors' network),
76
Mendocino County (CA), 13, 30–31;
Colorado-style regulation opposed in,
167; crime in, 39–40; environmental
activism in, 32; federal crackdown in,
189–90, 208; indoor marijuana growing
in, 34, 43; marijuana economy in, 37; as
marijuana tourism hub, 151; medical
marijuana regulations in, 37, 40–42,
75, 190; pot culture figures in, 93;
Proposition 19 impact in, 139. *See also*
Emerald Triangle marijuana farming
Mendocino County Board of Supervisors,
40–41, 190
Mendocino County Farm Bureau, 41, 190
Mendocino County Sheriff's Department,
37–38, 40–41, 190
Mendocino Farmers Collective, 42
Mendocino National Forest, 38
MendoGrown (trade association), 41
Merced County (CA) Mental Health
Department, 70
Mexican drug traffickers, 153
Mexico, drug violence in, 153
Michigan, 164
Mikuriya, Tod H., 69–70, 126
Miley, Nate, 20
Mills, Evan, 93
Modoc National Forest, 30

Mohr, Anthony J., 88
money laundering, 169
Monson, Diane, 130–31
Montagnier, Luc, 46
Montana, 165
Moore, Eric, 90
Moorman, Ann, 39
Moskowitz, Barry Ted, 114
Mountain Democrat (newspaper), 130
Movement in Action (San Diego, CA),
110, 113
MSNBC, 34
Multidisciplinary Association for
Psychedelic Studies, 49, 51
murders, 39–40, 89
Murphy, Gene, 59–60
Musikka, Elvy, 135
My Mother Earth Co-op (Sand Diego
County, CA), 194

Naples, Matthew, 182–83
National Association for the Advancement
of Colored People (NAACP), 146–47
National Institute of Mental Health
(NIMH), 69
National Institute on Drug Abuse
(NIDA), 50–54, 61
National Institutes of Health, 51, 52
National Organization for the Reform of
Marijuana Laws (NORML), 112;
Berkeley conference (2011), 176–77;
California medical marijuana
regulations supported by, 166–67, 200;
California Proposition 19 supported by,
28; conferences of, 140; Lee's legalization
efforts opposed by, 27; online marijuana
service listings of, 74, 107; rallies held by,
17; WAMM raid and, 8
NBC, 98–99
Nederland (CO), 167–68
Neely, Bonnie, 36
Nevada, 165
Neves, Jeff, 128
New Age Canna (Garden Grove, CA), 182
New England Journal of Medicine, 54
New Hampshire, 165
New Jersey Compassionate Use Medical
Marijuana Act, 165

New Mexico, 165
New York Times, 84
Nguyen, John, 184
Nixon, Richard M., 11
NJ Today, 165
NoHo Caregivers (North Hollywood, CA), 188
No on 19 campaign, 138, 149, 154
Norris, Mike, 23
Norris, Mikki, 145
North Hollywood (CA), 188
Northstone Organics (Mendocino County, CA), 40, 41, 190

Oakland (CA): budget deficit in, 172; federal crackdown in, 7, 196–99; Lee's marijuana network in, 22–23; local marijuana tax passed in (Measure F), 26, 177–78; local regulations, 81, 170, 174; marijuana distribution program in, 21; marijuana economy in, 192; marijuana law enforcement priority in (Measure Z), 22; marijuana market in, 13; marijuana movement in, 22, 26, 31, 92; marijuana tax revenues in, 172; medical marijuana dispensaries in, 19, 81; Oikos mass shooting in, 198; USDOJ sued by, 201–2. *See also* Harborside Health Center (Oakland, CA); Oaksterdam University (Oakland, CA)
Oakland Cannabis Buyers Cooperative: city support of, 20–21, 114; federal lawsuit against, 20–22, 52, 114, 202; founding of, 19, 114, 138; Lee and, 19–20; medical users provided by, 20
Oakland City Council: industrial marijuana farm applicants to, 143, 144, 172–74, 175–76; industrial marijuana farms approved by, 170–72, 176–77; medical marijuana dispensaries authorized by, 178, 196; OCBC declared city's agent by, 20–21, 170; warnings given to, 172, 174–75, 178–79, 180
Oakland City Hall, 209
Oakland Patient I.D. Center, 139
Oakland Police Department, 198

Oaksterdam Blue Sky (Oakland, CA), 197, 199. *See also* Coffee Shop Blue Sky (Oakland, CA)
Oaksterdam University (Oakland, CA), 170; Coloradans as students at, 156–57, 158, 169; courses offered at, 23; faculty of, 29, 147, 151–52, 157; federal crackdown on, 197–99; founding of, 23, 27, 28; Lee as professor emeritus at, 206; as Proposition 19 campaign HQs, 28, 141–43, 144, 146, 166; reputation of, 170, 189
Obama, Barack, 113, 114, 153, 161, 171, 187, 188
O.D. Media (Oakland, CA), 22
Ogden (David W.) memo, 12–13, 113, 171, 183, 203–4
OG Kush (marijuana strain), 25
Oikos University (Oakland, CA), 198
O'Malley, Nancy, 175–76
One Love Wellness (Sacramento, CA), 104–5, 193–94
Operation Endless Summer, 108
Operation Full Court Press, 38
Operation Green Rx: Davidovich arrest, 106–10, 111–13, 119; defendant appearances at San Diego City Council meetings, 109; Jackson arrest, 110–11, 119–20, 210–11; media coverage of, 107, 108; Stacy arrest, 113–14
opiates, 61
Orange County (CA), 117, 184, 188
Ordinance 9.31 (Mendocino County, CA), 41, 190
Oregon, 164, 165
Oregon Measure 74, 164
Organica (Los Angeles, CA), 89–90

Pappas, Charlie, 194
Patel, Sona, 76
Peron, Dennis, 193; Lee as viewed by, 28; as medical marijuana activist, 16, 18, 48; as Oaksterdam lecturer, 147, 157; Proposition 19 opposed by, 147; as Proposition 215 proponent, 147; Rogers and, 157; as SFCBC founder, 7, 19
pesticides, 82–83
Peterson, Jeffrey, 100, 101

Pew Research Poll, 207
Pfeil, Suzanne, 4, 6, 7–8, 205
Pham, Theresa, 111–12
Pings, Anne, 131–32, 133, 134–35
Placerville (CA), 121
Polis, Jared, 161
Pope, Bruce, 181
Pot City, U.S.A. (TV documentary), 34
Pottenger, Frances Marion, 121
Prange, Donald, Sr., 182
Prettol, Seth, 204–5
Printz, Kyle, 96
Pro Grow Time Machine, 105
protease inhibitor drugs, 52, 61
Pumping Iron (film documentary), 152
Pure Blueberry Hash (hash type), 43
Pure Life Alternative Wellness Center
    (Los Angeles, CA), 79, 91, 210
Purple Hindu Kush (marijuana strain), 32
Pyhtila, Jordan, 39

Quan, Jean, 175, 196

R & R Wellness Collective (Sacramento,
    CA), 184–85
Raich, Angel, 40, 72, 130–31
Raich, Robert, 21, 145
Raiding California (TV documentary), 117
Rainbow Family, 30, 31
Randall, Robert, 51, 135
Rand Corporation, 151, 153
Rathbun, Mary Jane ("Brownie Mary"), 18,
    48–49
Reason TV, 117
Redding (CA), 82
Redman, John, 97
Redway (CA), 36
Redwood College (Eureka, CA), 34
Redwood Curtain, 33
Redwood Summer (1990), 32
Reid, Larry, 176
Reno, Janet, 68–69
Republican Party, 200
Reserve dispensary (Sacramento County,
    CA), 100
Rhode Island, 165
Rice, Ben, 8
Richards, Jaye, 35

Rio Dell (CA), 39
Rio Oso (CA), 187
Ritter, Bill, 163
River Rock marijuana store (Denver, CO),
    162
R. J. Reynolds Tobacco, 150
Robert T. Matsui United States
    Courthouse (Sacramento, CA),
    186–89, 192
Robinson, Joe, 68
Rochester (NY), 38
Rocky Mountain High Intensity Drug
    Trafficking, 169
Rodrigues, Danny, 10, 213
Rodriguez, Yolanda, 90
Rogers, Dan, 156–57, 158, 169
Rohrabacher, Dana, 113–14
Rolling Stone, 167
Romer, Chris, 159
Rose, Mark, 168
Rosenthal, Ed, 7, 29, 114–16
Ross, Gary, 154
Roxane Laboratories (Columbus, OH), 54
Rush, Dan, 140–42, 143–44, 145–46,
    154–55, 163–64, 191
Russo, John: federal marijuana policy as
    viewed by, 170; federal warning given
    to, 170–72; Holder contacted by, 175,
    177; as Oakland city attorney, 175;
    Oakland City Council warned by, 172,
    174–75; resignation as Oakland city
    attorney, 178–79

Sackett, Charles, 116
Sacramento (CA), 11, 36, 64, 78, 81, 123,
    144; federal crackdown announced in,
    186–89; federal crackdown in, 193–94;
    marijuana tax passed in, 155; medical
    marijuana dispensaries in, 180; medical
    marijuana tax revenues in, 180
Sacramento Bee, The, 66, 92–93, 94–96, 98,
    119, 130, 147, 150
Sacramento County (CA), 81, 177, 179–80,
    182–83, 193
Sacramento County Grand Jury, 182
Sacramento Press Club, 200
Sahagun, Vanessa, 101
Sai Center (Arcata, CA), 33

Samano, Elizabeth, 180
San Diego (CA), 81, 194. *See also*
  Operation Green Rx
San Diego Cannabis Providers, 109
San Diego County (CA), 194
San Diego County Courthouse, 107
San Diego County Superior Court, 106,
  120
San Diego Union-Tribune, 111
San Fernando Valley (CA), 85–87
Sanford, Dawn, 96
San Francisco (CA): AIDS epidemic in,
  46, 47, 131, 206; federal crackdown in,
  7, 194–95; federal crackdown protested
  in, 191, 199; local regulations, 81;
  marijuana legalization conference in
  (2013), 207–8; medical marijuana
  dispensaries in, 19, 20, 48, 81; medical
  marijuana initiative in, 48, 49
San Francisco Bay Area, 93–94, 100–101,
  143, 171, 186. *See also* Oakland (CA)
  entries; specific place
San Francisco Cannabis Buyers Club, 19,
  20, 48, 122
San Francisco Chronicle, 115
San Francisco City Hall, 199
San Francisco Community Consortium, 50
San Francisco District Attorney's Office,
  195
San Francisco General Hospital, 46,
  48–50, 51, 61
San Francisco Giants, 98–99
San Francisco Public Health Department,
  53
San Jose (CA), 81, 155, 166, 192
San Jose Convention Center, 13–14
San Jose Federal Building, 10
San Jose Police Department, 155
San Juan Capistrano (CA), 95
San Leandro (CA), 174
Santa Cruz County (CA), 4. *See also* Wo/
  Men's Alliance for Medical Marijuana
  (WAMM)
Santa Cruz County Sheriff's Department,
  9
Santa Monica (CA), 160
Schafer, Dale: arrest/trial of, 131–35; as
  cannabis celebrity, 126; conviction/

sentencing of, 135–36; as El Dorado
  County district attorney candidate,
  122, 130; imprisonment of, 211;
  marijuana delivery service offered by,
  126–27; as martyr, 135–36; media
  coverage of, 131–32; as medical
  marijuana activist, 122, 123; openness
  with local police, 125–26; undercover
  investigations of, 127–29. *See also*
  Whole Health Medical Marijuana
  Research Center (Placerville, CA)
Schafer, Donald, 70
Schafer, Geoffrey, 129, 136, 211
Schafer, Heather, 129, 133
Schafer, Jeremy, 133
Schlueter, Erik, 130
Schmidt, Paul, 163
Schopler, Andrew G., 114
Schorr, Kathryn, 83
Schroder, Mary M., 69
Schwarzenegger, Arnold, 145, 152–53, 207
Scruggs, Newy, 98–99
Scully, Jan, 140, 181
Scutari, Nicholas, 165
Seattle (WA), 164–65
Sebastopol (CA), 23
Serra, Tony, 132, 133–35
Service Employees International Union
  (SEIU), 145–46
Shalala, Donna, 68
Shambhala Healing Center (San
  Francisco, CA), 104, 195
Shawa, Al, 104, 195
Sherer, Steph, 115, 167
Shiva Skunk (marijuana strain), 20
Shore, Howard H., 120
Simply Pure (Denver, CO), 161, 168–69
Singing River Hospital (Pascagoula, MS),
  64
Sisco, Aimee, 183, 184
S. K. Seymour (Oakland, CA), 22, 139, 142,
  197
Skunk (stoner magazine), 14, 94
Smith, Alice, 6, 8
Smith, Bryan, 184–85
Smith, Catherine, 195
Smith, Cheryl, 164
Snoop Dogg, 154–55

Society of Cannabis Clinicians, 126
Sonoma County (CA), 41–42, 49, 190
Soros, George, 28, 155
Sour Best Shit Ever (marijuana strain), 43
Spiers, Curtis, 66, 77–78
SR-71 (Oakland, CA), 22
Stacy, James, 110, 113–14
Steadman, Pat, 159
Steep Hill Lab (Oakland, CA), 24–25
Sterling-Nichols, Alison, 168
Stevens, John Paul, 130–31
Stockton (CA), 155
Stoners Against Proposition 19, 139, 149
Substance Abuse and Mental Health
    Services Administration, 165
Sun Herald (MS newspaper), 64
Sutter County (CA), 177, 183
Sweet God (marijuana strain), 34

Talleyrand, Jean, 75, 149
Tandy, Karen, 205
Taylor, Stephanie. *See* De la Luz,
    Dragonfly
T-Beezle (marijuana grower), 43
Teamsters Local 70, 173–74
Tehama County (CA), 38
Teshara, Jeffrey, 133
tetrahydrocannabinol (THC), 24–25, 50,
    54, 56, 60–61, 63
THC, the (Arcata, CA), 35
Thicke, Alan, 85
Thicke, Brennan, 85
Thicke, Robin, 85
Thomas, Clarence, 22
tobacco companies, 150
Todd, Tamar, 166
Tracy, Mark, 9
Trim Scene Solutions (Redway, CA), 36
Trinity County (CA), 30–31, 35, 38. *See also*
    Emerald Triangle marijuana farming
Trutanich, Carmen A., 82–83, 88, 90, 108,
    210
Turner, Tony, 35
2 A.M Dispensary (Los Angeles, CA),
    86–87, 195–96

Uelemen, Gerald, 8
Ukiah (CA), 33

Ukiah Daily Journal, 37
United Food and Commercial Workers
    Union, 200; Local Number 5, 140, 141,
    142, 145–46, 163; Local Number 7,
    163–64
United Parcel Service (UPS), 126, 127–28,
    184
U.S. Attorney General's Advisory
    Committee, 187
U.S. Attorney's Office (Los Angeles,
    CA), 188
U.S. Attorney's Office (Sacramento, CA),
    129, 181–82, 183–84, 186–87, 199–200,
    211
U.S. Attorney's Office (San Diego, CA),
    188–89, 194
U.S. Attorney's Office (San Francisco,
    CA), 171, 174, 177, 178, 189, 199
U.S. Controlled Substances Act (1970), 6,
    7, 22, 67, 130, 154, 185, 204, 207
U.S. Courthouse (Sacramento, CA),
    186–89, 192
U.S. Court of Appeals (Washington, DC),
    209
U.S. District Court, 39
U.S. District Court (Rochester, NY), 38
U.S. District Court (Washington,
    DC), 51
U.S. Drug Enforcement Administration
    (DEA), 196–97; Domestic Cannabis
    Eradication/Suppression Program, 2;
    Emerald Triangle operations, 38;
    lawsuits against, 12–13, 14, 68–69, 203,
    209; Los Angeles raids conducted by,
    89; marijuana as classified by, 18;
    marijuana doctors distrusted by, 123;
    marijuana prices and, 42; Mendocino
    County raids conducted by, 189–90;
    NORML rallies against, 17; Oakland
    raids by, 114; Proposition 19 and, 153–
    54; public backlash against, 2, 7, 10–11,
    113, 130, 203; retirees from, as Colorado
    medical marijuana police, 162, 163; San
    Diego raids by, 110–11; WAMM raid
    conducted by (2002), 1–4, 6–11, 113,
    114, 123, 130, 203, 212. *See also*
    California medical marijuana
    dispensaries, federal crackdown on

U.S. Environmental Protection Agency (EPA), 83
U.S. Food and Drug Administration (FDA), 50, 51, 62, 135, 209
U.S. Health and Human Services Department, 68
U.S. Justice Department: Colorado medical marijuana industry ignored by, 159; Isleton Town Council warned by, 181–82; Oakland City Council warned by, 170–72, 174, 177; Oakland lawsuit against, 201–2; Ogden memo as explained by, 12–13; post-crackdown concessions hinted by, 211–12; Proposition 19 opposed by, 153–54, 157. See also California medical marijuana dispensaries, federal crackdown on
U.S. Marshals, 189, 196–97
U.S. Ninth Circuit Court of Appeals, 21–22, 69, 123, 136
U.S. Office of AIDS Research, 53
U.S. Office of National Drug Control Policy, 67, 68
U.S. Supreme Court, 22, 40, 69, 72, 114, 130–31, 190
United States v. Oakland Cannabis Buyers Cooperative and Jeffrey Jones, 22, 114
University of California, 13
University of California—Davis, 57, 59, 60
University of California—Irvine, 122
University of California—San Diego, 55, 57–59, 60–61
University of California—San Francisco, 45–46, 50, 57, 58, 61–62
University of California—Santa Cruz, 101
University of Mississippi, 50–51, 54, 59
University of Pennsylvania, 55
Upper Lake (CA), 74–75

Vapor Room (San Francisco, CA), 195
Varmus, Harold, 46
Vasconcellos, John, 12, 55, 56–57
VaVoom, Cha Cha, 101
Venice Beach (Los Angeles, CA), 72–74, 76
Venice Beach Care Center (Los Angeles, CA), 85

Vermont, 165
Veterans Administration Hospital (Sacramento County, CA), 59
Vianchini, George, 142–43
Vicodin, 60
Victory Outreach Church (Sacramento, CA), 103
video surveillance, 161, 167, 168
Village on the Delta (Isleton, CA), 179
Volberding, Paul, 46

Wade, John, 98
Wagner, Benjamin B., 181–82, 183, 199–200, 211
Wain, Harry, 5
Waldos, 100–101
Walker, John Melvin ("Pops"), 184
Wallace, Mark, 57, 60–61
Wallace, Vince, 23
Walsh, John F., 169, 199
Walter, Steve, 119–20
Walters, John P., 69
Ward 86 (San Francisco General Hospital), 48–49
War on Drugs, 16
Washington (DC), 25, 26, 164
Washington State, 164–65, 206, 211
Washington State Initiative Measure 502, 207
wasting syndrome. See HIV wasting syndrome
Webb, Shawna, 100
Weed Wars (TV documentary series), 191–92
weGrow (Oakland, CA), 172
Weil, William Stuart. See Cardillo, Sean
Werner, Clint, 55
West, Jonathan, 7, 48
West Coast Cannabis (magazine), 92, 94
West Coast Leaf (newspaper), 145
West Hollywood (CA), 7
Westword (Denver alternative weekly), 158
White House Office of Drug Abuse Prevention, 11
White House Office of National Drug Control Policy, 153, 165, 207
Whitman, Meg, 145, 155

Whole Health Medical Marijuana Research Center (Placerville, CA), 121; full-spectrum services offered at, 123, 126–27, 129; opening of, 123, 136; police investigations of, 124–25, 127–29; police raid on, 129–30

Wicken, John, 161

Wilcox, Jeff, 143–44, 148, 171, 172, 175–76, 196

Wilde, Mikal Xylon, 39–40

Wilkinson, Lee, 45

Williams, Montel, 117, 164

Willits (CA), 33

Willits News, 37

Wilsey, Barth, 57, 59–60

Wilson, Ora Mae, 64

Winkle, David ("Papa Winky"), 38

Witemyre, Matthew, 142–43, 198

Wofsy, Connie, 46

Wo/Men's Alliance for Medical Marijuana (WAMM): consciousness engendered by, 14; DEA raid on (2002), 1–4, 6–11, 113, 114, 123, 130, 203, 212; DEA sued by, 12–13, 14, 203; Design for Dying Project, 6, 213; emergency "phone tree" of, 8; founding of, 3, 16, 123; medical marijuana federally permitted at, 12–13; membership of, 5–6, 48, 68; post-crackdown existence of, 203–6, 212–13

Woody Kush (marijuana strain), 84

World Series (2010), 98–99

Wright, Perry, 111

Wu, George H., 117–18

Yee, Betty, 181

Yes on 19 campaign, 138

Young, Francis L., 18

Youth International Party, 25

YouTube, 155

Yuba County (CA), 183

Zimmerman, Doreen, 128

Zimmerman, Todd, 128, 133

Zine, Dennis, 87–88, 91

Zugsberger, Matt, 75